THE
NEW ORLEANS
VOODOO
HANDBOOK

"To understand a spiritual practice one must understand both the history and culture in which it flourished. In *The New Orleans Voodoo Handbook*, Kenaz Filan begins with the critical eye of a historian before investigating New Orleans Voodoo as both a spiritual science and religion. He strips away myth and fallacy, leaving us with fact, and gives us an insider's view of the faith's deepest mysteries. It is the first book I've read by an experienced houngan dealing with one of the South's most enduring, powerful legacies. This volume is a welcome addition to both the casual historian's and active practitioner's library."

OCHA'NI LELE,
AUTHOR OF *DILOGGÚN TALES OF THE NATURAL WORLD*,
TEACHINGS OF THE SATERÍA GODS, AND
THE DILOGGÚN: THE ORISHAS, PROVERBS, SACRIFICES, AND PROHIBITIONS OF CUBAN SANTERÍA

THE
NEW ORLEANS
VOODOO
HANDBOOK

KENAZ FILAN

Destiny Books
Rochester, Vermont • Toronto, Canada

Destiny Books
One Park Street
Rochester, Vermont 05767
www.DestinyBooks.com

Destiny Books is a division of Inner Traditions International

Library of Congress Cataloging-in-Publication Data
Filan, Kenaz.
    The New Orleans voodoo handbook / Kenaz Filan.
        p. cm.
    Summary: "A guide to the practices, tools, and rituals of New Orleans Voodoo as
well as the many cultural influences at its origins"—Provided by publisher.
    Includes bibliographical references (p.   ) and index.
    ISBN 978-1-59477-435-5 (pbk.) — ISBN 978-1-59477-798-1 (ebook)
    1. Voodooism—Louisiana—New Orleans. 2. New Orleans (La.)—Religious life
and customs. I. Title.
    BL2490.F545 2011
    299.6'750976335—dc23
                                                                        2011024155

Printed and bound in the United States by Versa Press, Inc.

10   9   8   7   6

Text design and layout by Virginia Scott Bowman
This book was typeset in Garamond Premier Pro with Bembo and Gill Sans used
as display typefaces

Photographs in the color insert by Chanc VanWinkle Orzell
Plates 7–14 and 16–22 were taken at and with the permission of the New Orleans
Historic Voodoo Museum

To send correspondence to the author of this book, mail a first-class letter to the
author c/o Inner Traditions • Bear & Company, One Park Street, Rochester, VT
05767, and we will forward the communication.

CONTENTS

INTRODUCTION

Many people will tell you that there is no such thing as New Orleans Voodoo. According to them, the whole thing started as a marketing campaign to woo tourists. Later, a few bored white folks created a "tradition" by reading some books on African and Afro-Caribbean spirituality, then combining that information with African American folk magic, Wicca, hermeticism, and just about anything else they could find that was suitably "mysterious" and "spooky." Those criticisms aren't entirely without merit. And yet they miss the greater point: New Orleans Voodoo has become for many a powerful and meaningful religious tradition.

The critics may have a point. There may not have been a survival of Haitian Vodou that persists to the present day in the Louisiana backwoods and bayous. But, like most creation myths, the stories point to a deeper truth. There is *something* magical in the Crescent City, some force that powers New Orleans Voodoo and that draws people to its holy land for pilgrimages and parties (which have often been closely linked, despite what you may have heard in Sunday school). The explanations may not be literally true, but that's not important. What's important is that the creation myths point to something that must be explained.

The French philosopher Jean Baudrillard has spoken of *simulacra*—signs, symbols, and simulations that are treated as and become reality. As he puts it, "Simulation . . . is the generation by models of a real without origin or reality: a hyperreal. The territory no longer precedes the map, nor does it survive it. It is nevertheless the map that precedes the territory—*precession of simulacra*—that engenders the territory."[1]

Perhaps the legends created New Orleans Voodoo. If so, that creation has long since taken on a life of its own. The myth has sired many children and has called others to listen and to learn beneath the city's wrought-iron balconies. But many believe something else is behind the stories. They have felt the reality behind the magic; they have drunk from the water of Lake Pontchartrain, and now the city has claimed them for her own.

You may feel her calling out to you in your dreams. You may long for her brightly colored shotgun cottages and the jazz bands playing in her streets. Or you may just be looking for a new spiritual diversion. Your motivations are your own; whatever you want, you'll find that New Orleans is happy to oblige you. But be careful. Those who know the city will tell you that there's plenty of danger to go with the beauty. If you don't watch yourself, you may just wind up sucked into something you never bargained for. She's a sweet mistress, but she can be a harsh one too. Take her joyfully, take her lovingly, but don't you dare take her lightly.

Because, you see, that's the way real magic is. Real magic is as joyful and sad as a jazz funeral, as pretty and as dangerous as white oleander. If you want to experience the spirit world, be ready for beauty that will bring tears to your eyes and for terrors that will scare you witless. There's plenty of both in New Orleans, and those who will share in her dreams had best be prepared to face her nightmares too. Lots of visitors who overindulged in Bourbon Street's bars have awakened without their wallets and cell phones, and many spiritual tourists who took New Orleans Voodoo for a harmless game found themselves face to face with things they hadn't expected. Those who escaped alive rarely got out unscathed. Like many who came before them, they left with scars as souvenirs of their journey to the Big Easy.

Unlike Haitian Vodou or other more organized Afro-Caribbean traditions, New Orleans Voodoo is a freeform system of worship. You can incorporate whatever works for you into your personal practices, and nobody will tell you that you're doing it wrong. On the other hand, no one is going to tell you that you're doing it right. Like any conjure person, you'll have to judge that by how your magic does or does not work. New Orleans Voodoo is not about adherence to a doctrine or a script; it's about working with the spirits to bring about changes on the material plane.

For those coming to New Orleans Voodoo from a more structured tradition, this can be simultaneously exhilarating and terrifying. You can declare yourself a conjure man, a root doctor, or a Voodoo Queen—but then you'll be expected to deliver the services appropriate to your self-proclaimed title. You'll be judged not by who initiated you or how well you have memorized the proper prayers, but by whether you can do the work for your clients and yourself. If you can't, you're just an empty title, a poor deluded soul pretending to have power you'll never have.

I have provided you with introductions to some of the spirits most commonly honored in New Orleans Voodoo, as well as safeguards that may help you to avoid psychic or physical injury. But, in the end, the instructions I've provided here are merely guidelines. It's up to you to make the acquaintance of the spirits, and it's up to you to accept responsibility for the changes they may bring into your life—and you can rest assured they *will* bring changes. When you call on the lwas, don't be surprised when they answer.

PART ONE

HISTORY

To understand New Orleans Voodoo, you must first understand the city. New Orleans is a conglomeration of races, classes, and cultures unlike anyplace else in the world. Its terrain, its history, and its people have all contributed to its triumphs and tragedies, and have helped to shape its religious and magical practices.

History should not be treated as a dull collection of names, dates, and events, but as a celebration of the achievements of those who have gone before us. (Besides, only a truly determined historian could make the story of New Orleans boring.) With that in mind, let's pay a joyous, if sometimes somber, tribute to the people who made the Big Easy what it is today.

1

BORN ON THE BAYOU

The Rise of New Orleans

As the Mississippi flows south from Minnesota's Lake Itasca, it joins with other great streams like the Ohio, the Arkansas, and the Missouri rivers. Each of these brings with it a payload of rich Midwestern soil. By the time the river reaches its mouth, the waters of the "Big Muddy" are heavy with silt. Flowing into the Gulf of Mexico, it deposits the sediment in the brackish area where salt- and freshwater meet. The result is a fan-shaped landform that resembles the Greek letter "D" and that is hence called a *delta*. The delta fills in the river channel as it grows, and water pressure digs out a new path through the soft earth as the old one becomes clogged. Rivulets are born and die to be reborn again; limpid pools and creeks form amid the bogs and marsh grasses. The Choctaw called these small, slow-moving streams *bayuks*; the settlers who came after them called them bayous.

This swampy delta ecosystem teems with life—not all of it friendly to humans. Venomous cottonmouths and copperheads lurk amid the reeds, and what looks to be a fallen log might be a sleeping alligator. The swarms of mosquitoes are a torment at best and potential carriers for malaria and yellow fever at worst. And while avoiding the native fauna, one also needs to look out for quicksand and pitfalls hidden beneath the verdant undergrowth. But those who are able to overlook these drawbacks will find many treasures in the marshes. Thanks to their waterproof fur, beaver skins can be used to make weather-resistant hats and coats. The bayous teem with crayfish, and the marshes and estuaries are home to many shrimp, turtles, and fish.

But New Orleans has something more important going for it—as real estate professionals say, it has "location, location, location!" New Orleans is the natural port of the Mississippi Valley. Goods produced throughout the Midwest can be shipped down the wide river to the Gulf of Mexico, and from there to markets around the world. In exchange, items from Latin America can be sent up the river to reach consumers in America's heartland. Throughout its reach from New Orleans to the Gulf Coast, the Mississippi is both wide and deep, so large vessels can land there without difficulty. Like many ports, New Orleans is a multicultural city—but its multiculturalism (and its magic) has a pronounced French accent.

La Salle's Expedition

In 1677 French explorer René-Robert Cavelier, Sieur de La Salle, received a commission from King Louis XIV to find a water passage through North America. La Salle had made many sallies throughout New France, including explorations of Lakes Michigan, Huron, Ontario, and Erie. Building upon the expeditions of Louis Jolliet and Father Jacques Marquette, who had mapped the northern reaches of the Mississippi River, he set out to find what he believed to be a short cut to the lucrative markets of China.

After several setbacks (including mutinous soldiers, sunken ships, and burning forts), La Salle finally succeeded in reaching the Mississippi on February 6, 1682. By April 9 he reached the river's mouth. There, near modern-day Venice, Louisiana, he erected on the shore a cross and a column engraved with King Louis' name and claimed the territory of "La Louisiane" for France. Returning to Canada and thence to France, he asked the king for support in colonizing this vast new territory. In July of 1684 he set sail with four vessels and 250 men. But once again La Salle ran into difficulties, this time from pirates and hostile Indians. Instead of French Louisiana, they landed on the coast of the Spanish lands that now make up part of Texas.

By 1687, after multiple failed efforts to locate the Mississippi River, La Salle's remaining men grew tired of his leadership. The supplies were running out and starvation was looming. Bad weather made travel difficult, and of the original crew, only thirty-seven men remained alive. Finally, on March 19, 1687, La Salle was killed in an ambush organized by his surviving troops. Seven troops who remained La Salle loyalists set out for Fort Saint Louis in Illinois, ruled by La Salle's ally Henri de Tonti. When they got there they stayed mum about their leader's untimely demise. They needed to borrow money from Tonti to return to France and were afraid he would not provide a loan if he knew his friend had been killed. It would be several years before anyone outside of La Salle's troops learned of his death and decades before a long-term settlement would be established in La Salle's Louisiana.

Governor Bienville's Crescent City

As the eighteenth century dawned, France was facing its own challenges from England and Spain. Responsibility for the governance of Louisiana rested with administrators residing in Quebec. But while the French royals preferred to concentrate on their holdings in the Caribbean, the Quebecois establishment saw lucrative potential in the furs, timber, and fertile soil of the Mississippi Valley. In 1699 an eighteen-year-old Montreal native named Jean Baptiste le Moyne, Sieur de Bienville, accompanied his older brother Pierre d'Iberville on an expedition down the Mississippi in an effort to reclaim La Salle's discovery and set up a bulwark against Spanish and English encroachments.

Arriving on the coast of modern-day Mississippi, they set up a fort in what is now Biloxi. Continuing on, Iberville and Bienville rediscovered La Salle's river. Journeying upward, they discovered a maypole on which the native Indians had hung fish and game, and they honored that bloody sight by naming the area "Red Stick," or in French, "Bâton Rouge." After returning to Quebec, Iberville left for France, while his younger brother stayed on to take charge of the colony. Not quite twenty-one, Bienville was now in charge of a bedraggled colony of 150 survivors, the rest of the men having perished of malnutrition and disease.

Upon his return from France, Iberville had the seat of the colony transferred to Fort St. Louis de la Mobile along the coast of modern-day Alabama. But then, in 1706, he died of yellow fever during a campaign against British colonies in the Caribbean. With Iberville's death, the colony lost its most influential lobbyist with France. The colonists were already neglected, and with the loss of Iberville, their situation became even more perilous. Yet Bienville rose to the challenge and kept his people alive despite all difficulties.

Concerned about hurricanes, Bienville had moved the St. Louis de la Mobile colony inland to the site of modern-day Mobile. But he soon realized that the Biloxi and Mobile forts were precariously located and vulnerable to attacks from hostile Indians or troops from Britain or Spain. Remembering a crescent bend in the Mississippi that he had seen while traveling with his late brother, Bienville resolved to set up the Louisiana colony's new capital there on the high ground overlooking the river. In 1718 he set off to start construction on La Nouvelle-Orléans in what is today the French Quarter.

> *[T]his wild and desert place, which the reeds and trees do yet almost wholly cover, will be one day, and perhaps that day is not far off, an opulent city, and the metropolis of a great and rich colony. . . . Rome and Paris had not such considerable beginnings, were not built under such happy auspices, and their founders did not find on the Seine and the Tiber the advantages which we have found on the Mississippi, in comparison of which these two rivers are but little brooks.*
>
> FATHER PIERRE FRANÇOIS XAVIER DE CHARLEVOIX, JANUARY 10, 1722[1]

But while the soil around New Orleans was fertile and the climate well suited for growing sugar, cotton, tobacco, and rice, the colony faced a serious labor shortage. To meet those needs, the colonists began importing African slaves. While most of the African captives brought to the

East Coast of America were of Bantu and Kongo origin, two-thirds of the slaves brought to Louisiana before 1730 came from the Senegambian area of West Africa (modern-day Senegal and Gambia). They brought with them the knowledge of rice cultivation and helped make rice the most successful food crop cultivated in French Louisiana. They brought the *bamboula* dance and beat, which has become associated with Mardi Gras (chapter 6). They brought the *nkombo* (okra), which later became an integral part of New Orleans gumbo. They also brought with them Malian melodies and scales, which evolved into the Delta blues (chapter 7), and *gerregerys* (charms), which later generations would call gris-gris bags (chapter 23).

Still, prosperity did not come immediately to the new Crescent City. In 1717 French plutocrat Antoine Crozat, who had purchased a charter to administer the Louisiana Territory, resigned after his efforts to establish trade with the Spaniards in Mexico failed. Then a Scotsman named John Law, financial advisor to the Duc d'Orleans, came up with a scheme to turn the desolate wilderness into a thriving colony. Orleans, as regent to the young Louis XV, was struggling to meet the huge debts that were the legacy of Louis XIV. Law proposed that an entity called the "Mississippi Company" assume the French Crown's debt in return for the charter to operate Louisiana. To finance this, Law proposed selling shares in the company to the French public in exchange for dividends on the Mississippi Company's profits.

At first Law's scheme was wildly successful as he preached of the fortunes to be made in Louisiana's gold mines and fertile land. Speculators across France invested their savings into the Mississippi Company. But alas, there was no gold to be found in Louisiana, and efforts to attract farmers to the colony were undone by (accurate) reports of the heat, humidity, mosquitoes, and disease. The Mississippi Company tried settling "volunteers" from jails and debtors' prisons, along with convicted "ladies of ill repute," but this only served to saddle New Orleans with a reputation for lawlessness and prostitution that persists to this day.

By 1720, when the promised dividends failed to materialize, the "Mississippi Bubble" burst. Thousands of French investors were ruined, and the French currency was destabilized. While the Crown resumed control of the colony, "Louisiana" was a curse word for many French nationals, and the trickle of immigration nearly ceased. A shortage of labor in Louisiana encouraged the importation of slaves, and the shortage of eligible French women led to mixed marriages and a growing mulatto population. These "free people of color" developed a culture of their own, but also had dealings with both white and black society. They helped to establish the three-part social order (black, white, colored) that became a hallmark of New Orleans and encouraged the cultural interchanges that later became New Orleans Voodoo. Then, in the 1760s, the region saw another major influx of French-speaking settlers.

Louisiana Becomes Cajun Country

Seeking relief from the poverty and chaos of a country devastated by thirty years of civil war between Catholics and Huguenots, doughty French farming families took their plows to Canada's Maritime provinces. By 1603 a permanent French fishing and trading post was established at Tadoussac, where the St. Lawrence and Saguenay rivers meet in Quebec. By 1605 a settlement, Port Royal, was established in the Annapolis Basin in what is now called Nova Scotia. Because the region was known as L'Acadie, these French-speaking settlers were called Acadians. But while the French had claimed colonization rights between the fortieth and forty-sixth parallel (modern-day New England and Nova Scotia), the British had other ideas. In 1613 a band of British privateers led by Samuel Argall burned the Port Royal settlement to the ground. The surviving Acadians took to the wilderness, where they survived with help from their friends and trading partners, the Micmac Indians.

Acadia would pass between British and French control several times. For the most part the Acadians did their best to avoid contact with government officials on both sides. The Acadians became a clannish, self-contained society, isolated by the rugged terrain from major centers like Quebec and Boston. Within their settlements, dikes were built with ingenious sluice gates called aboiteaux, which allowed them to reclaim the salt marshes. These marvels of engineering allowed excess freshwater to escape through one-way valves during rainy periods, but closed shut during high tides. Within two to four years the ground was flushed free of excess salt and ready for farming. Cultivation, harvesting, barn-building, and hunting expeditions were also community affairs. This helped to reinforce group unity, as did raids from French and British forces, who were irritated at their scrupulously neutral stance in the ongoing conflicts.

In 1713 the French finally ceded Acadia to the British with the Treaty of Utrecht. Now residing in the newly named Nova Scotia, the Acadians agreed to pledge their loyalty to England, provided they were granted freedom to exercise their Catholic faith, to stay neutral in future Franco-English colonial wars, and to remain a distinct community. After waffling on the issue for several years, Governor Richard Philipps agreed to their terms in 1730—then brought their signatures back to England and claimed they had pledged unconditional obedience to the British Crown. This deception satisfied both parties. Philipps was able to return to England and turn the colony over to a series of lieutenant governors.

For some time life went on as usual for the Acadians. Attempts by the chronically undermanned English garrisons to gain greater control over their subjects were generally resisted by procrastination or argument. They also took advantage of their neutral position and encyclopedic knowledge of the terrain to run a brisk smuggling business with French and British merchants. But after Philipps's death in 1750, Edward Cornwallis, Nova Scotia's new governor, decided to take charge of the situation. Conflicts with soldiers from New France were increasing, and Cornwallis and other British leaders distrusted these French speakers despite their claims of neutrality. He demanded that the Acadians declare unconditional loyalty to King George III. When they resisted, he decided to expel any Acadians who would not submit to British rule and renounce their Catholic faith for Anglicanism.

Between 1755 and 1763 over fourteen thousand Acadians—three-quarters of Nova Scotia's Acadian population—were expelled, their homes burned, and their farms confiscated. Families were separated. Some were packed on ships and distributed from Massachusetts to Georgia;

others were taken to England as prisoners. By 1763 the Seven Years' War (better known to modern Americans as the French and Indian War) was over, thanks to the Treaty of Paris. Under the terms of that agreement, the Acadians were given eighteen months to leave the English colonies.

While the British were unwilling to let them return to Nova Scotia, Louisiana was more accepting. The territory had recently been given to the Spanish under the terms of yet another treaty, the Treaty of Fontainebleau. Spanish Governor Don Antonio de Ulloa hoped the Catholic refugees could provide a buffer zone between the English colonies and New Orleans. Accordingly, he provided them with land along the river and in the delta.

The New Orleans elite saw these Acadians, with their rough speech and clannish ways, as peasants. For their part, the Acadians had little use for the fancy people who ruled New Orleans. Settling in the bayou, they set about reclaiming farmland from the salt marshes using their aboiteaux and put their trapping, fishing, shrimping, and hunting skills to good use in the verdant wild country. The bayou region outside New Orleans became Acadian territory—or, in the Acadian dialect, "Cajun country"— but despite tensions between the Cajuns and the New Orleans Creoles, they would learn a great deal from each other. Acadian traditional healers (*traiteurs* and *traiteuses*) shared herbal and magical secrets with Creole root doctors and cunning folk. Cajun devotion to the saints and the Virgin influenced the religious practices of the Louisiana countryside and propagated the fervent folk Catholicism that would become an integral part of New Orleans spirituality.

Spanish Rule

While Spain accepted rule over the Louisiana Territory, the residents of Louisiana were not so quick to accept Spanish rule. Most still identified as French, and many had left the parts of the province ceded to Britain by the Treaty of Paris so they could hold on to their French identity. When Ulloa arrived in 1766, he brought only ninety soldiers with him. Lacking the military or financial clout to take power, he tried to engage in a joint rule with the current French leaders. Alas, he also tried to take control of commerce in the city and end the longstanding contraband trade between French colonists and English merchants. To stir up the common people, wealthy merchants said that Ulloa was going to ban the sale of Bordeaux and subject the populace "to drinking the wretched wine of Catalonia." Faced with crowds yelling, *"Vive le roi, vive le bon vin de Bordeaux!"* ("Long live the King, long live the great wine of Bordeaux!") Ulloa abdicated and retreated to Cuba.[2]

For nearly a year Louisiana remained independent, until Irish soldier of fortune General Alejandro O'Reilly arrived in August of 1769 with over two thousand Spanish troops. After quickly seizing control of New Orleans, O'Reilly summarily arrested and tried the rebellion's leaders, then offered amnesty and Spanish citizenship to the rest of the city's populace. Although he had five rebels executed, O'Reilly was generally a lenient governor. By 1770 Spanish control was firmly established. O'Reilly turned the reins over to the colonial authorities in Havana and returned to Spain.

For the next thirty years Spain ruled over the Louisiana Territory. After a March 21, 1788, fire destroyed 856 buildings, Governor Esteban Rodriguez Miro rebuilt the city in Spanish style, with courtyards, thick brick walls, arcades, and iron balconies. After another fire in December 1794 claimed another 212 buildings, most of the French Quarter's French architecture was gone. Today only the Ursuline Convent on 1114 Chartres Street survives from the French colonial period.[3] The remainders are largely in a "Creole style" that mixes African, French, Spanish, and Caribbean influences. It is not for nothing that New Orleans has been called "the northernmost city of the Caribbean."

The Spanish also left New Orleans with a "black code" that was considerably more lenient than surrounding areas. In New Orleans slaves could earn money with which to buy their freedom, they could buy and sell things at their own market, and they could circulate in town and attend public dances and meetings with other Africans and with free people of color. In addition to free whites and black slaves, Spanish and French authorities recognized free people of color, many of whom were of mixed blood. While these rights could be taken away at a moment's notice and racism still existed, there was also much more cross-racial interaction than in the British colonies.

But despite their best efforts, Spanish colonial authorities were never able to establish a Spanish presence and culture in Louisiana. The Spanish soldiers and sailors who served there may have enjoyed the brothels and taverns, but few of them put down roots. A contingent of *Isleños* (natives of the Canary Islands) settled in Louisiana between 1778 and 1783, and their descendants still reside in what is today St. Bernard Parish. Still, most New Orleans natives identified more with their French heritage—especially after the refugees from what was once France's wealthiest colony began arriving.

2

FROM SAINT-DOMINGUE TO WASHINGTON
Revolution Comes to Louisiana

It has become one of the great creation myths of New Orleans Voodoo: planters escaping the chaos of the slave uprising in Saint-Domingue came to Louisiana with their slaves in tow. There they re-created their plantation lifestyle—and their slaves re-created the Vodou religion that had developed in the "Pearl of the Antilles." Many scoff at this claim, stating that there is no evidence that Haitian Vodou ever took root in America before the Haitian diaspora of the twentieth century. Others speak of shadowy secret rituals that still persist in the inaccessible bayous, rites practiced only by the oldest families of New Orleans. The truth, as truth is wont to be, is somewhat more complicated.

The Haitian Revolution

The god who created the sun which gives us light, who rouses the waves and rules the storm, though hidden in the clouds, he watches us. He sees all that the white man does. The god of the white man inspires him with crime, but our god calls upon us to do good works. Our god who is good to us orders us to revenge our wrongs. He will direct our arms

*and aid us. Throw away the symbol of the god of the whites
who has so often caused us to weep, and listen to the voice
of liberty, which speaks in the hearts of us all.*

BOUKMAN DUTTY[1]

On a stormy night in August 1791, Boukman Dutty, a self-educated
slave, led some two hundred slaves in the now-legendary Bwa Kaiman
ceremony. While sacrificing a black pig and drinking its blood, he called
out to the attendees to overthrow their white masters or die trying. A
week later slaves working in the cane fields turned their machetes on their
overseers and then on the plantation owners. Within twenty-four hours,
over two thousand whites were dead and over one thousand plantations
were aflame. By November as many as eighty thousand of the colony's
five hundred thousand slaves were in active revolt. Then, in 1793, another
simmering conflict exploded: King Louis XVI was beheaded by revolutionaries who instituted the Reign of Terror in France. By 1794 slavery
had been abolished in all French territories, including Saint-Domingue.

Hoping to return once the various conflicts were settled, many of
the settlers left for the United States. Most stayed along the Atlantic
Seaboard. Louisiana was farther away and under Spanish control, and
since Spain was then at war with France, the Louisiana Spanish were
less than welcoming to an influx of French refugees. They were particularly leery of colonists bringing their slaves. They feared that the
Saint-Domingue planters would bring the insurrection along with their
domestic servants and infect American blacks with seditious ideas.

But although the Spanish government could keep out the slaves,
it could not keep out uprisings inspired by the successful French and
American revolutions. Baron François-Louis Carondelet, who took
the governor's office in 1791, expelled sixty-eight suspected Jacobins
(French revolutionaries), demanded a loyalty oath to Spain, and called
on English-speaking soldiers from Natchez—Tories who had fled the
American Revolution and pledged loyalty to Spain—to uphold order.
But despite this, tensions between French and Spanish speakers continued. Seriously outnumbered, the Spanish rulers lived as virtual prisoners

in their fortresses. By October 1, 1800, under pressure from Napoleon and from their restive subjects, the Spanish returned the Louisiana Territory to France, but the trade was kept secret for some time. Louisiana remained under Spanish control as France and the United States negotiated the terms of yet another exchange.

Occupied with the fighting in Saint-Domingue, and trying to keep the revolution from spreading to the colonies on Martinique and Guadeloupe, Napoleon had few resources to spare for the New World colonies. But the Americans needed access to the Mississippi and the Port of New Orleans in order to supply their new western territories in Kentucky and Ohio. Despite opposition on both sides, the Jefferson administration and the French government were able to work out the terms of a transfer. On December 13, 1803, France sold the Louisiana Territory for $15 million, and the young United States doubled in size.

Both the Francophone and growing Anglophone population of the territories welcomed this new development. The old French families welcomed the end of Spanish rule, and the Americans celebrated the triumphant growth of their nation. Both saw it as a great business opportunity. Both French and Spanish rulers had limited and heavily taxed trade between New Orleans and American merchants (although neither had much success in stamping out smuggling and black market transactions). Under American rule, the citizens of New Orleans expected an economic boom—and they were not disappointed. A city that had languished under the benign neglect of its former rulers would become an important strategic location in the development of the American West.

Saint-Domingue Comes to New Orleans

Many of the Domingans (refugees from Saint-Domingue, now the Free Black Republic of Haiti) had traveled to nearby Cuba, and between 1701 and 1800 some thirty thousand arrived in that Spanish colony.[2] After the destruction of Saint-Domingue's plantations, Cuba's sugar industry grew by leaps and bounds. Much of the new sugar industry was staffed by exiles from Saint-Domingue and worked by African slaves. Other Domingans lent their expertise to building up Cuba's coffee industry. By 1793, two years after the first refugees arrived, coffee production had increased tenfold. In 1804 alone Domingans established fifty-six coffee plantations and planted more than five hundred thousand coffee bushes.[3] Overnight, Cuba changed from a sleepy settlement of small towns and cattle farms into a land of massive plantations.

Then, in February 1808, Napoleon turned on his ally Spain. On the third of May, 1808, the French army shot hundreds of unarmed Madrid civilians in retaliation for the previous day's uprising. Saint-Domingue's refugees were suddenly personae non gratae in Spanish Cuba. Orders were issued expelling all French subjects and confiscating their property. Cast out from their new home, many of these once-again refugees found their way to Louisiana. Between 1809 and 1810, 9,059 Domingans arrived in New Orleans from Cuba: 2,731 whites, 3,226 slaves, and 3,102 "free people of color."[4]

As more and more English-speaking natives moved "uptown," or above Canal Street, downtown New Orleans became known as the "French Quarter." While Francophone New Orleans welcomed Anglophone money, they considered them barbarians. Many of the Anglophone residents came on the flatboats that traveled downriver to the port, and they retained many of the rough-hewn manners that were common to those living on the wild American frontier. After selling their goods, they frequently spent much of their income in the city's bars and brothels. More threatening to the old aristocracy were the English-speaking investors and speculators who came to New Orleans hoping to profit from its booming economy—and who were often wealthier than the city's old aristocrats.

While the Domingan refugees arrived with little money, they helped to preserve the city's French character in the face of Anglo-American influence. Although they lacked capital (at least upon arrival), they had a degree of sophistication that was frequently lacking in what was still a backwater city. Many of the once-wealthy Domingans, both white and colored, had been educated in Paris and brought a new intellectualism to New Orleans. Many others were skilled craftspeople who would become important furniture makers, carpenters, and artisans.

While most of the new Anglophone residents were Protestants, Francophone New Orleans was staunchly Catholic. Granted, they were not known for their piety or their observance of the commandments. Catholicism, however, served as yet another way to distinguish them from the uptown newcomers. Their floridly decorated churches and larger-than-life statues would play an important role in creating the aesthetic of New Orleans Voodoo. While most Southern and African American folk magic draws from Protestantism, New Orleans Voodoo, like Haitian Vodou, has a strong Catholic influence. Whether the Domingans brought Vodou with them to New Orleans is debatable, but there is no question that they helped to preserve New Orleans Catholicism.

In Saint-Domingue, marriages were uncommon. Unmarried white women were rare in Saint-Domingue, and whites were legally forbidden to marry people of color. Most white colonists hoped to someday return to France and use their newfound wealth to marry into a higher social class. As a result, concubinage was widespread. Attractive women of color would seek the attentions of wealthy planters in long-term *plaçage* relationships or short-term sexual affairs. This would be replayed in New Orleans. At a time when miscegenation was looked upon with horror in most of the United States, it was not uncommon for white men to have open relationships with mulatto mistresses.

These meetings were encouraged at quadroon balls, similar to today's debutante affairs. There attractive young ladies of color could meet potential white "protectors." Should there be a mutual attraction, the gentleman could speak with the girl's parents to make suitable arrangements. The young lady was typically provided with a home of her own, along with suitable furnishings and servants. Any children of the union would be provided for and educated in France or in local convent schools. These unions might end upon the man's marriage to a white woman or last through the lifetimes of both parties.

The residents of Saint-Domingue were noted for their superstitious proclivities and their adherence to any interesting fad that came their way. Mesmerism, the science of "animal magnetism" founded by visionary physician Franz Anton Mesmer, had been wildly popular in the pre-revolutionary colony. Upper-class residents had flocked to see the healing exhibitions of Count Antoine-Hyacinthe-Anne de Puységur, a student of Dr. Mesmer and a great showman. (Their interest had spread to the slaves. In May 1786 an edict prohibited the practice of magnetism by any nonwhite Saint-Domingue resident, because it "is easy to abuse and is apt for the tricks of jugglers who are common among the blacks and respected by them.")[5]

The Domingans were also known for their love of Freemasonry. By some accounts as many as one out of three French colonists in Saint-Domingue were active Freemasons. The Cercle des Philadelphes, a Masonic society dedicated to developing the arts and sciences, claimed many of Saint-Domingue's most prominent white residents as members, as well as foreign notables like Benjamin Franklin. Many of the wealthy affranchis (free blacks) were also Masons. The oldest lodge in New Orleans, Perfect Union No. 1, was founded as "Parfaite Union" by Laurant Sigur and thirteen other Masons who had fled from Saint-Domingue.

Finally, Domingan refugees also contributed to the city's racial mixture. By 1809, 63 percent of the population of New Orleans had a greater or lesser percentage of African ancestry. The multiracial nature also helped to redefine the word *Creole*. Hitherto it had been used primarily to describe New Orleans natives who could trace their ancestry to France. Many of the free people of Saint-Domingue also had African ancestry, and in time, *Creole* would come to describe New Orleans' mixed-race people of color. Light-skinned blacks whose families came from the city called themselves Creole to distinguish themselves from the "colored" blacks. This three-caste society, which had developed in New Orleans during the years of French and Spanish rule, was upheld by Domingan refugees on all sides of the color line.

As had been the case in Saint-Domingue, certain trades were almost exclusively the province of free people of color. In New Orleans most mechanics, carpenters, shoemakers, barbers, and tailors were free blacks. Capitalizing on knowledge acquired in Saint-Domingue, the wealthy cigar manufacturers George Alcées and his uncle Lucien "Lolo" Mansion employed as many as two hundred workers in their factories. Many took up residence in the Faubourg Marigny (Marigny suburb), a tony neighborhood that even today is noted for its "Creole cottages." And free black Domingans would play an important role in one of the most famous battles of the War of 1812.

The Battle of New Orleans

By 1814 things were looking grim for the fledgling United States. Now that Napoleon had been defeated at Waterloo, the British were able to focus on their American campaign. In August British troops set the nation's capital aflame. Meanwhile, some ten thousand veterans from Jamaica set their sights on the Crescent City. Their leader, Sir Edward Michael Pakenham, was a much-decorated military man and brother-in-law to the Duke of Wellington. He hoped to claim New Orleans and take control of the Mississippi River trade.

For protection, the citizens of southern Louisiana looked to Major General Andrew Jackson, known as Old Hickory. Jackson had a reputation for toughness, courage, and a deep and abiding hatred of the British. While Jackson was a prisoner of war during the American Revolution, a British officer ordered him to shine his boots. The fifteen-year-old Jackson refused. In retaliation the officer slashed him across the face and hands with his sword. Since that time Jackson had borne deep scars and a deeper grudge; indeed, the citizens of New Orleans worried that if worse came to worst he would burn their city down rather than surrender.

On December 23, 1814, he was informed that the British army had discovered an unguarded waterway and set up camp an easy day's march from New Orleans. Unruffled, Old Hickory launched a nighttime surprise attack, gaining valuable time for his outgunned and outnumbered American forces. Jangled by their opponent's valor, the British delayed advancing to New Orleans until they could bring in all their troops. But while they waited, Jackson's troops built a fortified mud rampart between the Mississippi River and a cypress swamp. There he dug in with his forces—a motley crew that combined regular U.S. Army units with frontierspeople, Choctaw Indians, buccaneers led by the legendary

French pirate Jean Lafitte, and a sizeable contingent of free blacks who had fought for the French in Saint-Domingue.

Pakenham made a number of sorties against the fortified line in late December, but Old Hickory's troops stood their ground. On January 8, under cover of a thick morning fog, the British troops began an advance toward the fortifications and on to New Orleans. But they had not counted on the marksmanship of the American troops—nor had they expected the fog to lift early. Behind their mud and cotton-bale barricades, Jackson's soldiers fired shot after shot at the advancing British soldiers. By the end of the battle, the British had been decisively routed, with 291 British troops dead (including General Pakenham), 1,262 wounded, and 484 captured or missing. The American losses totaled 13 dead, 39 wounded, and 19 missing. New Orleans and the Louisiana Territory had been saved—and Andrew Jackson would use his newfound popularity as a war hero to become a senator and later the seventh president of the United States.

New Orleans Voodoo, Haitian Vodou?

Many of the elements found in Haitian Vodou today are not seen in New Orleans. This, however, may be misleading. After two centuries, both traditions have been transformed by the vicissitudes of history. The symbols that we have come to associate with Haitian Vodou—the beaded *asson* rattle of the priesthood, the sequined *dwapo lwa* (lwa flags), the *regleman* of the rada rite—gained popularity in the 1920s as Haiti's increasing urbanization pulled many peasants away from their ancestral farms and religious practices. We would not expect to find them in traditional New Orleans, and indeed we do not see them until the revival and reinvention of New Orleans Voodoo in the latter half of the twentieth century.

The original Haitian Vodou was almost exclusively practiced by the slaves—and there were few slaves brought to America from Saint-Domingue. The Haitian Revolution struck terror into the hearts of slaveholders across the Americas. Few countries would welcome an influx of rebellious slaves to their shores. Laws were passed prohibiting the importation of blacks from the French Antilles long before the troubles started, since Saint-Domingue's slaves had a reputation for being unmanageable and seditious. (Given the brutality of the colony's plantation system—most Africans died of malnutrition and overwork within a few years of landing on the island—it is little wonder that they were inclined to rebel.)

After the revolution, these concerns became a panic. Writing in 1793, one concerned citizen said, "The NEGROES have become very insolent, in so much that the citizens are alarmed and the militia keep a constant guard. It is said that the St. Domingo negroes have sown these seeds of revolt, and that a magazine has been attempted to be broken open."[6] That same year Thomas Jefferson warned the governor of South Carolina of two Saint-Domingue free blacks who were allegedly headed to Charleston "with a design to excite an insurrection among the negroes."[7]

A few Domingans managed to bring some of their slaves with them, but they were in the minority. Whereas slaves vastly outnumbered affranchis and whites alike in Saint-Domingue, the majority of Domingans in America were free. Their ties to the slave religion and revolutionary practices were more tenuous, underplayed by socially insecure newly liberated and wealthy free blacks alike. In New Orleans, as in contemporary Haiti, Vodou was a folk religion; admitting your practice was to mark yourself a member of the folk, not the educated elite.

Some Vodouisants definitely made their way from Saint-Domingue. Later in the book, tantalizing traces of their practices are described. But most slaves in New Orleans, like the majority of slaves in the United States, were brought to the city by Anglophone masters and traced their descent from the Kongo (also known as "Congo") regions of central and southern Africa. Kongo practices form the major African influence on both Hoodoo (African American folk magic) and New Orleans Voodoo. The veneration of the dead, mojo hands, and homage to "Li Grand Zombi," among other traditions, can all be traced to the Kongo. (And of course we have the famous clearing in the Tremé neighborhood where slaves and free blacks would gather on Sundays to sell their wares and dance, Congo Square!) The Dahomey traditions that informed Haitian Vodou and the Yoruba practices that would later become popular in Cuba played a less prominent role in traditional New Orleans customs.

While the Domingans did not bring Haitian Vodou with them, they did help create the conditions in which New Orleans Voodoo was born. They provided a French-speaking and Catholic bulwark against the flood of Anglophone Protestants. This helped to ensure that many folk practices in the city would have a Catholic flavor, as opposed to the Protestant-inspired Hoodoo found in most of the South. And they brought with them mores in which interaction between the races was far more common than in the more rigidly segregated Anglophone regions. All this was instrumental in forming the culture that gave us the folk customs of New Orleans—a culture that would come under attack as Louisiana faced American prejudices.

3

KING COTTON, LADY LIBERTY, AND JIM CROW

As American settlers continued moving westward, the Mississippi became the lifeline by which goods were transported. By 1840 New Orleans challenged New York as the country's leading exporter. What had been a tiny backwater town at the edge of a barely charted frontier was now the nation's fourth largest city—and one of the biggest party towns in the world—thanks to a few major inventions that changed the face of New Orleans, and the United States.

Steamboats and Cotton Gins

At first products were shipped on flatboats, glorified rafts that were generally broken up for lumber once they reached their destination. Traveling upriver involved pushing your craft with poles, pulling on overhanging bushes and trees ("bushwhacking"), or walking along the shore while dragging the boat by rope. This was backbreaking labor, and the people who plied this trade were said to be "half alligator and half horse."

Then in 1812 the first steam-powered boat—appropriately named the New Orleans—reached the Crescent City. Steamboats were faster than flatboats, especially when traveling upstream. Traveling upriver, a flatboat might make fifteen miles in a day under ideal conditions; the trip between New Orleans and St. Louis would typically take three months or more. By the 1830s steamboats were making the same journey in twelve to fourteen days. They were also relatively inexpensive. Half the steamboats on the Mississippi were owned by groups of one to four men and funded with local capital. By 1820 sixty-nine steamboats traversed the Mississippi; between 1820 and 1860 that number increased a hundredfold.[1]

New Orleans profited from another invention as well. In 1794 Eli Whitney perfected a cotton engine (or cotton gin, for short) that separated cotton fibers and seeds. What had once been an arduous manual process was now mechanized. The price of cotton fabric dropped precipitously, and the demand for raw cotton grew apace. Throughout the southern United States, cotton farming became a major industry, and the demand for labor resulted in a corresponding boom in the slave industry. In 1790 approximately 650,000 slaves inhabited the Southern states; by 1850 there were 3.2 million, 1.8 million of whom were laboring on cotton plantations.[2]

The hands are required to be in the cotton field as soon as it is light in the morning, and, with the exception of ten or fifteen minutes, which is given them at noon to swallow their allowance of cold bacon, they are not permitted to be a moment idle until it is too dark to see, and when the moon is full, they often times labor till the middle of the night. They do not dare to stop even at dinner time, nor return to the quarters, however late it be, until the order to halt is given by the driver.

The day's work over in the field, the baskets are "toted," or in other words, carried to the gin-house, where the cotton is weighed. No matter how fatigued and weary he may be—no matter how much he longs for sleep and rest—a slave never approaches the gin-house with his basket of cotton but with fear. If it falls short in weight—if he has not performed the full task appointed him, he knows that he must suffer. And if he has exceeded it by ten or twenty pounds, in all probability his master will measure the next

day's task accordingly. So, whether he has too little or too
much, his approach to the gin-house is always with fear
and trembling. Most frequently they have too little, and
therefore it is they are not anxious to leave the field. After
weighing, follow the whippings.

SOLOMON NORTHRUP, FORMER SLAVE (1853)[3]

During the nineteenth century, 75 percent of the world's cotton supply was produced in the southern United States—and most of it traveled
through the Port of New Orleans. Two hundred and fifty thousand acres
of sugar were planted in southern Louisiana by Saint-Domingue refugees,
along with comparable acreages of rice. The city also profited from the
slave trade: its slave market was the largest in the South. In 1850 twenty-
five major slave depots were within a half mile of the St. Charles Hotel,
where slaves could be bought and sold.

Along with those unfortunates who came to New Orleans in chains
were those who arrived to take advantage of its booming economy.
Between 1820 and 1860 over 550,000 immigrants came to New Orleans,
and by 1850 about one-quarter of Louisiana's and the majority of New
Orleans' white population was foreign-born. New Orleans was home
to sizeable communities of Germans, Spaniards and Spanish Creoles,
Italians, and Jews. Still other immigrants saw New Orleans as a gateway
to the burgeoning West. Traveling on a steamboat was cheaper and far
more comfortable than the arduous overland routes from New York. As
they headed out for their final destination, they often crossed paths with
an ever-growing number of tourists.

Feasting and Carousing in the Crescent City

For the young men of sleepy frontier villages or cotton towns, a trip to
New Orleans was often a rite of passage. Its music halls, gambling dens,
taverns, and whorehouses offered excitement and danger. "The Swamp,"
an area of cheap rooming houses and saloons located on Tchoupitoulas
Street, was notorious for its ladies of ill repute, but the city offered

brothels to fit every budget. While technically illegal, the police recognized the profits to be made from the world's oldest profession—and many of the city's rulers were on a first-name basis with the madams who operated the city's many fancy houses.

While taverns in other parts of Louisiana faced numerous laws forbidding sales to Indians, slaves, and soldiers, New Orleans was a free-for-all zone where any thirsty traveler could wet his whistle. In the early 1800s, Creole apothecary Antoine Peychaud distilled aromatic bitters from an old family recipe and served them with brandy, water, and sugar for ailing clients. Other tavernkeepers began using Peychaud's Bitters in what is arguably the first mixed drink on record, the Sazerac. Barkeeping also provided an income for many of the city's widows and enterprising women, allowing them an unprecedented degree of social and economic freedom for the time.

Those who were more culturally inclined might explore the Crescent City's many artistic offerings. The theater scene in New Orleans featured a number of venues, including what many considered the finest theater in America, the St. Charles. Built in 1835, the St. Charles could seat five thousand. Ten Corinthian columns decorated its exterior, along with statues of Apollo and the seven muses. Inside was a massive chandelier illuminated by 176 gas jets, 26 dressing rooms, and 4 tiers of boxes.[4] (Alas, the St. Charles burned to the ground in 1842 and was rebuilt in a more modest fashion. In 1965 it was torn down altogether to make way for a parking lot.) And thanks largely to thespians from Saint-Domingue, including some quadroon actresses noted for their beauty and talent, a viable French theater continued alongside English productions.

Actors who couldn't find work in the Crescent City might have better luck on the various showboats that stopped at New Orleans. River communities that were too small to support a resident theater company could see melodramas and minstrel shows when the showboat docked in their town. While many of these were modest craft run by acting families, some were ornate gilded palaces with massive stages and casinos. The largest showboat, the Floating Circus Parade, could seat over three thousand people and featured animal acts and an equestrian show.

New Orleans also became one of America's major opera centers in the nineteenth century, premiering more than four hundred operas. But performances in the Crescent City were frequently marked by clashes between high and low culture. Drinking, gambling, and prostitution were frequently found in the cheaper gallery section, and the audience was wont to yell out requests. During an 1835 performance of *The Marriage of Figaro,* the audience grew tired of Mozart's old-fashioned music. The lead soprano was compelled to sing such popular numbers as "The Light Guitar," "Come Prithee Kneel to Me," and "Bright Eyes" to avoid a riot.

And since travelers cannot live by drink alone, New Orleans also offered fine dining. African okra, Native American filé (powdered sassafras leaves), and French roux (flour browned in fat) all were used to thicken one of the city's signature dishes, gumbo. In 1840 Antoine Alciatore opened his pension and restaurant, Antoine's. Later his descendants would go on to create signature dishes like Oysters Rockefeller and Pompano en Papillote (pompano cooked in a parchment sack with a creamy sauce). Hardworking Sicilian immigrants laboring on the docks would often feast on muffalettas, thick ham sandwiches garnished with liberal helpings of olive relish. Those with a sweet tooth might enjoy pralines, candies made with butter, brown sugar, and pecans, or beignets, a deep-fried pastry sprinkled with powdered sugar and served with coffee and chicory.

The American frontier was a lawless place, but also a devoutly religious one. Camp meetings and revivals vied with the showboats as community entertainment. Frontier preachers railed against the evils of drinking, whoring, gambling, and dancing—all of which were prominent New Orleans attractions. The frontier was also an area that feared immigrants, foreigners, and Catholics (this was the era of the militantly anti-Papist Know-Nothing party). But, as is often the case, all this strident moralizing only served to increase the Crescent City's allure.

New Orleans became the epitome of foreign decadence and moral decay, a place where anything could be had at a price and where swarthy people whispered charms and spells in strange tongues. The legends of Voodoo practices spread because they seemed plausible: What could one expect from a city of foreign idolaters? These legends had more than a little basis in fact. By the 1840s John "Doctor John" Montaigne (chapter 10) and Marie Laveau (chapter 14), among others, had become prominent New Orleans citizens, thanks to their alleged magical abilities. And while many sought to enjoy the pleasures of New Orleans, still others sought to clean up this hive of pestilence, prostitution, and Papism.

The Civil War: New Orleans under Occupation

When the Civil War broke out, a number of the prominent free blacks of New Orleans volunteered for military service in the new Confederate government. While at first Confederate authorities praised their patriotism, they soon decided that a regiment of black troops would give the lie to slavers' assertions that blacks were inherently inferior to whites. Accordingly, they rejected the Louisiana Native Guards.

Then, on April 26, 1862, combined U.S. Army and Navy forces captured New Orleans. Short on reinforcements, Major General Benjamin Franklin Butler decided to raise troops among local black men. Stung by their earlier rejection, the Louisiana Native Guards answered Butler's call. On September 27, 1862, they became the first black regiment in the Union Army.

During the war, the Native Guards fought at Port Hudson, Mansura, and Mobile. They also guarded prisoners, built fortifications, and contributed to the Union efforts despite continued prejudice from white officers. Their efforts paved the way for other black soldiers, and by 1865 some 180,000 blacks—over 20 percent of the adult male black population under forty-five—had served in the Union Army.[5]

It was astounding that this negro brigade would assault such a place. But they came on in splendid form, bayonets glistening like silver in the bright June sun, uniforms spick and clean, and the Commanding Officers riding close behind them. When they got within 150 yards of the front of this bluff, every cannon, heavy and light, double shotted, and every rifle turned loose on them. They stopped, and at once fell to pieces in this terrific fusillade playing havoc and death among them. They stampeded, and every man, not on the ground, took to his heels for the woods, the guns meanwhile playing on them, and, after the ones fortunate enough to escape reached the heavy timber, the 100 heavy cannon continued to pour a volcano of shot and shell into the timber producing a terribly crashing noise. About 500 or 600 of the Negro Federals were left dead and wounded on the ground which they traversed.

THOMAS R. MYERS, CONFEDERATE INFANTRYMAN,
RECALLING THE BATTLE OF PORT HUDSON[6]

But while Butler had his admirers among the free blacks of New Orleans, he and his troops faced vituperative abuse from patriotic Confederate women. Their resistance ranged from derisive comments and loud renditions of Confederate songs to spitting on passing soldiers or emptying chamber pots on their heads. Finally Butler issued General Order No. 28, which proclaimed,

As the officers and soldiers of the United States have been subjected to repeated insults from the women (calling themselves ladies) of New Orleans, in return for the most scrupulous noninterference and courtesy on our part, it is ordered that hereafter when any female shall, by word, gesture, or movement, insult or show contempt for any officer or soldier of the United States, she shall be regarded and held liable to be treated as a woman of the town plying her avocation.[7]

The "Woman's Order" provoked criticism throughout the Confederacy and in Europe from people who considered Butler's proclamation an unpardonable affront to the good women of New Orleans. Jefferson Davis, president of the Confederacy, issued a proclamation branding Butler and his officers outlaws who would be hanged if captured. But Butler's order achieved its desired effect: the insults largely stopped when high-born women learned they would be treated as common whores should they demean Union soldiers. Throughout his eight-month term, Butler distinguished himself in his efforts to maintain order in a city that was unruly even under friendly governments. He also distinguished himself in his efforts to enrich himself and his cronies on the spoils of war. New Orleans locals called him "Spoons," since they said if he visited their home he was sure to steal their silverware.

Reconstruction and Its Aftermath

Since Louisiana had been under Union control for much of the Civil War, it was one of the first regions to experience Reconstruction. It was also a hotbed of Confederate sympathy. New Orleans had not suffered the fate of Atlanta or other cities burned during Sherman's March, nor did it experience the privation and suffering that marked the Confederacy's latter years. Sheltered from the worst of the war, many white New Orleanians still expected a Southern victory and a return to what they saw as the natural order of things—meaning a world where whites ruled and blacks served.

The free (and newly freed) black and colored population of New Orleans fought vigorously for their rights. The *New Orleans Tribune,* founded in 1864 by three free black men whose families came from Saint-Domingue, was a tireless critic of the federal government and its refusal to defend the rights of black citizens. Its front page was printed in the French spoken by New Orleans Creoles and free blacks, with the reverse side printed in English, which was more commonly read and spoken by freed slaves. The Convention of Colored Men in January 1865 called for commanding military authority to integrate streetcars and pressed for voting rights for all black men.

Alas, their efforts proved to be in vain. On July 30, 1866, Louisiana's Radical Republicans, a group that favored civil rights and black enfranchisement, met at the Mechanics Institute, an educational faculty for technical workers. Outside was a large, enthusiastic crowd of black men, women, and children. They were attacked by a mob of white citizens, aided by New Orleans police and firefighters. By the time federal troops arrived, the mayhem had run its course. Official figures listed thirty-seven persons (thirty-four black and three white) killed and 146 wounded. Contemporary witnesses believed the numbers to be much higher.[8] As the Andrew Johnson administration took charge after Lincoln's assassination, it became increasingly clear that emancipation did not mean equal rights. A Southerner himself, Johnson showed far more sympathy for ex-Confederates than ex-slaves and routinely vetoed efforts by the Republican-led Congress to give blacks the vote or protect them from Black Codes, which imposed restrictions on freed slaves and people of color.

> *Everyone would, and must admit, that the white race was superior to the black, and that while we ought to do our best to bring them up to our present level, that, in doing so, we should, at the same time raise our own intellectual status so that the relative position of the two races would be the same.*
>
> ANDREW JOHNSON TO BENJAMIN B. FRENCH,
> FEBRUARY 8, 1866[9]

White gangs roamed the streets of New Orleans, intimidating blacks and breaking up Republican meetings. Commanding General Lovell Rousseau, a friend of President Johnson, urged blacks to stay away from the polls for their own protection and crowed that the "ascendance of the negro in this state is approaching its end."[10] In 1874, 3,500 members of the Metropolitan Police Force of New Orleans fought a pitched battle with 5,000 members of the White League, a paramilitary group made up of well-armed Confederate veterans. For three days they occupied the State House and New Orleans City Hall until federal reinforcements arrived.

But there were triumphs alongside these tragedies. In 1874 the manager of the Academy of Music was fined $1,000 for ejecting Peter Joseph from his seat after he had purchased a ticket, and C. S. Sauvinet was awarded $1,000 in damages after a saloon keeper refused to sell him a drink. On June 13, 1874, local newspaper the *Louisianan* asserted that

New Orleans' "Catholicity of spirit . . . has expressed itself by the recognition in our midst of the civil and public rights of the colored race more fully than has been the case in any other Southern city."[11]

Then, in 1877, Reconstruction ended. Across the South, various Jim Crow laws were enacted to keep blacks and whites separate. While segregation existed in Louisiana, it was not so pervasive, far-reaching, or consistently applied as in other Southern states. Many blacks came to New Orleans to find a freedom they could never achieve in the more rigidly segregated cities of the American South. Some took up residence in the city. Others came as tourists to enjoy the food and music—and to seek spiritual advice from the city's many rootworkers in the black neighborhood of Algiers (chapter 10). This helped to establish a thriving spiritual trade that would later become one of New Orleans' most popular and profitable industries. But the forces that sought white supremacy throughout the nation were still active, as an octoroon shoemaker named Homer Plessy would discover.

Plessy v. Ferguson

In 1890 Louisiana's Act 111 required separate accommodations for white and black railway passengers, although it insisted that the accommodations must be kept equal. On June 7, 1892, Homer Plessy was jailed for sitting in the "White" car of the East Louisiana Railroad. Although Plessy was only one-eighths black and seven-eighths white, he was expected to sit in the "Colored" car. Unbeknownst to the railroad officials, Plessy was carrying out an act of civil disobedience on behalf of the New Orleans Comité des Citoyens, a group of educated free people of color. They knew the light-skinned Plessy could purchase a first-class ticket without difficulty. Once on the car, he announced his African ancestry in the hopes of challenging the Separate Car Act in court.

When he was found guilty of violating the act, he challenged the case in *Homer Adolph Plessy v. The State of Louisiana,* arguing that the Separate Car Act violated the Thirteenth and Fourteenth Amendments to the Constitution. Judge John Howard Ferguson, who had earlier ruled separate cars unconstitutional on trains that crossed state lines, decided that the state had the right to regulate rail companies that operated only within Louisiana and found Plessy guilty for refusing to leave the white car.

Plessy appealed to the Supreme Court of Louisiana, which upheld Ferguson's decision. Then, in 1896, the Supreme Court of the United States heard Plessy's case and found him guilty once again. The doctrine of "separate but equal" was now enshrined as law, and segregation became endemic south of the Mason-Dixon Line. While blacks and whites still mingled at many New Orleans taverns and entertainment houses, there was a growing push for "freedman's boxes" and "Negro seats." Integrated neighborhoods were separated, by law and sometimes by racist mobs, into "white" and "black" areas. Public schooling for black students was inadequate at best and nonexistent at worst. As opportunities diminished—and as the railroads replaced the Mississippi steamboats—New Orleans became increasingly poor and run-down. Yet amidst its crumbling grandeur some old-timers still held on to tradition as newcomers arrived to search for its mysteries.

4

THE (RE)CREATION OF "NEW ORLEANS VOODOO"

As the twentieth century dawned, New Orleans had seen better days. The railways had supplanted the Mississippi River as the primary mode of transport to Middle American towns and cities. The port where most of America's cotton was shipped to the world felt the effects of the boll weevil infestation of the 1920s, and as the prominence of cotton declined, so too did the American trade. Struggling amid the prosperity of the Roaring Twenties, the Crescent City was then clobbered by the Great Depression.

For a time it looked as if Louisiana might come back with the rise of Huey Long, a larger-than-life radical with a magnetic speaking ability and a knack for down-and-dirty political infighting. Elected governor of Louisiana in 1928, Long was then elected to the Senate in 1932. But his effectiveness did not always match his talent for oratory, and his penchant for grandstanding alienated many potential allies. In 1935 the man the people called the Kingfish (after a character in his favorite radio comedy, *Amos and Andy*) was gunned down, leaving behind big dreams and even bigger problems. New Orleans sank further into economic despair; crime rates increased and opportunities declined. To escape this endless cycle of poverty and violence, many of the city's residents joined the exodus north and west, making their way to California, Chicago, or other communities in search of a better life.

Only the entertainment and tourist industries remained strong. For those businesses the New Orleans brand was still profitable, and the city's culture remained chic despite her reduced circumstances. Crawfish, zydeco, and *"Laissez les bon temps rouler!"* ("Let the good times roll!") became marketing symbols for entertainment and easy living—and old stories of ghosts, rituals, and curses were a great way to create atmosphere and bring in much-needed income. The stage was set for New Orleans Voodoo to attain national prominence. Once it had been seen as a potential tool in a slave uprising; now it became the focus of a promotional campaign. But while this may have inspired some charlatans, it also cast a light on the folk practices of New Orleans and attracted the attention of some serious scholars.

Zora Neale Hurston

The Harlem Renaissance had no shortage of larger-than-life characters, but few were as charismatic or flamboyant as Zora Neale Hurston. Her irreverent wit and penchant for colorful storytelling soon made her a leading figure among New York's black intellectuals and writers—or as she coined her circle, the "niggerati." (This distinguished them from the solemn, sometimes pompous reformers she scorned as "Negrotarians" and members of "the sobbing school of Negrohood.")

But her easy glibness belied her Herculean efforts to better herself. After the death of her beloved mother in 1904 and her father's subsequent remarriage, thirteen-year-old Hurston was shuffled among various relatives. While her mother had encouraged her to get an education, her father saw little reason for a poor black girl to go to school. Cast out into a cold world, Hurston supported herself through various menial jobs. Finally, in 1917, Hurston was able to register in the Baltimore public schools by claiming she was sixteen rather than twenty-six. This audacious gamble paid off. Within a year Hurston had earned her high school diploma. Soon after this she began studies at Howard University, and later she received a bachelor's degree from Barnard College, where she worked with legendary anthropologist Franz Boas.

Most scholars of the time took the innate superiority of European culture and the white race for granted. Boas, by contrast, declared that "The old idea of absolute stability of human types must . . . be given up, and with it the belief of the hereditary superiority of certain types over others."[1] He encouraged Hurston to apply her considerable talents to studying African American folk culture. With his help, she was able to secure grants for fieldwork in Florida and Louisiana. Later she would turn this work into *Mules and Men,* a book that described African American folk customs throughout the deep South, paying particular attention to New Orleans. She wrote:

> New Orleans is now and has ever been the hoodoo capital of America. Great names in rites that vie with those of Hayti in deeds that keep alive the powers of Africa. Hoodoo, or Voodoo, as pronounced by the whites, is burning with flame in America with all the intensity of a suppressed religion. It has its thousands of secret adherents. It adapts itself like Christianity to its locale, reclaiming some of its borrowed characteristics to itself, such as fire-worship as signified in the Christian Church by the altar and the candles. And the belief in the power of water to sanctify as in baptism. Belief in magic is older than writing. So nobody knows how it started.[2]

Hurston would return to black folk customs in other works. Her 1928 trip to Haiti inspired her to write a sympathetic study of Vodou, *Tell My Horse* (1937). In her 1934 *Jonah's Gourd Vine,* Deacon Harris says of Moses, "He's de greatest hoodoo man dat god ever made. He went 'way from Pharaoh's palace and stayed in de desert nigh to forty years and learnt how tuh call god by all his secret names and dat's how he got all dat power."[3] Her 1939 *Moses, Man of the Mountain* took this idea and ran with it, presenting Moses as a Hoodoo man leading his black Israelites to the promised land.

But her writings did not sit well with many in the black establishment.

Following activist W. E. B. duBois, many black leaders wished to focus on the "talented tenth" within the community. By presenting examples of educated, intelligent, and successful blacks, they hoped to counter the stereotypes of the lazy, ignorant, and superstitious "darky." Hurston, by contrast, focused on life among the black poor; what's more, she often wrote in black dialect. Richard Wright, the author of *Native Son,* accused Hurston of using a "minstrel technique" that pandered to "a white audience whose chauvinistic tastes she knows how to satisfy."[4]

To add insult to injury, Hurston frequently expressed skepticism about integration and assimilation. Inspired by her early childhood in the all-black community of Eatonville, Florida, she feared that integration would threaten black cultural traditions. In August 1955 she criticized *Brown v. Board of Education* in a letter to the *Orlando Sentinel.* Instead of forcing black students to go to white schools amid violent resistance, she advocated improving the quality of education in segregated black schools. This letter shocked many black leaders—and many white liberals. Black scholars criticized her for pandering to white audiences, while many white readers were uncomfortable with her ingratitude for their efforts to better the lot of oppressed Negroes.

In the face of this controversy, Hurston's writing became increasingly unfashionable. As in the hardscrabble days of her youth, she was again forced to support herself as a maid. After an October 1959 stroke she was moved to the St. Lucie County Welfare Home, where she died the following January. Buried in an unmarked grave, Hurston was forgotten for over a decade as her books and stories went out of print. Then a young black writer named Alice Walker chanced upon her work and found a kindred spirit.

In 1973 Walker made a pilgrimage to the Garden of Heavenly Rest and purchased a headstone for Hurston's grave. Her article "In Search of Zora Neale Hurston" appeared in *Ms. Magazine* in March 1975 and sparked a revival of interest in Hurston. Her once-shocking ideas about black culture were more palatable to Afrocentric scholars and activists, and her writings on black folk spirituality helped influence authors seeking to create a black culture based on African roots. Hoodoo and Voodoo would play important roles in the writings of Walker and other black writers, like Toni Morrison and Ishmael Reed. And a growing number of African Americans would come to see the folk and magical practices of New Orleans and the American South not as embarrassing superstitions to be overcome but as valuable survivals of their lost African heritage.

Robert Tallant

Like many in New Orleans, Robert Tallant didn't find his career so much as he drifted into it. After stints as a bank teller, ad man, and clerk, Tallant decided he would try his hand as a writer. And, like many in New Orleans, he was able to find work thanks to the kindness of an influential friend—Louisiana journalist and bon vivant Lyle Saxon. From 1935 to 1941 the Works Progress Administration, a New Deal agency tasked with providing jobs for writers and artists, brought forth the American Guide Series, which featured over four hundred volumes on every state, several territories, and various thematic and regional volumes. Saxon, state director of the Louisiana Writers' Project, hired Tallant to work on *The New Orleans City Guide* (1938) and *Louisiana: A Guide to the State* (1941).

Later Saxon would use Tallant's work in a massive 1945 compilation of Louisiana folklore gathered while compiling the city and state guides. The end result, *Gumbo Ya-Ya,* took its name from a tasty stew made from leftovers or a Creole discussion where everyone talks at once. *Gumbo Ya-Ya* is still considered a landmark collection of Louisiana folk tales and customs, and it helped to establish Tallant as a New Orleans literary figure. He would later say fondly of Saxon, "As a writer, I owe him everything."[5]

Following in his friend's footsteps, Tallant focused on New Orleans history and culture. Between 1948 and his death in 1957, he published eight novels and six full-length works of nonfiction. His 1951 *The Pirate Lafitte and the Battle of New Orleans* won the Louisiana Library Association award for best book of the year. Young adult works like *The Louisiana Purchase* (1952) and *Evangeline and the Acadians* (1957) gave juvenile readers an entertaining and educational look at Louisiana, while adults could enjoy his lurid tales of infamous New Orleans murders in *Ready to Hang* (1952). But he is remembered best today for his works on New Orleans Voodoo—*Voodoo in New Orleans* (1946) and his novelization of the life of Marie Laveau, *The Voodoo Queen* (1956). *Voodoo in New Orleans* offers the following insights:

> If the white man inspects these he will see candles of various sizes and colors, incense and strange-looking roots and herbs, usually reduced to white or brown powders. He will see the empty vials and small bottles these vendors sell, and he will wonder at the sight of the queer old women who stop to buy them. He may even speculate on whether or not these people are Voodoos. He will get no satisfaction asking questions. Here he has reached a barrier.[6]

Tallant used the ethnographic skills he had honed working on the Louisiana Writers' Project. In many cases in his later work, he used interviews that had not found their way into *Gumbo Ya-Ya*. But he never made any effort to go beyond the "barrier" that separated him from practitioners. For him, Voodoo was a curious set of folk superstitions that added to the city's local color. Like ghost stories, they were good for spooky fun but hardly something to be taken seriously. Tallant interviewed many practitioners and believers, but was not averse to editing their stories or adding exciting details to appeal to a wider audience.

This has led to claims that Tallant was a hack journalist, a sensationalist, and a racist. These criticisms are not entirely unwarranted. At times his speculations on "negroes" and their exotic beliefs can come across as patronizing to modern audiences. And his blending of fact and fiction makes his work almost useless for scholarly purposes. But for all his flaws, Tallant's sensitivity and willingness to cross the color line and explore their lives was unusual for a gentleman of his background. While northern academics like Melville Herskovits and Harold Courlander were also exploring African American culture, few Southern whites of the time would have thought it worth the effort. And his love of New Orleans and its customs shone through in his Voodoo works as it did in his other books. His errors were generally caused by overexuberance rather than cynicism.

While *Voodoo in New Orleans* may fail as an anthropological text, it succeeds as entertaining literature. Tallant introduced readers to Doctor John (chapter 10) and other unforgettable Crescent City characters, and helped transform Marie Laveau (chapter 14) from a New Orleans heroine into a world-renowned witch who triumphed over sexism and racism. He helped to put the city's folk traditions on the map for white tourists who wanted to experience the "real" New Orleans. Those tourists, like Tallant himself, sometimes had trouble distinguishing between truth and tall tales, but in time those tall tales became their own truths. And in time, an industry would grow up that catered to their vision of Voodoo—and that would take on a life of its own.

Charles Massicot Gandolfo

According to one of Charles Massicot Gandolfo's favorite family legends, his great-great-great-great-grandfather died at the 1791 onset of the bloody Haitian Revolution. Riding up to his plantation, the mortally wounded Germain Daubert lived just long enough to warn his wife of the oncoming slave army. The widow and her son would have joined him in death were it not for a loyal slave named Jacquinette. Jacquinette hid them in barrels until the rampaging rebels had moved on, then smuggled them onto a refugee ship. Jacquinette later accompanied the widow and child to the Faubourg Marigny district. When Mme. Daubert married and moved to France with her new husband, Jacquinette raised young François in New Orleans. There he became a prominent citizen, and she became a famous Voodoo queen who passed down much of her knowledge to her young charge.[7]

As was often the case with Gandolfo, his story contained a good deal of truth and a fair bit of romantic fiction. While Germain Daubert was indeed a Saint-Domingue privateer, he survived the revolution, and before dying in Cuba in 1806, he wrote a lengthy account complaining of the blacks who "repudiated the benefits that had been offered to them and, deploying the blood-stained flag of revolt, transformed this country into a dreadful theater of devastation."[8] An artist at heart (he held degrees in fine and commercial art), Gandolfo was never shy about embellishing a story for dramatic effect. This led many to dismiss his New Orleans Historic Voodoo Museum as a sensationalist tourist trap. But those who turn their noses up at his collection of alligator heads and dusty skulls underestimate his passion for the Crescent City and his influence on modern-day New Orleans Voodoo.

In 1972 Voodoo stores were largely confined to the city's poor black neighborhoods, where "drug stores" sold roots, herbs, perfumes, and other spiritual supplies. But Gandolfo decided to share his interest with the public nonetheless. In the early days his exhibition of paintings, altars, and a twelve-foot albino Burmese python named "Zombie" saw an average of thirty visitors a day. By 1999 those numbers had risen to 180 guests of the museum and its affiliated curio shop.[9]

Like many rootworkers before him, Gandolfo supplemented his income by doing readings and magical work for clients. Like them, he had his share of unusual requests. "A man wanted to die being eaten alive by women," he recalled. "He looks at women's stomachs and wishes he was in them. I thought he was a prankster but he phoned so many times, I told him: 'I don't do that kind of ritual.'"[10] But in between the cranks and kooks, he was able to make a tidy living serving his spiritual clientele. Others followed his lead, in their stores or on Jackson Square, where tourists can still seek the services of various counselors, readers, and intercessors.

Mambo Sallie Ann Glassman, Santeria priestess Ava Kay Jones, drummer and occultist Louis Martinié, and Voodoo Spiritual Temple founder Oswald Chamani all have done rituals at the New Orleans Historic Voodoo Museum. Gandolfo was among the first to begin the now-popular practice of "mixing and matching" various African diaspora traditions. Yoruba practitioners, Paleros (practitioners of the Kongo-derived Cuban tradition Palo Mayombe), and Spiritualists were welcomed and presented as Voodoo priests. Today many practitioners follow his lead, happily blending Santeria, Haitian Vodou, and other traditions into their practice. Lukumi (Santeria) spirits like Exu and Oshun are honored alongside Haitian lwa like Erzulie Freda and New Orleans "Hoodoo saints" like St. Expedité.

Gandolfo worked on *The Big Easy, Eve's Bayou,* and other movies in which Voodoo played a key or a supporting role. He also sat for numerous interviews with journalists and curious students. This helped to popularize his vision of New Orleans Voodoo and make it the standard for those who came after him. As his museum grew in popularity, others set up their own curio shops and Voodoo events. Some hold him responsible for the "Voodoo dolls" and vévé shot glasses that can be found throughout the French Quarter. While there may be some justice to that charge, we should also give him credit for the public face of New Orleans Voodoo.

One of the main attractions of the New Orleans Historic Voodoo Museum is the Voodoo altar featured in one of its two rooms. Originally built by Charles and his brother Jerry, the shrine has grown as visitors have brought candles, statues, notes, and other offerings to the spirits. As Elizabeth Thomas Crocker says in her master's thesis,

> The space was created to represent the owners' idea of what a Vodou altar should be in order to attract tourists. Interestingly, if this is true, the visitors have appropriated it as a legitimate religious space and have remodeled it to fit their own conceptions of what a Vodou altar should entail.[11]

Charles Gandolfo died on February 27, 2001—on Mardi Gras. His brother Jerry presently runs the Voodoo Museum at its location on 724 Dumaine Street. But many say Gandolfo still remains involved in his creation. Many have said that he haunts the museum. Other practitioners honor him for his contributions to the religion, paying homage to him as "Voodoo Charlie."

These and other figures helped to develop a new Voodoo in New Orleans, one that drew upon the old practices and added material from new traditions. While some scorned it as an affectation for jaded tourists and bored white folks, others recognized the power of the spirits who were born in the Crescent City and of those who took root in its fertile delta soil. New Orleans became a place of pilgrimage, a magical kingdom as synthetic and resonant as Disneyland. Then, on August 29, 2005, everything changed. . . .

5

WHEN THE
LEVEE BREAKS
Hurricane Katrina

You do live with the belief that some day the big one's going to get you. You're almost fatalistic, which is part of the reason New Orleans has that mixture of frivolity and fatalism. Living in a soup bowl will do it to you, like Romans dancing while Nero fiddled and the city burned.

NEW ORLEANS RESIDENT
PATRICIA McDONALD GOMEZ, 1992[1]

Of the 273 hurricanes making landfall on the American Atlantic coast between 1851 and 2004, forty-nine struck New Orleans.[2] As the city cleaned up after each storm the question arose: When will the Big One finally hit the Big Easy? In June 2002 the New Orleans *Times-Picayune* stated, "It's only a matter of time before south Louisiana takes a direct hit from a major hurricane. Billions have been spent to protect us, but we grow more vulnerable every day."[3]

But while occasional work was done to shore up the levees and maintain the pump stations, there were few overarching plans for dealing with the inevitable. When New Orleanians spoke of hurricanes, they were most likely to be discussing the sweet rum cocktail made famous by Pat O'Brien's, a famous French Quarter club. Life continued on in the bowl between Lake Pontchartrain and the Mississippi River; today the skies were clear and tomorrow was in the hands of God.

> AT 5 PM EDT . . . 2100Z . . . THE GOVERNMENT OF THE BAHAMAS HAS ISSUED A TROPICAL STORM WARNING FOR THE CENTRAL AND NORTHWEST BAHAMAS. THIS INCLUDES CAT ISLAND . . . THE EXUMAS . . . LONG ISLAND . . . RUM CAY . . . SAN SALVADOR . . . NORTHWESTERN BAHAMAS . . . THE ABACOS . . . ANDROS ISLAND . . . BERRY ISLANDS . . . BIMINI . . . ELEUTHERA . . . GRAND BAHAMA ISLAND . . . AND NEW PROVIDENCE. A TROPICAL STORM OR HURRICANE WATCH MAY BE REQUIRED FOR PORTIONS OF SOUTHERN FLORIDA LATER TONIGHT.
>
> TROPICAL DEPRESSION TWELVE ADVISORY
> NUMBER 1, CORRECTED
> NWS TPC/NATIONAL HURRICANE CENTER (MIAMI,
> FLORIDA) 5 P.M. EDT, TUESDAY, AUGUST 23, 2005[4]

On August 23, 2005, an atmospheric trough (an elongated area of relatively low air pressure) combined with the scattered thunderstorms that remained from Tropical Depression Ten to form Tropical Depression Twelve. As it passed over the Caribbean, it grew in intensity, and by the morning of August 24 it had sustained winds over 39 miles per hour and was upgraded to Tropical Storm Katrina. Two hours before reaching Florida on August 25, it was upgraded to a Category 1 hurricane, with sustained winds between 75 and 94 miles per hour.

During its six-hour trip over southern Florida, Katrina left twelve people dead and one million residents without power. It toppled trees, overturned mobile homes, and dumped over a foot of rain. But it also lost a good deal of its force, as it was cut off from the ocean waters that fueled it. By the time it crossed over into the Gulf of Mexico, it had been downgraded once again into a tropical storm. Expecting it to continue on its northerly trail, the residents of the Florida Panhandle braced for heavy rains and strong winds.

But as it returned to the sea, it began moving west and gained strength in the warm Gulf waters. An eyewall replacement cycle began as Katrina's eye broke up and reformed. This slowed the winds but caused the storm to nearly double in size. By August 28 the larger storm had regained its force. Katrina was now a massive Category 5 hurricane, with maximum sustained winds of over 175 miles per hour. And though it had spared the Panhandle, it was now headed for New Orleans.

MOST OF THE AREA WILL BE UNINHABITABLE FOR WEEKS . . . PERHAPS LONGER. AT LEAST ONE HALF OF WELL CONSTRUCTED HOMES WILL HAVE ROOF AND WALL FAILURE. ALL GABLED ROOFS WILL FAIL . . . LEAVING THOSE HOMES SEVERELY DAMAGED OR DESTROYED.

THE MAJORITY OF INDUSTRIAL BUILDINGS WILL BECOME NON FUNCTIONAL. PARTIAL TO COMPLETE WALL AND ROOF FAILURE IS EXPECTED. ALL WOOD FRAMED LOW RISING APARTMENT BUILDINGS WILL BE DESTROYED. CONCRETE BLOCK LOW RISE APARTMENTS WILL SUSTAIN MAJOR DAMAGE . . . INCLUDING SOME WALL AND ROOF FAILURE.

HIGH RISE OFFICE AND APARTMENT BUILDINGS WILL SWAY DANGEROUSLY . . . A FEW TO THE POINT OF TOTAL COLLAPSE. ALL WINDOWS WILL BLOW OUT. AIRBORNE DEBRIS WILL BE WIDESPREAD . . . AND MAY INCLUDE HEAVY ITEMS SUCH AS HOUSEHOLD APPLIANCES AND EVEN LIGHT VEHICLES.

SPORT UTILITY VEHICLES AND LIGHT TRUCKS WILL BE MOVED. THE BLOWN DEBRIS WILL CREATE ADDITIONAL DESTRUCTION. PERSONS . . . PETS . . . AND LIVESTOCK EXPOSED TO THE WINDS WILL FACE CERTAIN DEATH IF STRUCK.

POWER OUTAGES WILL LAST FOR WEEKS . . . AS MOST POWER POLES WILL BE DOWN AND TRANSFORMERS DESTROYED. WATER SHORTAGES WILL MAKE HUMAN SUFFERING INCREDIBLE BY MODERN STANDARDS.

URGENT WEATHER MESSAGE
NATIONAL WEATHER SERVICE, NEW ORLEANS,
LOUISIANA 1011 A.M. CDT, SUNDAY, AUGUST 28, 2005[5]

On Saturday night (August 27), New Orleans Mayor Ray Nagin declared a state of emergency. Residents in low-lying areas were encouraged to evacuate. By 6:00 that evening, the National Weather Service was predicting a 45 percent chance that New Orleans would sustain a direct hit from Katrina. Many New Orleanians piled what possessions they could carry into their cars and headed out on the jammed expressways leading out of the city. Others greeted the warnings with skepticism. Since Hurricane Betsy in 1965 and Camille in 1969, there had been numerous near misses and false alarms. And still others had no choice in the matter: they had no transportation and no money to pay for a hotel.

By Sunday, as the situation worsened, Nagin took the unprecedented step of ordering a mandatory evacuation of the city. "We are facing a storm that most of us have long feared," he warned. "The storm surge most likely will topple our levee system." For those who could not escape, the Louisiana Superdome was opened as a shelter of last resort. This was not the first time the facility had been pressed into service during an emergency. In 1998 fourteen thousand people stayed in the Superdome as Hurricane Georges approached, while over one thousand homeless people waited out the storm during Hurricane Ivan's near miss in 2004. Lines began forming outside the Dome almost immediately after Nagin's press conference as many residents realized the gravity of their situation. Other residents boarded up their houses, stocked up on ammunition, and vowed to defend their property against both hurricanes and looters.

At 6:10 a.m. CDT Katrina made her second landfall in Plaquemines Parish, Louisiana. The storm had weakened from its fearsome Category 5 rating and was now a Category 4 on the Saffir-Simpson Scale, with sustained winds of 145 miles per hour. But though its winds had diminished slightly, its size had not. The massive hurricane pushed a wall of water before it, a storm surge that inundated the coastline in a fast-moving flood. St. Bernard Parish, which borders New Orleans, was entirely underwater. Out of 26,900 homes, fewer than half a dozen remained habitable. As the surge traveled up the Mississippi and into Lake Pontchartrain, water flooded over the retaining walls. For a time the levees held, but within hours breaches were spotted at multiple locations. By August 31, 80 percent of the city was submerged beneath a soup of stagnant water and toxic chemicals.

This is mass chaos. To tell you the truth, I'd rather be in Iraq. You got your constant danger, but I had something to protect myself. [And] three meals a day. Communications. A plan. Here, they had no plan.

NATIONAL GUARD SERGEANT JASON DEFESS, 27,
AUGUST 31, 2005[6]

In 1998 during Hurricane Georges, refugees housed in the Superdome stole approximately $8,000 worth of barstools and artificial plants and did some $46,000 in damage. To encourage residents to evacuate—and to avoid further damage to the Dome—city officials wanted to ensure that the lodgings weren't too comfortable. Nagin told evacuees to show up at the Superdome with enough food and drinks to last three or four days, or at the very least to "eat a full meal before arriving."[7] The National Guard arrived with seven truckloads of food, enough to feed fifteen thousand for three days. As the floodwaters rose and the Dome filled up with people rescued from their homes, it soon became clear that the supplies would be stretched exceedingly thin.

While the Dome had held up during Ivan and Georges, Katrina's winds in excess of 100 miles per hour were a more serious affair. Seventy-five percent of the two-inch-thick foam and rubber membrane that protected the roof was torn to shreds and blown across the local business district. The roof itself was breached in half a dozen places. Water poured in through the holes, destroying the carpets and ruining the giant scoreboard. "You didn't know if you were going to be drowned," said evacuee Phyllis Johnson. "There was smoke in the dome. You didn't know if you were going to burn up or if the building was going to fall down around you."[8]

More immediate was the problem of electricity. Like most of Louisiana, the Superdome was without power. A backup generator quickly failed, and with it the air conditioning. When the city's water pumps went out, so did the Superdome's flush toilets. Feces and urine piled up in the bathrooms, and the smell of sweat and waste and rotting garbage filled the stale, swampy air. Barricades were put in place to ensure nobody left the Superdome, while five hundred gun-toting National Guard troops tried to maintain order over a growing and increasingly restless crowd.

Local and state officials waited for guidance from the Federal Emergency Management Agency (FEMA). FEMA head Michael Brown did not act until hours after Katrina's landfall. Federal officials barred the Red Cross from bringing food to the Superdome, blocked a five-hundred-boat flotilla of private citizens from delivering aid, and turned away Coast Guard boats carrying much-needed diesel fuel—all in the name of "securing the city." "We wanted soldiers, helicopters, food and water," said Denise Bottcher, press secretary for Governor Kathleen Blanco of Louisiana. "They wanted to negotiate an organizational chart."[9] Meanwhile, the Superdome refugees waited for buses that would take them out of their filthy prison to new shelter. Instead, rescue boats and helicopters brought in more evacuees plucked from their rooftops.

Since the lines of communication had been severed by the storm, the wildest rumors passed as facts. A seven-year-old girl was raped and murdered in a Superdome bathroom; armed mobs of New Orleans refugees were hijacking cars and engaging in robbery sprees in towns from Houston to Baton Rouge; bodies were piling up as New Orleans locals preyed on those tourists unfortunate enough to be stranded among them. As a result, many of the recovery efforts were aimed at containing the refugees rather than helping them. Police in neighboring (and largely white) Gretna guarded the bridge leading into their town, driving back evacuees at gunpoint to ensure their city didn't "become another New Orleans." Louisiana Governor Kathleen Blanco reassured worried citizens that she had called for more troops who "know how to shoot to kill . . . and I expect they will."[10] Only after the last of the thirty thousand Superdome refugees were evacuated on September 3 would it become clear that the reports of rape, anarchy, and violence had been greatly exaggerated.

> *New Orleans now is abortion free. New Orleans now is Mardi Gras free. New Orleans now is free of Southern Decadence and the sodomites, the witchcraft workers, false religion—it's free of all of those things now. God simply, I believe, in His mercy purged all of that stuff out of there—and now we're going to start over again. . . . It's time for us to stand up against wickedness so that God won't have to deal with that wickedness.*
>
> REVEREND BILL SHANKS, SEPTEMBER 2005[11]

New Orleans had acquired worldwide fame (or notoriety) for its vice. Now that it lay underwater, many speculated that God's patience had finally worn thin. An Al-Qaeda spokesman congratulated "the whole Islamic nation for the prophesized and awaited destruction of the infidel's head." An Iranian blogger bragged that "the soldier Katrina joins us to fight against America." A senior Kuwaiti official suggested that American intervention in Afghanistan and Iraq led to the city's destruction in an article entitled "Katrina Is a Wind of Torment and Evil from Allah Sent to This American Empire."[12]

In Israel, Rabbi Ovadia Yosef, spiritual leader of the ultraorthodox Shas movement, said of Katrina, "It was God's retribution. God does not shortchange anyone." He blamed Bush for supporting the withdrawal of Jewish settlers from the Gaza Strip, warning, "This is his punishment for what he did to [Gaza settlement] Gush Katif, and everyone else who did as he told them, their time will come, too." (He also suggested that New Orleans *Kushim*—a derogatory Hebrew term for black Africans—didn't study the Torah and had no God.)[13] Meanwhile, many Christian leaders commented that Katrina had occurred right before Southern Decadence, an annual gay festival that regularly attracted over one hundred thousand attendees.

Among those who didn't blame divine intervention, many blamed the people of New Orleans. One observer described a widely held view of the Katrina refugees: "They lived in a silly place, they didn't get out when they should, they stole, they shot at each other and they shot at rescue workers."[14] Talk radio host Neal Boortz called New Orleans "a welfare city, a city of parasites, a city of people who could not and had no desire to fend for themselves. You have a hurricane descending on them and they sit on their fat asses and wait for somebody else to come rescue them." He added, "When these Katrina so-called refugees were scattered about the country, it was just a glorified episode of putting out the garbage."[15]

While there may have been theological differences, there was near-universal agreement that the Katrina rescue efforts were grossly inadequate. Before his appointment as FEMA head, Michael Brown had been the leader of an Arabian horse organization. At first Bush supported him, saying, "Brownie, you're doing a heck of a job" in a Houston news conference on September 2. ("He's done a hell of a job, because I'm not aware of any Arabian horses being killed in this storm," Kate Hale, former Miami-Dade emergency management chief, noted dryly.)[16] But in the face of growing criticism, Brown offered his resignation on September 12. On September 13 Bush said, "to the extent that the federal government didn't fully do its job right, I take responsibility."

Federal officials claimed that they had been hog-tied, unable to offer support until help was requested by state and local officials. Governor

Blanco claimed she had asked for firefighting support, military vehicles, generators, medical supplies, and personnel days before the storm hit. But her office also appeared overwhelmed by the storm and unable to coordinate relief efforts. She left the specifics of evacuating New Orleans and providing for survivors to local officials and failed to file the necessary paperwork to send National Guard troops from other states into the disaster area until after the hurricane had already struck. And Louisiana's widespread culture of corruption also played a role in the disaster. Much of the money that had been sent to retrofit property and improve flood control went missing. An amount of $40.5 million was sent to state emergency-management officials for hazard mitigation, but there were no receipts for 97 percent of a $15.4 million allocation awarded to subcontractors on nineteen different projects.[17]

> *If you've never been here, maybe you've read our books or listened to our music. You've always loved the romantic idea of us, but maybe now you think it would be smarter, kinder, certainly cheaper to let us die. We will not die easy. We will not be driven away from the places that are in our blood, because any of us can die any damn minute of any damn day of our lives. If you're ever lucky enough to belong somewhere, if a place takes you in and you take it into yourself, you don't desert it just because it can kill you. There are things more valuable than life.*
>
> POPPY Z. BRITE, AUTHOR OF SEVERAL BOOKS SET
> IN NEW ORLEANS, SEPTEMBER 2006[18]

After the city was evacuated, some wondered if rebuilding would be worthwhile. Representative Dennis Hastert of Illinois suggested that it didn't make sense to rebuild a city that was largely below sea level and said, "It looks like a lot of that place could be bulldozed."[19] Former First Lady Barbara Bush, the president's mother, felt that most of the evacuees wanted to stay in Texas. Since they were underprivileged before the storm, she thought that Katrina was "working very well for them."[20] Some argued that aid to New Orleans would only encourage people to continue living in a hurricane-prone, crime-ridden, poverty-stricken city—and on the taxpayer's dime to boot.

While rich and poor alike suffered from Katrina's wrath, the worst flooding took place largely in low-lying poor and largely black neighborhoods. These residents were most often renters rather than homeowners. But the massive destruction wrought by Katrina meant that apartments and homes were in short supply, and the cost of renting doubled or tripled from pre-Katrina rates. Wealthy New Orleanians could rebuild their homes with the help of private insurance policies and their personal savings. Those who had no such cushion found themselves living in FEMA trailers or in badly damaged mold-choked homes.

The relative boom in construction (which has persisted even through the real estate downturn) led to a growing population of Latino immigrants. As the tourism industry began to revive, the restaurants and bars began hiring. But the shortage of well-paying careers, which had always plagued New Orleans, remained and was now joined by a shortage of inexpensive housing. By 2007 less than 50 percent of the population of New Orleans was black, down from nearly 70 percent pre-Katrina.[21] Poor blacks had relocated to Texas, while wealthier and more educated black New Orleanians found better opportunities in Atlanta and other cities. In 2003 three hundred New Orleans–area "disadvantaged" companies (companies owned by women or minorities) were certified to work at the New Orleans airport. In 2009 that number had dwindled to 164.[22]

Many outsiders are drawn to the imagery and practices of New Orleans Voodoo; fewer have an interest in the impoverished but culturally rich areas from whence it sprung. The modern mélange of African traditions continues to flourish in the French Quarter and on the high grounds. It is unclear when, or if, the African American folk magic that has been practiced in the Crescent City for centuries will recover.

PART TWO

TRADITIONS

The cultural mélange that gave us New Orleans Voodoo also produced many other strange and wonderful traditions. Many of them inspired—and were inspired by—the city's folk-magical practices. All have helped to ensure that New Orleans isn't just a city—it's a way of life. There's plenty of magic to be had in the Crescent City; its charms and spells can be found in all the expected places and in a few corners where you might never have thought to look.

6

MARDI GRAS

The pre-Lenten celebrations that end with Ash Wednesday are found in many places around the world, but as so often happens, New Orleans has put a special spin on the event. The feast of Mardi Gras (Fat Tuesday) has become an emblem of the city, and each year people make their way to New Orleans to get their fill of sin before the long weeks of repentance. Women bare their breasts for beads, while drunkards, masked and unmasked, engage in various and sundry acts of debauchery.

But amid all the celebrating one might ask: When did this party begin? It turns out Voodoo isn't the only Crescent City custom that combines Catholic imagery and traditions with pagan rituals and beliefs. To understand Mardi Gras we must go back to the agricultural magic practiced in pre-Christian Europe.

Before Easter—and After

For our ancestors the turning of the seasons was a matter of the utmost urgency. A late spring could mean famine for the entire tribe. To ensure the ice would melt, the beasts would mate, and the plants would bloom once more, ceremonies were performed. By appeasing the gods who held sway over the weather, they hoped to avoid the ever-looming threat of starvation. The gods received offerings and praise. In return, the congregation expected their blessings for the crops and the community. The bigger the ritual, the greater the rewards they could expect, and so these ceremonies involved not only priestly or shamanic castes but people from all walks of life.

In those days seasonal eating wasn't an affectation for foodies; it was mandatory. When the ground was blanketed with snow, there were no more greens to be had. The produce put up after the harvest had to last through the cold, lean months. The frozen ground would produce no more root vegetables and the icy fields gave no more grain. Spring was a cause for celebration and relief. It was a sign you had made it through the winter alive and a promise that your bland winter diet would soon be augmented with fresh fruits and vegetables. And so it was not surprising that these rituals involved a great degree of merriment.

This revelry often took on a decidedly sexual character. This was in part due to the high spirits attendant upon a good party, but there was a deeper meaning as well. Millennia before Freud, our ancestors recognized the connection between the sexual urge and the force that drove the cattle into rutting and set the flowers blooming. They hoped that their own licentiousness could encourage their farms and hunting grounds to mate and produce the resources to keep the village fat and happy through the warm times and well stocked against the inevitable barren months.

By the time of the Roman Empire, these customs were already ancient. The Romans celebrated Lupercalia on February 15 even though they no longer remembered the god or gods to whom it had originally been dedicated. Noble youths clad in loincloths (garb more suited to shepherds and peasants) ran through the streets lashing passersby with whips made of goatskin. Instead of running from these floggings, people (particularly young women) crowded to receive their blows, since they believed they would encourage fertility and easy childbirth. The whole event was marked with much drinking and merrymaking.[1]

After the rise of Christianity some efforts were made to stamp out these heathen customs, but to little avail. The wealthy and educated may have turned up their noses at the local superstitions, but the peasantry weren't about to put their crops at risk—or give up the year's best party! At last the Church bureaucracy decided that if you can't beat them, you might as well join them. As was often their wont, Church officials reinterpreted the tradition in the light of Christian mythology. The holiday that marked the earth's return to life became the Easter feast of Christ's death and resurrection, and the riotous fertility festivals became a last celebration before the austerities of Lent. Since meat was forbidden during that period of purification and mortification, the rites became a last chance at indulgence, a *carne vale,* or "farewell to the flesh."

The carnival season officially ran from January 6 (the Feast of the Epiphany, when the Three Kings brought their gifts to Jesus) to the Tuesday before Ash Wednesday. Revelers wore masks, which allowed them to gamble, carouse, and break social barriers anonymously. While the festival first became popular in Italy (so popular that Pope Gregory XIII made Mardi Gras an official holiday in 1582), it later spread throughout the Roman Catholic parts of continental Europe.

Then, with the dawn of the colonial era, Carnival spread through much of the New World as well. Portuguese settlers brought the festivities to Brazil and Goa, India. French colonists invited to Trinidad by the Spanish established a carnival tradition that continues to this day. And on March 3, 1699, Lord Iberville and his troops celebrated the holiday by holding the first Mass of record in French Louisiana and naming their campsite (about sixty miles from present-day New Orleans) Point du Mardi Gras.

Mardi Gras Comes to New Orleans

The first official mention of Mardi Gras in New Orleans comes from a 1781 Spanish report that expressed concerns about slaves wearing masks during celebrations. By 1806 masked balls were banned by the New Orleans City Council in an effort to tame the unruly and sometimes violent partying that was already a staple of the city's pre-Lenten celebrations. Alas, the councilors learned that passing a law in the city was one thing, enforcing it quite another. By 1823 masked balls were once again permitted, and by 1827 masked and costumed revelers were once again making their way through the city streets.

From the start Mardi Gras in New Orleans was known for the large number of black and Creole participants. Writing in 1823, a Protestant minister described the proceedings:

> The great Congo-dance is performed. Everything is license and revelry. Some hundreds of negroes, male and female, follow the king of the wake. . . . All the characters that follow him, of leading estimation, have their peculiar dress, and their own contortions. They dance, and their streamers fly, and the bells that they have hung about them tinkle. Never will you see gayer countenances, demonstrations of more forgetfulness of the past and the future, and more entire abandonment to the joyous existence of the present moment.[2]

This led to many calls for the banning of these pagan rites, especially with the continuing problems of violence and street crime during the celebrations. A solution came from six businessmen who had been involved in similar celebrations in Mobile, Alabama. Forming together as the Mystick Krewe of Comus, they organized a torchlit parade and ball. Comus started many Mardi Gras traditions that are still held today, particularly the floats that throw trinkets to the crowds. Unlike the wild black celebrations, membership in their secret society was limited to white people of the appropriate social class. The only blacks who marched with their floats were hired torch-bearers, and the only blacks at their balls were servants.

But black revelers were not so easily denied their chance at a party. Since 1783 the Perseverance Benevolent and Mutual Aid Association had served as a form of insurance and social aid for free blacks in New Orleans. It would be followed by many other similar groups that would sponsor their own krewes, carnival organizations, and Mardi Gras parties. Membership in these groups meant more than just a ticket to the best balls; it provided a network whereby unemployed or injured laborers could find work and deceased members could be guaranteed a decent burial. While the white krewes marched through the French Quarter, the black krewes made their way through the African American neighborhoods.

Another Mardi Gras tradition would soon arise: the Black Indian "tribes." Since the earliest African presence in the New World, blacks and Indians had interacted. Many maroons (escaped slaves) found a home among the Indian tribes living in the inaccessible swamplands beyond the plantations. To pay tribute for their aid, blacks formed "tribes" or "gangs" named after their neighborhoods. Members of these organizations were known for their intricately beaded costumes, complete with plumage, sparkling rhinestones, and moccasins. The feathers hearkened back to Indian ceremonial costumes, while the beading was inspired by West African artwork. The Indian tribes became especially popular after a New Orleans visit by Buffalo Bill's Wild West Show in 1884.

In the beginning, tribes frequently engaged in turf wars, with regular fights between "uptown" and "downtown" tribes that often devolved into gunfights, hatchet attacks, and stabbings. Since the New Orleans police were generally occupied with keeping order in the white sections of town, these gang wars raged with impunity in the poor black areas. Today the Black Indians remain an important part of Mardi Gras celebrations, but their conflicts are much more ritualized and less bloody. When two tribes pass each other on the street, each "chief" will demand of the other "You humba" (pay your respects to me) and respond "Me no humba, YOU humba." This will then be greeted by a series of war whoops and intricate dance maneuvers. At the end of this display, each will acknowledge the other's skill and the quality of the tribe's costumes. (Some say the cost and skill involved in costume designing contributed to the peace between rival tribes. No one who has spent hundreds of hours and thousands of dollars designing a suit wants to risk ruining it in a fight!)

Another black krewe, formed by the Zulu Social Aid and Pleasure Club, first marched in 1909. Its king wore a lard can as a crown and carried a banana stalk scepter. The Zulus were one of the first krewes to bring in a celebrity king, when Louis Armstrong was accorded the honor in 1949. They are still the lead krewe in the largely black Zulu parade that takes place alongside the historically white Rex parade. The Zulus have attracted some controversy for their grass skirt and blackface costumes, but have risen above that to become one of the most popular and famous Mardi Gras krewes. The organization's choir, the Zulu Ensemble, performs at local churches, gospel concerts, schools, funerals, and the Jazz and Heritage Festival. During the Christmas season Zulus provide baskets to needy families and donate funds and time to various community organizations.[3]

Throws

After putting all that effort into building a fine float and fancy costume, you want to make sure the audience appreciates your handiwork. And as everyone in the Crescent City knows, a little *lagniappe* (extra free gift) will always win hearts and minds. To that end, "throws"—gifts tossed into the crowd—are an intrinsic part of Mardi Gras parades. (An earlier custom of throwing flour and pepper into the audience wasn't nearly so endearing.)

Sometime in the 1920s, the members of the Rex Krewe acquired a large number of inexpensive glass beads from Czechoslovakia, strung them into necklaces, and threw them from their floats as mementos. They were warmly received by the crowd and thus began a trend that has lived on: Mardi Gras beads. After World War II the beads were imported from Japan, and later, plastic replaced glass and China replaced Japan as the primary supplier. According to Fred Berger, owner of Mardi Gras Imports of Slidell, Louisiana, the average Mardi Gras krewe member spends approximately $800 on beads and "some people won't bat an eye at spending $2,000 or $2,500."[4]

In 1959 New Orleans artist Alvin Sharpe created another famous Mardi Gras tradition: the doubloon. The Rex krewe ordered eighty-three thousand of his intricately detailed aluminum doubloons. Unsure how they would go over, they asked him to leave off the date on all but a few, so that any left over could be used another year. But it turned out that they were a huge hit: between 1960 and 1970 Rex threw 2.75 million doubloons. Others soon followed suit, and today collectors strive to acquire complete collections of their favorite krewes at the parade or at various online and offline memorabilia stores.

Other krewes throw plastic toys or cups emblazoned with their logo. But few gifts are as prized as the Zulu krewe's hand-painted coconuts. Originally the Zulu krewe became famous for throwing "golden nuggets," or gold-painted walnuts. Although these were cheaper than glass beads, they were greatly appreciated by the crowd since they could be eaten while watching the parade or at the tavern afterwards. (Bar owners along the route were less thrilled about the walnut shells that inevitably littered their floor.) Later they began throwing coconuts that were painted gold and decorated with glitter. Most featured the Zulu blackface design, and some even featured hair and hats. After a number of lawsuits from people who were hit by thrown coconuts, the club briefly suspended the practice. But to keep the tradition alive, the Louisiana Legislature passed SB188 (the "Coconut Bill"), excluding the krewe from liability for injuries caused by coconuts handed off (as opposed to tossed) from the float. Over one hundred thousand coconuts are passed out during a typical Zulu parade.

But while the regular coconuts are treasured, those who are especially favored by the Zulus (or who wish to purchase one from their master engraver, Willie Clark) may get one of their special "Mardi Gras Coconuts." These are meticulously decorated and engraved; they may have as many as thirty-seven colors and sixty-eight color mixtures on their surface. As Zulu member Lester Pollard says, "Our organization centers around the coconut—the coconut is everything to us! Man, we've got laws passed concerning our coconuts!"[5]

Kings and Queens

For the 1872 Mardi Gras, the Crescent City had a noble visitor: Grand Duke Alexis Romanoff of Russia. To entertain him, a number of young New Orleans businessmen formed the Rex Organization. Unlike the Comus krewe's nighttime parade, the Rex krewe held their parade during the day. To honor Duke Alexis, they elected one of their members, Lewis Solomon, as king of the parade. Crowned and robed, riding a horse, and holding a scepter he borrowed from a traveling actor, Solomon became the first Rex, King of the Carnival. (He was also the first to march under the purple, green, and gold banner that has become emblematic of the New Orleans festivities.) Following in their lead, many other krewes elected their own kings, queens, and royal courts.

These royals are generally announced on King's Night—the twelfth night after Christmas, also known as the Feast of the Epiphany. While this ostensibly pays homage to the three magi who brought gifts to the Christ child, its roots stretch back to the Roman holiday of Saturnalia. In a sentiment familiar to many Mardi Gras revelers, the Roman poet Lucian had Saturn tell his devotees how to celebrate his party:

> During My week the serious is barred; no business allowed. Drinking, noise and games and dice, appointing of kings and feasting of slaves, singing naked, clapping of frenzied hands, an occasional ducking of corked faces in icy water—such are the functions over which I preside.[6]

During Saturnalia the family festivities were presided over by a Lord of Misrule, who ensured that his subjects were engaging in properly riotous behavior. This office was determined by lot: pieces of cake were passed out among the family, and the one whose cake contained a fava bean was raised to the throne until the festival was over. This is echoed today by the king cake, which is a staple of New Orleans Twelfth Night festivities.

A king cake is a pastry rather like a coffee cake, decorated with purple, gold, and green icing. Each weekend between Twelfth Night and Mardi Gras, slices are passed out at parties. The person whose slice contains a tiny plastic or ceramic baby is crowned king or queen—and is expected to pick up the tab for next week's party! Similar traditions exist in France (*gâteau de rois*), England (Twelfth Cakes), Portugal (*bolo rei*), Greece (*vasilopita*), and Catalonia (*tortell*).

Because the Mardi Gras royal offices are highly prestigious and sought after, the Twelfth Night Revelers, one of the oldest krewes, have resorted to yet another time-honored New Orleans tradition: rigging the elections. Instead of a real king cake, a wooden replica is presented at the climax of their ball. To the tune of "Thank Heaven for Little Girls," the debutantes seated in the call-out section are called forward and led to the wooden cake, which has many small boxes. Most of the boxes contain small pieces of cake, and a few contain beans on a chain. The girls who have been chosen to serve as maids in the court receive boxes containing silver beans, and the one who has been chosen as queen is given the box with a gold bean.[7]

The krewes have traditionally been segregated by race, gender, and social status. Popular krewes like Comus, Momus, Rex, and Endymion refused membership to blacks, Jews, Italians, women, and working-class people. Alternate krewes were established catering to these excluded groups, like Zulu (black), the Virgilians (Italian), Iris (female), and Petronius (gay).[8] Even canines had their own society, the Krewe of Barkus! Then, in 1991, the New Orleans City Council demanded the integration of the krewes. A law was passed prohibiting any club, marching society, or parade organization sponsoring public Mardi Gras activities from excluding anyone from membership because of race, color, sex, sexual orientation, national origin, ancestry, age, physical condition, or disability.

In response the old-line Comus, Momus, and Proteus clubs pulled out of the Mardi Gras parades altogether. Others allowed in a handful of minority members, while still others moved their parades out to the largely white suburban parishes. In the end, most of the old krewes—and new multicultural ones like Harry Connick Jr.'s Krewe of Orpheus—embraced new minority members. "New Orleans is a city that survives on its tourism industry and its reputation for hospitality," Norman C. Francis, president of the largely black Xavier University, explained. "For people around the country to think we were living in isolation, that we were shunning diversity, that would have been our death notice."[9]

7
MUSIC

New Orleans is a party that never ends—and you can't have a party without music! The cultural blending that produced Louisiana's unique cuisine has also given us some of America's most colorful and distinctive tunes. Many of these songs pay homage to the religion and magic of New Orleans, while others discuss the historical events that shaped the Crescent City. If you want to understand the Big Easy, you'll need to learn something about its soundtrack.

To give you some idea of the various influences on New Orleans music, consider legendary Cajun fiddler Dennis McGee. His grandfather was an Irish immigrant, and his mother was half Seminole Indian. (He still insisted McGee was a French name, since "I don't know anyone named McGee who doesn't speak French."[1]) He performed on some of the first recordings of Cajun music with Amédé Ardoin, a Creole singer and accordion player. Later he recorded many duets with his brother-in-law, violinist and furniture salesman Sady Courville.

Still another example is the New Orleans pianist and composer Louis Moreau Gottschalk. Born in 1829 to a Jewish businessman from London and a refugee from Saint-Domingue, young Gottschalk began teaching himself to play piano at the tender age of three. Schooled in Europe, he would later incorporate the French, Spanish, and African rhythms of his native city into compositions like "Bamboula!" and "The Banjo." Upon the elder Gottschalk's early death, Louis took responsibility for his five half-siblings by his father's quadroon mistress. Touring ceaselessly, he played to adoring audiences throughout South America until his death in Brazil in 1869.

New Orleans has always been a place of commingling musical styles. At a time when few American cities had one opera company, New Orleans had several. A visitor could hear Chopin played at a conservatory during the day, then listen to bawdy ragtime and barrelhouse at a local speakeasy or brothel at night. All these influences came together to create several styles of music that have become symbolic of the Big Easy in all its high-living, hard-partying glory.

Delta Blues

In Islamic West Africa, *griots* (or female *griottes*) preserve history and culture through their music. Accompanying themselves on stringed instruments, they sing tales of ancestors and their feats and ribald tunes about love and its various complications. Although their presence is required at celebrations and rituals, the griots frequently occupy a liminal place in their society. Admired for their talent and sometimes paid handsomely for their performances, they are also often shunned as sorcerers and men and women of dubious moral character. While some also hold day jobs in their community, others support themselves as traveling musicians, making their living by their voice and their instrument.

The stringed instruments used by the griots resemble the guitar and banjo commonly found in African American folk music. The griot melodies are based on a *pentatonic* scale—instead of the seven notes (Do, Re, Mi, etc.) found in a major scale, melodies are based on scales of five notes. The third and fifth notes of these scales are often flattened, played at a pitch below "just intonation" (equal divisions between each note of the scale). The griots frequently improvise on standard tunes, making up new lyrics on the spot to honor generous patrons or mock stingy ones.

These musical conventions can be found among the descendants of slaves brought from West Africa. Many blues songs are based on a pentatonic scale, and whenever flattened thirds and fifths appear in American music, they are generally called blue notes. In African American society blues artists have often held a place very like that of the griots. They provide entertainment for their audiences, and a lucky few can even earn a living at it—but many have also gained a reputation for heavy drinking, promiscuity, and drug use. And a few have even been accused of sorcery. Robert Johnson's legendary "deal with the Devil" at the crossroads is one example, but many other blues musicians have had reputations as "conjures" or "Hoodoo men."

Like griots, blues singers preserve the lives and cultures of their people. Their music could often be bawdy, with surprisingly frank discussions of sexuality. Blues musicians would brag about their sexual prowess (Skip James's "All Night Long") or complain about their impotence (Robert Johnson's "Dead Shrimp Blues"). Partners were lauded for their fidelity, or more often criticized for their cheating ways. But blues music also chronicled the lives of hardscrabble farmers and day laborers under Jim Crow. The blues gave a voice to anonymous convicts on the chain gang and celebrated legendary gangsters like "Stagger" Lee. It spoke of gin joints and prisons, of cotton fields and factories, of winning hands and hard times. And it described, often and in loving detail, the temptations, tribulations, and magic one might find in New Orleans and the surrounding countryside.

In 1925 Gertrude "Ma" Rainey sang in "Louisiana Hoodoo Blues,"

> *Going to the Louisiana bottom to get me a hoodoo
> hand*
> *Going to the Louisiana bottom to get me a hoodoo
> hand*
> *Gotta stop these women from taking my man.*[2]

Later, male blues singers like Alger "Texas" Alexander and George "Little Hat" Jones followed in her footsteps, traveling to the Crescent City to win back their lady love with a mojo bag prepared by some of the best Hoodoo doctors in the South. New Orleans was a place where the broken-hearted might find love magic—or, more precisely, the power to make a wandering lover return. The blues were more a feature of the rural delta than urban New Orleans. Most blues songs about New Orleans are sung by outsiders looking to visit for business or pleasure.

One classic blues saga, "House of the Rising Sun," began as a Kentucky folk tune. Told by a young woman brought to New Orleans and forced into prostitution (or, in other versions, a dissipate gambling man on his last legs), this archetypal tale of sin without salvation cast New Orleans in the role of Sodom on the Mississippi—a role that would have been all too familiar, and alluring, to folk growing up on the frontier and dreaming of city life. Like many a blues song, "Rising Sun" wagged its finger at sin while making it as attractive as possible. Grand Ole Opry founder Roy Acuff made a recording of this folk standard that became a country classic, and in 1948 Huddie "Leadbelly" Ledbetter gave us his version in one of his last studio sessions. Later other black musicians like Nina Simone and Miriam Makeba reclaimed this song in a blue mode.

A soulful rendition by the Animals topped the charts on both sides of the Atlantic in 1964. This version combined blues riffs with electronic instrumentation and vocal stylings reminiscent of the untrained singers of the Delta blues. This combination had for several years fueled the development of a movement that took its name from an old blues euphemism for sexual intercourse: rock and roll. A whole new generation came to know New Orleans as a hospice where morals and good character could die in a suitably entertaining fashion. But this was hardly the first time blues had shaped popular music—or vice versa. Generations before, New Orleans had seen another movement wherein West African song styles and scales had met contemporary standards and formed a new, enduring music that attained worldwide popularity.

Dixieland Jazz

In 1896 a young New Orleans newsboy named Emile "Stale Bread" Lacoumbe attracted attention (and newspaper sales) with his virtuoso harmonica playing. Gathering a troupe of young musicians around him, he soon gave up the newspaper business for a life as leader of Stale Bread's

Spasm Band. At first they played on soapbox guitars and washtub bass fiddles, but as they attracted attention they added cornets, clarinets, and other store-bought instruments to their instrumentation. Whooping and hollering in time with their songs, they soon became a local sensation and played at many local taverns, theaters, and brothels.

Then in 1905, Jack Robinson, owner of the Haymarket Restaurant, hired a band of experienced musicians to copy the sound of Stale Bread's street urchins, a group he billed as the Razzy Dazzy Spasm Band. Alas, the original Spasm band took umbrage at their competition and protested by heaving rocks and bricks through the Haymarket's windows. To placate them, Robinson quickly repainted his placards to feature the Razzy Dazzy Jazzy Band—one of the first recorded usages of the word *jazz*.

Other historians date the beginning of jazz to 1898 and the end of the Spanish-American War. As military bands returned from Cuba and decommissioned, the city was flooded with used band instruments. Black musicians who had hitherto been unable to afford cornets, tubas, and trombones quickly bought up these and other bargain-priced instruments and taught themselves how to play.

These self-taught musicians used unconventional playing techniques and developed unusual renderings of popular tunes. They also incorporated the complex rhythms of African musical traditions. Where most brass bands of the time emphasized the first and third beats of a measure, African music tended to concentrate on the backbeats—resulting in a distinctive oom-PAH oom-PAH sound. Since many were unable to read sheet music, they generally learned tunes by ear, rehearsing together until they achieved the desired sound. And since these ensembles frequently changed personnel, their tunes tended to be more loosely structured and improvisational than traditional brass band music.

Soon many white bands were emulating the sounds and techniques of the New Orleans jazz bands. As the recording industry dawned, many promoters hired white bands to play sanitized versions of popular New Orleans tunes, then released them for a nationwide audience. The first jazz hit, 1917's "Livery Stable Blues" by a white group called the Original Dixieland Jazz Band, had little of the ragged rhythm and free-form improvisation that marked the best of New Orleans jazz. Still, it went on to sell over a million copies.

Not until 1922 would a black jazz band be featured on record, when Louisiana trombonist Edward "Kid" Ory recorded "Ory's Creole Trombone" in a Los Angeles studio. Later Ory moved to Chicago, where he played alongside New Orleans jazz legends like cornetist Joe "King" Oliver. Meanwhile another trumpet player from the poor side of New Orleans was making his name in dance halls and riverboats—Louis "Satchmo" Armstrong. Raised by his beloved grandmother, a conjure woman, Armstrong maintained a healthy respect and fear of Voodoo throughout his life. Many of his peers whispered that he, like Robert Johnson, owed much of his success to bargains with supernatural powers.

Another legendary jazz pioneer, pianist Ferdinand "Jelly Roll" Morton, was also deeply involved in Voodoo. In a 1938 interview with folklorist Alan Lomax, Morton described how notorious killer Aaron Harris was able to avoid prosecution despite his many crimes, thanks to a Hoodoo woman named Madame Papaloos:

Madame Papaloos is supposed, that is . . . from certain evidences, to tumble up Aaron's house. Take all the sheets off the bed. Tumble the mattresses over. Put sheets in front of the glasses. Take chairs and tumble 'em all over. That is said and known to . . . discourage the judge from prosecuting.

And . . . of course the different witnesses . . . have all their tongues supposed to be tied. They supposed to tie 'em with . . . lambs' tongues. And . . . beef tongues and veal tongues out of the markets. And stick 'em full of needles. That is what I understand. I don't know, 'cause I've never seen 'em stick pins and needles all through 'em. And take some . . . we'll say twine in order to make it real secure. And tie these tongues up.

And that's supposed to have the prosecuting attorneys and the judges and the jurors and so forth and so on, have their tongues tied that they can't talk against whoever the victim's supposed to be. Not the victim, but . . . the one that's arrested, the prisoner. So Aaron Harris was always successful in getting out of all of his troubles.[3]

Morton was raised by his godmother, conjure woman and Voodoo Priestess Laura Hunter. But although their relationship was by all accounts a loving one, Morton always feared she had sold his soul to the Devil and that he would die soon after she did. When she passed on in 1940, Morton told several of his close friends that his time had come. A few months later he died of heart failure.

Unfortunately for the New Orleans jazz scene, its best black musicians (like many other black citizens) were joining the exodus north to Chicago and other Midwestern cities, where well-paying factory work was easy to come by. Ory made a name for himself in California; Armstrong became a sensation in Chicago and later New York City. During the Great Depression even the best musicians found it difficult to earn a living with their instruments. Kid Ory put down his trombone and took up chicken farming, while King Oliver worked at a roadside fruit stand, and legendary clarinetist Sidney Bechet opened a tailor shop in Harlem after gigs for his New Orleans Feetwarmers dried up.

When the economy improved, interest in Dixieland jazz returned, but traditional players faced new competition from swing, big band, and later bebop players. Dixieland jazz was seen by many new performers as old-fashioned and stodgy. Louis Armstrong's charismatic stage patter was disparaged by some young black musicians as "Uncle Tomming" for a white audience. New Orleans jazz became yet another tourist attraction for visitors, as sanitized and preserved as a ride at Disneyworld. In the words of eminent jazz critic Gary Giddins:

> Some of the music froze in a kind of Dixieland wax museum, complete with straw hat and sleeve garter, as compared to the original innovators, who were usually dressed to the nines—like hustlers, gamblers, sharp-looking guys. Somehow a culture of John Stetson hats and tailored threads was transformed into a culture of beer and peanuts and garters and vests, playing the same goddamn tunes every

night. When it is done well that kind of music can still be electrifying. . . . But more often, it has become a predictable exercise.[4]

But while time may have passed much Dixieland jazz by, it influenced yet another style of music that has become indelibly connected with the sound of New Orleans.

Zydeco

One popular Louisiana folk song, "Les Haricots Sont Pas Salés" ("The Snap Beans Aren't Salty"), describes hard times when the larder is empty and you can't even afford salt pork to spice up the beans. In the local dialect, *les haricots* (pronounced "lay zarico") became *le zydeco*. When it was recorded by Clifton Chenier in 1965, his bluesy, soulful version became a regional hit and gave its name to a whole new genre of music—zydeco. But this new sensation had deep roots in Louisiana Creole—and a pedigree stretching back to the first African slaves and Acadian settlers.

In the remote bayous and swamps, the Cajuns had to entertain themselves. Many learned to play music, making their own fiddles and stomping and clapping to provide rhythm at dance festivals. Since illiteracy was common, stories and legends were often passed down through ballads and songs. But though they were isolated, the Cajuns were not alone. Their songs were influenced by the music of neighboring blacks and various European immigrants. All would come together at house parties where musicians played till the wee hours of the night for a whooping and hollering audience.

African call-and-response informed the Cajun tradition of vocal improvisation. *Juré,* the syncopated field songs of black workers, added rhythmic complexity to the Cajun reels and two-steps. After World War II, rhythm and blues music inspired black and white musicians, and horn sections and electric guitars ultimately became part of many Cajun and Creole bands. Country music and Western swing had a similar influence, introducing pedal steel guitars to many lineups. But two instruments became particularly associated with zydeco.

When Germans arrived in New Orleans, they brought accordions with them. At first Cajun musicians shunned the new instrument. Its musical range was more limited than the violin, and it was tuned in keys that did not match well with the tunings used by Cajun fiddlers. By about 1925 accordion makers began producing instruments tuned in C and D—keys that were often used in Cajun songs. Although the accordion was not as versatile as the fiddle, it could be played more loudly, and its sound carried well through even the most rambunctious crowd. The accordion soon became part of the region's signature sound.

Folk musicians have long used washboards not only to clean their clothes but as a rhythm instrument. By tapping the washboard or scraping its ridged surface, a washboard player can produce a backbeat and emphasize particular passages. Traditionally an actual washboard is used. But in the late 1940s Cleveland Chenier (Clifton's brother) had a specially modified instrument produced by a local tinsmith. This board dispensed with the wooden frame, producing a distinctive rasp. Soon other musicians were hanging these *vests frottoirs* (vests for rubbing) around their necks and playing them by running spoons, bottle openers, or thimbles across their ridged surface.

In the 1950s the Chenier Brothers burst out of Opelousas, Louisiana, with "Hey, 'Tite Fille" ("Hey, Little Girl"). Signed to blues label Chess Records, their peppy, infectious grooves attracted nationwide attention from blues and jazz fans. Combining Cajun music with influences from musicians like Fats Domino and Professor Longhair, they helped to make zydeco a national phenomenon. Clifton Chenier won a Grammy Award in 1983 for his album *I'm Here!* In 1989, two years after his death, he was inducted into the Blues Hall of Fame.

Perhaps the most popular zydeco artist is Stanley Dural Jr., better known by his stage name, Buckwheat Zydeco. From 1971 to 1976 Dural led a funk band, then decided to concentrate on traditional Louisiana music, which his father, accordionist Stanley Sr., had played back in the 1940s and '50s, when it was called "la la." Trading in his Hammond organ for an accordion, Dural became the frontman for the Ils Sont Partis (They're Off!) band. Adding funky grooves to traditional zydeco,

Buckwheat Zydeco signed a major deal with Island Records. Later he toured with Eric Clapton and Willie Nelson and contributed tunes to movies like *The Big Easy* and to national commercials for Lincoln Mercury, Toyota, Cheerios, and Budweiser.[5]

Today a number of bands carry on the zydeco tradition. Experienced musicians like Grammy winner Ida Lewis "Queen Ida" Guillory and C. J. Chenier (Clifton Chenier's son) play alongside newcomers like Keith Frank and the Soileau Zydeco Band and twelve-year-old accordionist Guyland Leday. Chris Ardoin carries on the tradition started by his ancestors Amédé and Alphonse "Bois Sec" Ardoin, but adds a touch of hip-hop to the mix. Geno Delafose gives a nod to country and western in his "nouveau zydeco." In paying tribute to zydeco's roots while incorporating new influences, all these musicians continue to reflect New Orleans—a city that has always been quick to mix and match the traditional and the modern.

8

FOOD

New Orleans is legendary for its unique cuisine, and foodies from around the world come to the Big Easy to do some big eating. Well-heeled epicures can go to famous establishments like Brennan's, Commander's Palace, and Antoine's to feast on deliciously decadent culinary delights. Those on more modest budgets can enjoy beignets and chicory coffee or nosh on buttery-sweet pecan pralines after a hearty bowl of jambalaya or some dirty rice at one of the city's many less fancy but no less satisfying restaurants. While New Orleans caters to all seven of the deadly sins, gluttons will find the Crescent City a particularly delightful stop on their travels.

Beyond the sensual pleasures of a good repast, there are many lessons to be learned in the culinary history of New Orleans. The tale of any civilization can be told at its table, and many legends and interesting facts can be found behind the meals and beverages that make New Orleans a gourmand's paradise. If we're going to study New Orleans Voodoo, let us take a side trip through some New Orleans kitchens. The results may stimulate your intellect and will certainly stimulate your appetite.

Jambalaya

According to one story, this classic New Orleans dish originated when a hungry traveler showed up late one night at an inn. Alas, the innkeeper,

Jean, told him that nothing was left. Undeterred, the traveler told him "Jean, balayez!" ("Jean, sweep something together!") The innkeeper complied, and was so delighted by the rice-based mix of available scraps and leftovers that he named the dish "Jean balayez." Others claim the name derives from the word *jambon* (ham in French) and *ya* (purportedly an African word for rice), while still others claim it dates from the Spanish occupation of New Orleans and is a portmanteau of *jamón* (Spanish for ham) and paella, the famous Spanish rice dish.

Perhaps the most plausible explanation comes from culinary scholar Andrew Sigal. He notes that ham is not a particularly prominent ingredient in most jambalayas, and that pilau au jambon or paella con jamón would be a more likely name for these dishes in French or Spanish. But in the Provençal dialect of French there is a word that describes a mishmash or a rabble and also describes a stew of rice, vegetables, and various meats—*jambalaia*.[1] But while the word's origins may be European, the spicy seasonings that are common to many New Orleans jambalayas show a definite African influence. Ceebu jën, a popular Senegalese dish, combines tomatoes, rice, fish, and vegetables with abundant amounts of hot chile peppers. When meat is used instead of, or in addition to, fish, the dish is known as Wolof Rice (after the Wolof people of modern-day Senegal) and is served throughout Western Africa. Its fiery flavor has been preserved in Louisiana, where many like their jambalayas hot and some like them even hotter.

Just about every cook in Louisiana has the recipe for the One True Jambalaya and will swear that everyone else's is just a pale imitation. Creole (or red) jambalaya includes tomatoes and tomato paste, while Cajun (brown) jambalaya shuns tomatoes and gets its brown coloration from the bits of browned meat scraped from the bottom of the pan. The other ingredients used will vary. Cajun cooks typically include andouille, *tasso,* or smoked sausage, while Creole cooks generally add shrimp, but after that just about everything is fair game. Jambalaya can be made with chicken, boar, shrimp, fish, crawfish, alligator, beef, or just about any other meat you have around the larder. Onions and bell peppers are generally sautéed along with the meats and other vegetables. Stock is then added along with rice and, near the end, fast-cooking items like shrimp or crawfish. Cayenne pepper and Tabasco sauce are often added, although some prefer milder jambalaya.

Jambalaya became especially well known after the release of the 1952 Hank Williams Sr. hit "Jambalaya." Taking the melody to a classic Cajun tune, "Grand Texas," Williams added new lyrics celebrating life on the bayou, where one could enjoy "Jambalaya, a-crawfish pie and-a file gumbo." His version of the Cajun classic reached number one on the country music charts and remains one of Williams's most popular tunes. And when Luisah Teish wanted to name her now-classic 1988 collection of African-inspired women's charms and rituals, the most evocative title she could think of was *Jambalaya*.

Gumbo

Like Texas chili and New England clam chowder, gumbo has become an emblem (some would even say a cliché) of the Crescent City table. Gumbo has a long history: in 1803 it was served at a gubernatorial reception in New Orleans, and in 1804 the dish made an appearance at a Cajun gathering.[2] When Robert Tallant and Lyle Saxon compiled their leftover tales of New Orleans history and folklore, they called it *Gumbo Ya-Ya*. But what exactly is gumbo anyway?

At its simplest, gumbo is a thick soup served over rice. This soup most often contains vegetables along with some kind of meat or seafood. In 1832 Théodore Pavie wrote about consuming squirrel gumbo (which he described as a "delicious stew") during his journey to Louisiana and Texas, while other writers have described owl and muskrat gumbo. Today the most common gumbos are seafood gumbo (which generally contains some combination of oysters, shrimp, crawfish, and crab) and chicken and andouille sausage gumbo. The "holy trinity" of Louisiana cooking—diced celery, onions, and bell peppers—is often included, and bay leaves and cayenne pepper are commonly used for seasoning. But what separates a gumbo from a mere soup is the thickening agent.

One of the most common thickeners comes from Africa: okra. Many people loathe its slimy texture, but properly cooked okra is not only delicious but also good for you. Okra is high in vitamin B_6 and fiber. It helps stabilize blood sugar, as it curbs the rate at which sugar is absorbed from the intestinal tract, and helps ensure intestinal health, while its mucilage binds cholesterol and bile-acid-carrying toxins and helps feed probiotics.[3] That mucilage—called "slime" by those who dislike okra—also thickens many gumbos. In Africa hearty okra soups are an integral part of many West African diets, and the plant that Kongo peoples call *quingombo* or *ngombo* has given its name to Louisiana's signature dish.

But the other classic gumbo thickener comes not from Africa but from the Choctaw Indians. After their soups were done cooking, they would throw in a pinch of finely ground dried sassafras leaves. This thickened the broth and added a spicy herbal flavor and aroma reminiscent of eucalyptus. The settlers came to call this filé powder and used it in their gumbos. But while okra had to be boiled to release its mucilage, filé powder could be added only after the gumbo had been removed from the heat lest it turn the dish into a gluey, stringy mess. Today gumbos are thickened either with filé or okra, but never both. Traditionally seafood gumbos are made with okra while gumbos made with game are thickened with filé (since okra was not available during the fall and winter hunting seasons).

Those who can't get over their okra prejudices and who can't find filé needn't despair. In addition to Indian and African thickeners, New Orleans cooks often rely on a French roux. Combining equal parts flour and oil or butter, they whisk the combination over high heat until it begins to darken. This produces a rich, nutty flavor but requires patience: a roux-in-progress must be whisked constantly lest it burn and become unpalatable. Some Cajun cooks will keep a dark roux cooking for nearly an hour, whisking away all the while.

And vegetarians and even vegans can get in on the gumbo game by making a traditional New Orleans Good Friday dish, gumbo z'herbes. Catholics traditionally celebrate Good Friday by fasting and abstaining from meat. This gumbo is made by combining a variety of different greens—seven, nine, or fifteen, depending on whom you ask. (Tradition says that the number of greens you use will be the number of new friends you make in the coming year.) They are slow-simmered and then drained, reserving the cooking liquid. The pot liquor (reserved liquid) is used to cook rice, and the simmered greens are added to a mix of dark roux and the ever-popular onion, celery, and bell pepper. The greens are then served over a bed of the green rice, giving you a fast that many would call a feast!

Pralines

Not only was he a noted seventeenth-century French diplomat, warrior, and statesman, César de Choiseul du Plessis-Praslin was a great lover of almonds and sweet things. To oblige Plessis-Praslin, his chef, Clement Lassagne, came up with a special recipe—almonds coated with caramelized sugar. These delicacies were popular with Plessis-Praslin's friends as a digestive aid, and were especially loved by the ladies. Recognizing a good thing when he tasted one, Plessis-Praslin grew rich investing in sugar. Chef Lassagne showed a similar flair for business. Upon retiring from his master's employment, he opened a shop in Montargis, France, entitled Maison de la Prasline and became a wealthy man too.

In 1751 Jesuit missionaries planted sugarcane in what is now downtown New Orleans (their Immaculate Conception Jesuit Church still stands on 130 Baronne Street). At first production was modest at best, as sugarcane is very susceptible to the frosts that occasionally occur even in steamy Louisiana. But by 1795 Etienne de Bore, with expert advice from Antoine Morin, a Saint-Domingue sugar maker, succeeded in producing one hundred thousand pounds (forty-five thousand kilos) of sugar, earning him a $12,000 profit. The Louisiana sugarcane industry was under way—and the subsequent arrival of former plantation owners from Saint-Domingue after the Haitian Revolution only encouraged its growth.

But while sugar was widely available, almonds were more difficult to come by. In their stead, confectioners turned to North America's only native tree nut. During the fall and winter season, these nuts had provided a major food source for Native American tribes, including the Algonquins, who called them pecans. After combining pecans and caramel, they then went one step further than Lassagne by adding heavy cream and butter. The result was a rich, sweet, crunchy confection that has become a favorite New Orleans delicacy—pralines.

During the nineteenth century, pralines became a cottage industry for pralinières, women who sold their pralines on the streets of the French Quarter. Today a number of praline specialty shops offer their wares to tourists and locals throughout that area. Laura's Candies (established in 1913) sells its sweets at 331 Chartres Street, while the Evans Creole Candy Factory (established in 1900) has a shop at 848 Decatur Street, down the street from Aunt Sally's Praline Shop (established in 1930) at 810 Decatur.

Sailors and businesspeople visiting New Orleans brought these treats back home with them, and before long similar candies could be found throughout the Gulf Coast and the southeastern United States. But epicures know that the best pralines can be found in the Crescent City. Nonnatives are cautioned that they are "prah-leans," which have "pih-cahns" as one of their major ingredients. Mispronouncing this will forever mark you as an outsider. "Pray-lean" is something one does against a church wall, while "pee-cans" are something one keeps by the bedside.

While the basic praline recipe is simple enough—sugar, pecans, cream, and butter—there is considerable variation in the finished product. Some confectioners make thin, flat pralines filled with pecan bits; others turn out great dollops of creamy goodness with pecan halves inside. Some gild the lily by adding further flavorings to the basic recipe, like shredded coconut, rum, vanilla, chocolate, sweet potato, or peanut butter: Aunt Sally's has even combined two seemingly disparate local favorites in a Tabasco-spiked praline! But most New Orleanians and visitors feel there's no improving on perfection; they like their sweet pecan-studded decadence just the way it is.

Coffee with Chicory

Fearful of the Royal Navy's strength, Napoleon decided to defeat Britain through economic means. In 1806 he banned the import of British goods into French-controlled countries, hoping to starve out the "nation of shop-keepers" and destroy the British economy. But while Napoleon's blockade caused some hardship to English merchants, it caused even more suffering to French coffee lovers. As their beloved beverage became increasingly scarce, they stretched out their java with roasted chicory. But even after the Little Emperor was exiled to St. Helena, his erstwhile subjects continued to drink "café à chicorée," believing that it mellowed the drink and improved the taste.

Creole settlers in the Louisiana Territory had long supplemented their expensive imported coffee with chicory and were only too happy to continue after their beverage of choice became fashionable in France. Then, during the Civil War, Union naval blockades cut off the Confederacy's supply of caffeine. Forced to make do, Confederate civilians and soldiers followed Louisiana's lead and utilized roasted wild chicory root. But after the South's surrender at Appomattox, most Southerners turned their backs on chicory and returned to consuming their coffee neat. The citizens of New Orleans, however, upheld French tradition and continued to drink their bittersweet coffee-chicory brew.

The French believed that the chicory added to coffee served as a contrastimulant, and not entirely without reason. Chicory contains no caffeine, so a chicory admixture is less stimulating than pure coffee and easier on the digestive system. A 1940 study found that two of the compounds found in roasted chicory root, lactucin and lactucopicrin, are mild sedatives that counter the effects of caffeine in rabbits and mice.[4] Herbalists have prescribed chicory root decoctions as a general appetite stimulant and liver tonic, and for jaundice, liver enlargement, gout, and rheumatism. So chicory coffee may be that rarest of items—a New Orleans culinary delight that is actually good for you!

New Orleans chicory coffee is traditionally served au lait, mixed half and half with hot milk. This combination was popularized largely by Café du Monde, which has been catering to tourists and locals from its shop in the French Market (1039 Decatur Street) since 1862. Along with their beignets (fried dough squares dusted with powdered sugar), their café au lait has become a New Orleans tradition for breakfast or any other time.

The store is open twenty-four hours a day, seven days a week, except for Christmas and during hurricane warnings. And if you can't make it to the Big Easy, don't panic. The shop's coffee-chicory blend is available in many supermarkets. (It has also become popular with Louisiana's growing Vietnamese community, who combine it with condensed milk for their legendary Vietnamese drip coffee.)

Today, New Orleans is the number one coffee port in the country. In 1995, around 241,000 tons of green coffee beans came into New Orleans; that's 27.8 percent of the coffee that entered the United States that year.[5] And New Orleans may also be the origin of another great American tradition. Writing in 1928, Lyle Saxon stated:

> It is no unusual thing for a business man to say casually: "Well, let's go and get a cup of coffee," as a visitor in his office is making ready to depart. It is a little thing perhaps, this drinking of coffee at odd times, but it is very characteristic of the city itself. Men in New Orleans give more thought to the business of living than men in other American cities. . . . I have heard Northern business men complain bitterly about these little interruptions for coffee or what-not.[6]

While we cannot say for certain that the coffee break originated in the Crescent City, it is an interesting hypothesis, and one that deserves careful consideration—preferably over several café au laits and a plate of beignets!

Crawfish

According to Thibodeaux Comeaux, a rice farmer living in Ville Platte, Louisiana, crawfish have only been around since the latter part of the eighteenth century:

> You see, people up in Nova Scotia really liked lobster. So it was only natural that when the Acadians made their move to South Louisiana,

they brought their Lobster with them. The problem was that the lobsters lost their appetite along the way and shrunk up quite a bit. Since this smaller lobster didn't really look like a lobster any more, the Acadians, now known as Cajuns, called this small crustacean a Crawfish.[7]

Biologists, alas, disagree with M. Comeaux. They say the crawfish is a freshwater decapod crustacean related to the lobster, but one that has been found in the bayous since time immemorial. But scholars and Cajuns alike can agree on one thing: when it comes to good eating, there's nothing quite like the sweet, delicate flavor of crawfish meat. Crawfish boil, crawfish pie, crawfish étouffée, crawfish gumbo, crawfish sausage—all these and more can be made with Louisiana's state crustacean. Yet until recently crawfish were considered a dish only fit for poor bayou dwellers and a few brave souls who wanted to go slumming with the Cajuns. The fine folk in New Orleans would have turned up their noses at any restaurant that would dare put "mudbugs" on its menu.

Attitudes changed after the Great Depression, when improved transportation and cold storage allowed crawfish harvests to reach markets in New Orleans and Baton Rouge. Once they got a taste of fresh crawfish, the city dwellers knew what they had been missing. And as the demand grew, Cajun fishing folk worked diligently to meet the supply. Rice farmers began reflooding their paddies after harvest to produce crawfish for harvest during the autumn, winter, and early spring. This practice of crawfish farming eventually spread to closed-in woodlands and marshland as well. Crawfish farming allowed a more consistent supply of crawfish, as wild harvests varied widely, with years of abundant crawfish separated by years when the crustacean was difficult to come by. As crawfish became more readily available, the markets grew even greater.

By the mid-1960s, the amount of land devoted to crawfish farming had increased to approximately 10,000 acres of managed ponds. At this point, an industry based on peeling crawfish became established, and the new markets for crawfish meat allowed both crawfish farming and wild harvests to increase even more. Today more than 1,600 Louisiana farmers produce crawfish in approximately 120,000 acres of ponds, with over 800 commercial fishers harvesting crawfish from natural wetlands. Their combined annual yield ranges from 75 million to 105 million pounds—over 90 percent of the domestic crop! More than 7,000 people depend directly or indirectly on the crawfish industry, and it is estimated to add over $120 million each year to Louisiana's economy.

But this industry has faced a number of threats. By mid-1997, some 80 percent of the frozen crawfish sold in America were coming from private farmers in Jiangsu Province, China. Louisiana's crawfish industry took its case to Washington, where Senator John Breaux argued, "Crawfish to Louisiana is like cars in Detroit—it's very important to our economy and our culture, and we must do whatever is necessary to preserve the industry." Tariffs ranging between 97 percent and 202 percent were placed on the Chinese imports after the International Trade Commission found that "to upset the crawfish industry would not only put thousands of Louisianans out of work, but it would seriously jeopardize a way of life for a culture."[8]

Today the crawfish industry is still struggling to recover from the damage wrought to the bayous and farms after Katrina. The hurricane sent waves of saltwater into the region, devastating the freshwater-loving crawfish. But though times remain tough, Louisiana's crawfishers remain unbowed. "If there's any industry that'll come back, it's the seafood industry," says Ewell Smith, executive director of the Louisiana Seafood Promotion and Marketing Board. "We've been down before. Katrina is the biggest blow we've ever faced, but we'll come back."[9]

9

VOODOO TEMPLES AND CURIO SHOPS

New Orleans Voodoo, like its Haitian cousin, is resource intensive. Your local greengrocer is unlikely to have the makings for a gris-gris bag, a bottle of Bend Over Drops, or images of your favorite saint. And whenever you have a demand, you inevitably will find someone to supply it. As a result, a number of stores have sprung up to provide Voodoo queens, root doctors, and curious tourists with all the fixings for rituals, spellwork, and spooky magical souvenirs.

And much as there is a brisk business in supplies, so too is there a demand for finished products. Those who wish to experience the religion firsthand can attend services held at various temples. There Christian imagery is combined with Kardecian Spiritualism (a method of communing with the dead made famous by Frenchman Alain Kardec) and African drumming and dancing for a potent spiritual experience—and if you want more personal attention, gris-gris and magical services are also on sale! While Leafy Anderson's Eternal Life Christian Spiritualist Church (chapter 18) is probably the most famous of these Spiritualist churches, there are many other smaller groups that have provided counsel and magical aid to a satisfied clientele. All of these businesses have become an integral part of the city's landscape—and as New Orleans Voodoo has shaped them, so too have they shaped New Orleans Voodoo.

The Cracker Jack Drugstore

Dr. George Thomas started out as just another physician and pharmacist plying his trade at his Cracker Jack drugstore on Rampart Street. But as time went on he found that many of his black customers were more interested in botanical extracts, herbal preparations, and Voodoo supplies he started selling around 1919. Never one to turn away customers, Thomas began offering spiritual merchandise along with his powders and pills. His strategy paid off, and by 1919 he was able to move his family from the rooms above his store to a large house in one of the city's most prestigious neighborhoods.[1]

Thomas soon expanded his clientele by sending out mail-order catalogues advertising his various wares. But soon his national business attracted the attention of post office inspectors, who took a dim view of his good luck charms and magical potions. In 1927 New Orleans newspapers reported on an investigation into a "Voodoo practice . . . founded on the superstitions of Marie Laveau."

> The inspectors found the organization manipulated by an aged white physician. His practice . . . has been entirely confined to Negroes whose superstitious nature has enabled him to found a drugstore dealing in such articles as "goofer dust," "eagle eyes" and other charms for good and evil. . . . Assistant U.S. Attorney Edmond E. Talbot said that he had requested the physician to appear at his office [but] he had not determined what form the prosecution would take.[2]

But the investigation apparently came to naught. The Cracker Jack continued selling Hoodoo and Voodoo supplies to practitioners throughout the New Orleans area. These goods were generally kept hidden and sold only to black patrons. (There was no way of distinguishing a white tourist from an undercover policeman looking to file a fraud complaint, but law enforcement showed little interest in protecting black people from con artists.) Clients would arrive with "prescriptions" written by root doctors and reverend mothers. The druggist would then provide them with the requested powders, oils, and roots.

The Cracker Jack Drugstore also produced a well-known occult pamphlet, *Black and White Magic,* attributed to Marie Laveau and compiled by "Bivins N. D. P." While Bivins's identity remains a mystery, it is clear that he or she had some familiarity with Hoodoo and Spiritualism. It is also clear that the compiler knew something about marketing, as "Marie" recommended many of the products that were for sale at Cracker Jack. For promoting peace in the home, the reader was advised to

> sprinkle every room of your house with "Peace Water" and burn the "John the Conqueror Incense" mixed with the "Helping Hand Incense." Sprinkle some "Jinks Removing Salt" all around the outside of your house. Apply to your body daily the "Peace Powder" and anoint your head and clothes with "Bend Over Drops." Burn for one hour each day or night the "Peace Candle" until you have burned three of them.[3]

In 1972 the original Cracker Jack building at 435 South Rampart Street was torn down. Efforts were made to keep the store open at a new location on Prieur Street, but to no avail. By 1974 the Cracker Jack Drugstore closed for good. Today the site of the original location is a parking lot that serves the nearby Superdome.

The Temple of Innocent Blood

In 1922 Catherine Seals suffered a paralytic stroke. Desperate for a cure, she solicited the services of a white faith healer. Alas, the woman refused to help because she didn't work with colored folks. But the spirit told Seals that she didn't need anyone else's services; she could heal herself through prayer—and would become a noted healer in her own right once she was well. As soon as she was up and about again, Seals (now "Mother Catherine") began the process of founding her church. Her faith proved strong enough to overcome all obstacles, and soon she had a Temple in the

Ninth Ward, near the Industrial Canal, which joins Lake Pontchartrain with the Mississippi River. Some dispute this story, claiming that Mother Catherine was originally a student of Leafy Anderson, who parted ways with her due to personal differences and brought a small coterie of followers along. But whatever the circumstances behind the founding of Mother Catherine's organization, no one disputes that she soon garnered a reputation for prophesying, healing, and charity.

Seals was particularly devoted to unwed mothers and adamantly opposed to the abortionists who did a thriving (if illegal) business in the Crescent City. To honor these unborn children, she named her church the Temple of Innocent Blood. Mother Catherine took in women who had been injured by crude coat hanger abortions and nursed them back to health. Many of these charges turned away from their lives of prostitution and sin and became dedicated followers. Mother Catherine's church was predominantly female, and she made no apologies for taking charge of her flock. "It is right that a woman should lead," she told Zora Neale Hurston. "A womb was what God made in the beginning and out of that womb was born time, and that fills up space. So says the beautiful spirit."[4]

Mother Catherine also attracted notice for her intriguing art. A statue named *Jehovah God*, sculpted by Seals in fourteen days, graced the grounds. A large cylindrical object above the main altar, made shortly before her death, was called *Key to the World*. According to Mother Rita, her successor, Seals designed the key on instruction of the spirits, using soil, salt, and herbs in its construction. The four faces at its top stared out over statues of other saints provided to the church by grateful beneficiaries of Mother Catherine's healing. (Given that her healing rituals typically involved ingesting quantities of castor oil, their gratitude is especially noteworthy!)

Two weeks before her death, Mother Catherine was told by the Holy Spirit that she had only a short time to live. Rising from her sickbed, she returned to her birthplace in Kentucky. There, on August 9, 1930, she died. According to her successor, Mother Rita, she said, "Ah's gonna rise again. Ah's gonna continue ma good wuk."[5] She may not have attained her bodily resurrection, and her Temple of Innocent Blood may have crumbled to dust long before Katrina wiped out most of the Ninth Ward, but Mother Catherine's influence remains powerful within the black Spiritualist community of New Orleans—and many of today's reverend mothers claim that Mother Catherine still visits them in spirit to provide guidance and wisdom.

The Voodoo Spiritual Temple

At the age of eleven, Miriam Williams was baptized in the spirit in a Christian church. In her own words:

> I remember kneeling, and Rev. Jarret, he came and laid his hand on my back and I remember when he put his hand on my back, sort of like spirit of electrifying forces went through me and I was like lifted in a rapture. . . . And so it's from those times, I felt a presence.[6]

But Williams grew increasingly uncomfortable with the hypocrisy, self-righteousness, and power-tripping she saw in the organized church. Ultimately she found her way to the Spiritual Church Movement, an African American undertaking that combined Pentecostal revivalism with the teachings of Spiritualism. From 1982 to 1989 she was a bishop in Chicago's Angel Angel All Nations Spiritual Church. There she gained experience in ministering to a congregation and working directly with the spirits—skills that would serve her well when she began the next phase of her mission.

In 1989 she met Osman Chamani. Chamani had studied herbalism, drumming, and divination with the Obeah men of his native Belize. After a whirlwind courtship, they were married. Soon thereafter the Chamanis moved to New Orleans and, on the advice of the spirits, founded the Voodoo Spiritual Temple (see plate 15). In 1994 the temple was established at its present location, 828 North Rampart Street, opposite Louis Armstrong Park, or what was once called Congo Square. The Voodoo Spiritual Temple combined Osman's training in Afro-Belizean spirituality with Miriam's experience in Black Christian Spiritualism. Offering African bone readings, oils, baths, and other healing services, the Voodoo

Spiritual Temple soon became a major center for New Orleans natives and tourists interested in the more spiritual side of Voodoo.

Then, in 1995, Osman Chamani died. Although tragic, this was not entirely unexpected. When they first met he had told Miriam, "I will die a long time before you, but when I die the Temple will be completely formed and you will do what is necessary to carry the Temple."[7] With the training she had received from her late husband, Chamani continued their work, offering consultation and healing to those souls who came to her in need.

Visitors to the Voodoo Spiritual Temple may be struck with sensory overload upon entry. Most of the available space is taken up by various brightly colored and heavily decorated altars. West African Orisha and Haitian lwa are prevalent, but there are also shrines in honor of the ancestors, including one containing the ashes of Fred "Chicken Man" Staten (chapter 10), and a large statue of Buddha, which watches serenely above a collection of herbs and instruments. This eclecticism is in keeping with Chamani's belief that all properly functioning spiritual systems seek to heal the wounded and to align worshippers with the Spirit that is the fount of all life and energy.

Like other Voodoo practitioners in the city, Chamani offers spells and charms for those who are only interested in the magical side of Voodoo. But the temple also offers a place of worship for those who wish to explore the deeper spiritual realities behind the magic. While there are no formal initiations (Chamani prefers to concentrate on knowledge acquired and openness to Spirit rather than symbolic rituals), continuing involvement in the temple's activities will generally result in greater responsibilities and ceremonial duties. Through both public and private rituals, the temple continues to serve its stated purpose—to train and develop the spiritual and mental powers lying dormant in each of us—for members and guests alike.

The Island of Salvation Botanica

So how does a nice Jewish girl from Maine wind up a Voodoo priestess in New Orleans? "I don't really have a good excuse," says Sallie Ann Glassman, "except to say that it was a spiritual calling that brought me here. Initially, I just thought Vodou was interesting. The more I studied it, the more fascinating and rich the subject became for me."[8] But Glassman's modesty belies the determination she showed in her quest. When she first came to New Orleans in 1977, she found little spiritual nourishment amid the tourist traps and Voodoo shows. But still she persisted in her studies and her work with the spirits, until in 1995 she traveled to Port-au-Prince, Haiti, to undergo initiation in the house of respected houngan (priest of Haitian Vodou) and artist Edgar Jean-Louis.

Her store, the Island of Salvation Botanica, is located at 835 Piety Street in the Bywater neighborhood. It is difficult to miss: just look for the enormous paintings of the Stella Maris, St. Jacques Majeur, and Mater Salvatoris that hang from its front entrance. (They, like many of the art works sold at Island of Salvation, were created by Glassman.) Readings, candles, and gris-gris bags are among the store's offerings. Shoppers can also buy copies of Glassman's book *Vodou Visions* and her *New Orleans Voodoo Tarot* or commission her to do a visionary painting. And those who are interested in art may purchase sequined bottles made by Glassman or dwapo lwa (Haitian Vodou flags) made by Jean-Louis, one of Haiti's most famous flagmakers.

In addition to her public rituals (she regularly presides over Day of the Dead ceremonies on Halloween and other festivals throughout New Orleans), Glassman provides private instruction and ritual at her temple, La Source Ancienne Hounfo. Located near the site of Island of Salvation, La Source Ancienne has approximately twenty members who come together to serve the spirits as a community. La Source Ancienne provides training in drumming, dancing, and singing, and arranges opportunities for interested serviteurs (servants of the lwa) to seek initiation in Haiti.

While Katrina's wrath largely spared the Island of Salvation Botanica, it wreaked havoc on the surrounding neighborhoods, especially the nearby Ninth Ward. To help her city in its long recovery, Glassman founded the Hope and Heritage Project. Headquartered at Island of Salvation, Hope and Heritage combines community organizing with alternative modalities of healing like shamanic work and yoga. The failures of state, federal, and local officials during and after Katrina proved what poor folks in New Orleans have always known: if you don't do for yourself, ain't nobody else going to do for you. By leveraging her skills as a mambo, Glassman hopes to empower disenfranchised survivors and prepare for the next time a hurricane strikes New Orleans. When completed, the Hope and Healing Center will occupy a 55,000-square-foot building and involve $10 million in public and private financing. As Glassman says, this is "what a Vodou priest's work is all about—healing on every level."[9]

Some Vodou purists have criticized Glassman's innovations to traditional Haitian service. A vegan, Glassman does not sacrifice animals in her ceremonies. She has also incorporated services to the Orisha and elements of Thelema (the religious/mystical movement popularized by Aleister Crowley) into her rituals. "Vodou is a living tradition," she replies unapologetically. "You will absolutely encounter some aspects of ritual in my home that are not traditional to Haitian Vodou and yet are absolutely legitimate to the ongoing development of Vodou as a syncretic religion."[10] But no matter how far La Source Ancienne grows away from its Haitian roots, there is no question that it has developed into a vibrant and influential religious community in New Orleans.

The Westgate Museum

When she was four years old, Leilah Wendell encountered a spectral spirit who frightened her terribly, until he sat down beside her and put his hand on her shoulder. "The next thing I remember," says Wendell, "was never being afraid of Him ever again."[11] Her relationship with this angel of death who called himself Azrael grew closer as she matured. With a magazine called *Undinal Songs,* Wendell reached out to others interested in necromancy, necrophilia, and other long-tabooed views of death. Before long what had started as *Undinal Songs* grew into the Westgate Group, a conglomerate that consisted of a publishing house, art studio, and metaphysical information exchange.

Then, in 1990, Wendell spent four days in New Orleans and fell in love. In her words:

It seemed to have been chosen by Azrael Himself as a viable gateway through which He might emerge into the world. A city where many spiritual gates lie open. An unsettling threshold in its own right, where Life & Death merge behind a feathered mask. Where spectres weep in shaded courtyards, and magick recedes behind weathered shutters.[12]

Within a few months Wendell had pulled up stakes from her native Long Island and, along with her partner, Daniel Kemp, set up the Westgate Museum in an enormous black-and-purple house on 5219 Magazine Street. The museum functioned as a bookstore for tomes like Wendell's *The Book of Azrael* and *The Necromantic Ritual Book,* and Kemp's *The Book of Night,* as well as a gallery for Wendell's haunting art pieces. (These, unsurprisingly, generally focused on romantic death and featured gravestones, skeletons, and funeral floral arrangements.)

Even visitors who found the Westgate Museum's subject matter off-putting discovered that Wendell and Kemp were charming and knowledgeable hosts who were happy to answer questions about their art and their beliefs. While many in New Orleans have been known to work a spiritual angle for money, Wendell and Kemp were unquestionably sincere—at the risk of a bad pun, one might even say "dead serious." Like many other unorthodox mystics who had found a home in the Crescent City, Wendell, Kemp, and Azrael became a local fixture.

But as time went on, they grew increasingly dissatisfied with New Orleans. They felt that creeping gentrification was turning their once-bohemian city into a Disneyfied yuppie playground—and after the 9/11 attacks, even that wasn't enough to draw the tourists who supported their museum. When Hurricane Katrina struck, they decided enough was enough. After a bit of searching, Wendell and Kemp set up shop in Opelousas, a small central Louisiana city known as "The Spice Capital of the World" and home to the International Joke Telling Contest and the Holy Ghost Creole Festival. They have also established a presence on the Internet, selling their various wares at www.westgatenecromantic.com. And while the Westgate Museum is no more, Wendell has not ruled out the possibility of starting it up again, saying,

People still ask us if we will ever reopen the physical gallery ever again. I don't know. "Ever" is a long time. If I look back on all of the 30 years, one thing I DO know for sure, and have known for years, is that a moment truly does change all things, so it's best NOT to plan, but rather to let things unfold naturally.[13]

Boutique du Vampyre

Before the sparkly vampires of Forks, Washington, flew onto the scene, writer Anne Rice was holding court in New Orleans. Tapping into the themes of decadent Catholicism and sexual liberation—concepts long connected with her hometown—Rice became a one-woman cottage industry. Beginning in 1976 with *Interview with the Vampire* and continuing through books like *The Vampire Lestat* (1985), *The Queen of the Damned* (1988), and *Blood Canticle* (2003), Rice chronicled the afterlives of the beautiful and undead in lengthy bodice-rippers that are mocked by many and loved by many more.

Rice's androgynous, ethically conflicted bloodsuckers inspired a whole generation of fans to don plastic fangs, colored contacts, and monikers like "Nosferatu Nightlover." Some "psivamps" get their nourishment draining energy from others. Others, who identify as "sanguine," prefer to feed the old-fashioned way, by draining blood from a willing victim. (As Belfazaar, a sanguine who works at Voodoo Authenica, explains, "Even though the vampires are taking from someone there is an energy that we give off. . . . For some people, they describe it as calming, other people describe it as sensually arousing.")[14]

Many of these self-proclaimed vampyres made their way to Rice's hometown, a city as steamy, decadent, and overheated as her ultraviolet prose. Some came for the Endless Night festival, an annual Halloween event that attracts undead from around the globe. Others made the Crescent City their home base in the eternal search for victims and DJs willing to add Bauhaus and Dead Can Dance to their playlists. Whether they were nesting or just visiting, all found a warm welcome at Boutique du Vampyre.

Located at 633 Toulouse, the boutique provides everything a Child of the Night needs for a pleasant stay in the Crescent City. Wraparound sunglasses are provided for those occasions when one must go out before sundown, while coffin and bat mirrors are available for those who can still see their reflections. Custom fangs can be purchased, along with temporary bite tattoos for those wishing to mark those they have taken into their Dark Embrace. And if you're tired of transfusions, you can take home some Noctra Creole Mustard or Vampfire, a vampire hot sauce (made in Transylvania, Louisiana).

But amid the tourist merchandise one finds another New Orleans tradition: local artwork. The vampire aesthetic has inspired a number of talented craftspeople. Hand-blown glass chalices, vampire prints, ink drawings, and decorated candles are among the offerings on sale at the store. Local fragrance-maker Hové Parfumeur has created a special rose-scented "Bouquet du Vampyre," which is sold exclusively through Boutique du Vampyre. Local authors of vampire-related fiction and nonfiction frequently hold signings at the store, and members of the various clans meet over a glass of red (cabernet, that is) at the regular wine tastings.

While the vampyre affectations may seem silly to outsiders, they hold deep meaning to those who identify with the various reinterpretations of the old archetype. They may have been inspired by works of fiction and shop at stores that cater to tourists—but the same could be said of many other New Orleans traditions. Skeptics may scoff at them, as they scoff at those who profess belief in Voodoo. But it is clear that the vampyres, like those who have come to the city in search of the lwa, have created their own mythology and claimed New Orleans as one of their holy cities.

10

PRIESTS, PRIESTESSES, HOUNGANS, MAMBOS, AND CHICKEN MEN

There is no pope in New Orleans Voodoo. There is not even a governing body of presbyters to separate true from false practitioners. One becomes a priest or priestess by impressing potential clients and winning public attention. Charisma and showmanship are often more important than adherence to dogma, and entertaining stories often get greater attention than truthful ones.

While some may see this as a flaw, others see it as an opportunity. There has been no shortage of colorful characters who have set themselves up as New Orleans Voodoo priests and priestesses. And some of the accusations of exaggeration have themselves been greatly exaggerated.

Jean "Doctor John" Montaigne

Jean Montaigne had little trouble frightening people. Tall and broad-shouldered, with a scarred and tattooed face and fiery fierce eyes, he looked every bit the African prince he claimed to be. And if that wasn't enough to terrify his neighbors on Bayou Street, he was also a notorious medicine man known for his skill in casting curses and revealing secrets. Black and white patrons alike frequented his shop, making "Doctor John" one of nineteenth-century New Orleans' most powerful and successful conjurers.

Montaigne claimed to have been born in Senegal to the royal family. Captured by slavers, he was taken to Cuba and put to work on a sugar plantation. But his esoteric powers (or so he claimed) allowed him to charm his master into granting him his freedom. Once released, Montaigne traveled the world as a sailor and ship's cook before settling down in New Orleans and taking up work on the docks. His enormous physical strength and his personal magnetism led to him becoming a foreman over the other black longshoremen.

But here Montaigne began showing his talent as a seer. Rumor spread that he could foretell the future by reading the marks on a bale of cotton. Many black New Orleanians called upon this Senegalese prince to prophesy for them, and soon his reputation spread to the white community. White ladies who visited him for divination or love potions often went to his house veiled so that no one could identify them—but they still came, and still paid handsomely for an audience with him. In time Montaigne was able to give up his job on the docks and began working full time as "Doctor John."

As his fame grew, so did his prosperity. By the 1840s Doctor John was one of the wealthiest blacks in New Orleans. In his office (decorated with a picture of the Virgin Mary, some African shells for divination, and an elephant's tusk) he saw clients for $10 to $20 a session. Others would spend large sums of money on charms, gris-gris bags (chapter 23), or potions. Doctor John told a confidant that one of his potions was water in which some common herbs had been boiled. "I hurt nobody," he said, "but if folks want to give me fifty dollars, I take the fifty dollars every time!"[1]

Some whispered that Doctor John's perfidy went beyond fraudulent potions. They claimed that he had a network of slaves employed by the wealthiest families in New Orleans. These housemaids and manservants knew many of their employers' most intimate secrets—and so did Doctor

John. As a result, he was able to impress them with his fortune-telling skills—or make a tidy profit in blackmail. Others accused Montaigne of being a pimp. This may have been inspired at least in part by Doctor John's harem of fifteen wives (including at least one white woman) and his penchant for expensive clothing and fine wines. But for every critic Doctor John had many admirers who respected his magical powers and his generosity in distributing food during festivals and major holidays.

Whatever frauds Doctor John may have perpetrated, he was sinned against at least as often as he sinned. The man who taught him how to read and write had him practice his signature on a deed—then claimed a large part of Doctor John's property! His efforts to regain his fortune failed as his investment partners cheated him time and again. At his lowest point he squandered much of his money on lottery tickets. Were it not for his many children taking pity upon him, the once-wealthy Montaigne would have died homeless. As it was he retained the respect of black New Orleans, who always revered him as a great conjurer and Voodoo man who was said to have taught no less than the great Marie Laveau herself.

Long after Doctor John's death, a New Orleans musician named Mac Rebennack discovered that one of his distant ancestors, Pauline Rebennack, had allegedly been part of Montaigne's Voodoo and prostitution empire. Taking the stage name "Dr. John the Night Tripper," Rebennack released the visionary 1968 album *Gris-Gris*. Featuring songs like "Gris-Gris Gumbo Ya-Ya" and "Danse Kalinda Ba Doom," *Gris-Gris* combined psychedelic rock and progressive jazz with infectious New Orleans rhythms and Voodoo imagery. Fueled by Rebennack's bluesy piano stylings and swamp-thing growl, it was unusual and unforgettable even by the standards of the 1960s, what one critic called "a psychedelic Voodoo ceremony invading your living room."[2]

More than forty years later, Rebennack continues to tour and record songs like "Marie Laveau the Voodoo Queen" and "Black John the Conqueror." His recording of the New Orleans classic "Iko Iko" (a Mardi Gras standard that has roots in Ghana folk music) inspired the Grateful Dead to cover the song and make it a standard part of their live repertoire from 1977 onward. He continues to pay tribute to Montaigne and to Voodoo, stating in a 2006 interview that it is

> a beautiful part of New Orleans culture. It's such a blend of stuff; African, Choctaw, Christianity, Spanish. I just figured that if I wrote songs based on gris gris, it would help people. A lot of the people practicing it were dying off and the kids were not following it. I was trying to keep the traditions going.[3]

The Seven Sisters of New Orleans

If you go into a well-stocked botanica, you're sure to find the Seven Sisters of New Orleans. Their oils, sprays, and other spiritual offerings are distributed by Indio Products, one of the major players in the spiritual supply business. They inspired the Seven Sisters of Alabama, the Seven Sisters of Virginia, the Seven Sisters of North Carolina, and the Seven Hoodoo Brothers of New York, among other professional Hoodoo workers who wished to capitalize on their name. But who were the original Seven Sisters?

Some say they were daughters of Marie Laveau and have passed down their Voodoo knowledge through generations. Others say that there was only one sister, the seventh child in her family—but that her power made her one of the Crescent City's most feared and respected Voodoo queens. And still others say that their descendants still practice their craft today. While the gullible buy colored water and cheap incense, those who are diligent will find the real thing if only they know where to look.

A little research will reveal that the Seven Sisters allegedly made their home in the city's Fifteenth Ward, in the West Bank community of Algiers. Algiers had always had a prominent black presence. In the days of slavery, imported Africans were kept there in pens until they had recovered from the crossing and could be brought to the slave markets in the Vieux Carré (the French Quarter). Later it became home to many of the jazz musicians who worked across the river in Storyville, the city's red-light district.

And while it was famous for its musical residents, Algiers was even more famous for its rootworkers and spiritual professionals. Throughout the South the small community was known as Hoodoo Town and the home of "Algiers conjure." In his "Seven Sisters Blues" bluesman Boogie Bill Webb sang about the Seven Sisters of Algiers and how their gifts sometimes uncovered uncomfortable truths.

> *Well, they told me my fortune as I walked in their door.*
> *They told me my fortune as I walked in their door.*
> *She said: well, I'm sorry for you, Boogie,*
> *ooh, well, that little woman don't want you no more.*[4]

In 1931, Texas bluesman J. T. "Funny Paper" Smith gave us their names in his "Seven Sisters Blues":

> *Now, it's Sarah, Minnie, Bertha,*
> *Holly, Dolly, Betty and Jane*
> *Sarah, Minnie, Bertha,*
> *Holly, Dolly, Betty and Jane*
> *You can't know them Sisters apart,*
> *because they all looks just the same.*[5]

The Seven Sisters have also inspired Louisiana poet laureate Brenda Marie Osbey. Her "Faubourg Study No. 3: Seven Sisters of New Orleans," a thirteen-part poem, collects various stories and community narratives to paint a picture of holy women struggling to define themselves against a backdrop of racism, sexism, and religious prejudice. Some narrators scorn them as "run-down whores . . . come down into the city/to pass" and "foreigners or nations/island people most likely" who practiced "reading and healing and getting full of spirit." Yet by the end of the poem they have been transformed from motherless children into servants of the great goddess who is simultaneously the Virgin Mary and the Haitian lwa Erzulie, and the academic who came to study them "with camera and satchel" has recognized her own connection to the great feminine.[6]

Today the Seven Sisters remain controversial. The New Orleans Historic Voodoo Museum dismisses them as "a group of Black Women capitalizing on the legend of Marie Laveau's seven daughters having removed from New Orleans to Algiers. During the 1920's and 1930's they operated a Hoodoo business geared toward visitors."[7] By contrast, Cathi Smith operates the House of the 7 Sisters Musee & Gift Shop at 800 Brooklyn Avenue in Algiers Point. The museum's brochure claims the seven sisters were daughters of Marie Laveau and that they held meetings in Algiers for the Hoodoos and herb doctors from around the country.[8]

But while their story endures, finding the real Seven Sisters remains challenging. Boogie Bill Webb's 1937 paean to the Seven Sisters of Algiers was a rewritten version of an earlier tune dedicated to legendary root-worker Aunt Catherine Dye of Newport, Arkansas. No one has verified Smith's naming of the sisters, and Osbey's homage to Erzulie owes more to reconstructed New Orleans Voodoo than to the Hoodoo practiced in 1920s Algiers. As is so often the case in New Orleans, it is difficult to separate legend and reality—and perhaps those who try to do so are missing the point.

In many cultures the number seven is connected with good luck and mystical power. Gamblers consider seven a lucky number, so if you wanted a mojo hand to help your craps game, one made by seven sisters would be especially powerful. Rootworkers and conjure folk have long embellished their credentials to win customers. It could be that, in the best New Orleans tradition, the legend of the Seven Sisters originated as a marketing campaign that inspired imitators throughout black America and beyond.

Fred "Chicken Man" Staten

If you asked for his qualifications, Prince Keeyama would explain to you that he had been born in Haiti, where he learned the secrets of Voodoo from no less than François "Papa Doc" Duvalier. This explained his ability to paralyze a human with a single touch, his expert knowledge of snakes, and his general skill with animals. (He claimed that he had trained the lions on display at the New Orleans Zoo.) He would then offer to sell you some of his potions, incense, gris-gris bags, or blessed candles so that you too could benefit from his Voodoo powers.

Upon further research, many of Prince Keeyama's claims would prove to be a bit questionable. The New Orleans Zoo denied any knowledge of his lion-taming abilities, and his accent showed no trace of the classic Haitian lilt. (Later he changed his story and credited his Haitian-born grandparents with his Voodoo education.) A little more research would reveal that his birth name was the un-Haitian sounding Fred Staten, and his parents resided not in Port-au-Prince but Cleveland.

But you would likely forget all those details during his cabaret show. As a sign of his "God-given Voodoo powers," Staten handled snakes, ate fire, chewed on glass, and stuck pins through his throat. Then, as the grand finale, he "hypnotized" a live chicken, bit its head off, and drank blood from the spurting neck. This act earned him the sobriquet by which he would go down in New Orleans history—Chicken Man.

With his black top hat, dreadlocks, and long staff crowned with a plastic hand and a monkey skull, Chicken Man was an unforgettable character. The tourists loved him, but the "serious" Voodoo people were generally less impressed. To them he was a mere showman, a carnival geek who used Voodoo as a prop. According to one of his contemporary devotees, their scorn never bothered him:

He didn't mind being so put down in the public eye, because he knew he had the belief of the people that mattered to him, and he knew he was truly helping people every day. That is more than most people can claim, to say that they have helped at least one person every day they are alive.[9]

For a time Staten tried to get away from the Crescent City and take his Voodoo act elsewhere. There was a brief marriage in 1970 and an attempt to start a Voodoo museum in the small town of Blanco, Texas. The opening night went well. At the urging of the crowd, he even agreed to spare the sacrificial chicken. Unfortunately, his career ended in handcuffs, as a bounced Louisiana check came back to haunt him. "Toward the end, I felt the marriage wouldn't have worked, but he was fun and my kids loved him," said ex-wife Eleanor Forsythe. "There are a lot of kids and dogs around [Blanco] who'll miss the Chicken Man."[10]

Once released, Staten put down roots in New Orleans for good. With the aid of his new wife (who became known as the Chicken Woman), he set up Chicken Man's House of Voodoo on the 700 block of Bourbon Street. Staten generally left the store in her hands. He preferred working on the streets of New Orleans, doing readings, selling curios, and offering inspiration and advice to those in need. In time he even won over many of the skeptics of the New Orleans Voodoo establishment. (According to one rumor, even white supremacist David Duke called on Chicken Man for magical assistance during his unsuccessful 1992 gubernatorial campaign!)

Despite his chicken-decapitating ways, Staten was widely known for his kind and generous nature. Those who were short on cash often received his readings or gris-gris bags for free. He also mentored many black teens, encouraging them to stay away from drugs and avoid the gang violence prevalent in many of New Orleans' poor neighborhoods. Alas, this did little to ensure his financial success. His store closed and, as his health failed, he was less often seen in his beloved streets. When he died in 1998 at age sixty-one, his body sat in the morgue for over a month, since there was no money to bury him.

But then Earl Barnhardt returned home to New Orleans after a long business trip. In 1984 Barnhardt had been a struggling bar owner. In desperation, he hired Staten to bless his establishment. "He made the sign of the cross on all four walls," Barnhardt said. "Overnight, we became the bar of choice for the Tulane college crowd."[11] Upon hearing that Chicken Man was dead, Barnhardt not only paid for the burial, he hired a horse-drawn hearse and a brass band to send him out with a jazz funeral. Voodoo priestess Miriam Chamani and Santeria priestess Ava Kay Jones marched along with the coffin and hundreds of local residents. Much gin (Staten's drink of choice) was spilled in his honor and many more beverages were consumed by the crowd. "A rich man can have millions and a big funeral, but have no friends and have nothing," declared Barnhardt in his eulogy. "Chicken Man had many friends. He died a rich man."[12]

PART THREE

THE SPIRITS

As in Haiti, the spirits served in New Orleans come from many different African cultures. But things in the Crescent City are even more complicated than in Haiti. The Orisha of Cuban Santeria are honored alongside Haitian lwa, Catholic saints, African American folk heroes, and famous (or notorious) characters from the city's long and checkered history.

This section concentrates on the spirits who have long histories in New Orleans and those who are found there alone. To learn more about some of the other lwa who have taken root in the Crescent City, you may consult my *Haitian Vodou Handbook* (Destiny Books, 2006) or Sallie Ann Glassman's excellent *Vodou Visions: An Encounter with Divine Mystery* (Island of Salvation Botanica, 2007).

The *lois* (spirits) of New Orleans were not historically served with *vévés*, the beautiful cornmeal drawings that are used in Haiti. Instead they were honored with images of the saints and with prayers that were inspired by Roman Catholicism but with the addition of certain phrases and nuances. These would go undetected by outsiders but carried hidden meanings to those who knew their secrets. Instead of the vévés found in *The Haitian Vodou Handbook*, this book includes prayers that may be used to honor the saints and spirits of New Orleans.

11

THE OLD MAN AT THE CROSSROADS

Papa La-Bas

In Haiti Papa Legba is recognized as the guardian of the gate. Houngans and mambos believe that no lwa can come down without Legba's approval, and so he is saluted at the beginning of every *fete* (party) in order that the spirits may arrive and give their blessings. But while he is always given his due, he receives far less attention than some of the more popular lwa. Ghede's party is always one of the year's biggest and rowdiest festivals, and Ogou regularly receives offerings of rum and promises of marriage from women, while both Freda and Danto are pursued by men hoping to win their favor. Atibon Legba (Good Old Legba), by contrast, gets little but his regular offerings of cane syrup, rum, and an occasional rooster.

Outside Haiti the Master of the Crossroads is a far more popular fellow. Legba has become one of the most well known of the lwa, appearing in Grant Morrison's comic book series *The Invisibles* and William Gibson's science fiction novel *Count Zero,* and saluted in song by the Talking Heads and Elton John, among others. He has also long been an integral part of conjure and Hoodoo—and while many of the other lwa did not arrive in New Orleans until much later, Legba (under several different names) has been there all along, waiting by the roadside and opening the door for the spiritual activity that has made the Crescent City so famous.

St. Peter, Papa Limba, and Papa La-Bas

St. Peter, you hold the keys to the gates of the Celestial Kingdom; you open the door to those who are worthy and hold it fast against all others. Open the way for me so that I may partake of the blessings of heaven and shut out those who seek to do harm to me and to mine. Guide me that I may walk upon the road of righteousness and keep me from the wide and easy path that leads to perdition. May you who have known doubt lead me to certainty; may you who have known failure lead me to success.

In 1946 an octogenarian black woman named Josephine Green told Robert Tallant of the time her mother had seen Marie Laveau leading a procession.

> All the people wit' her was hollerin' and screamin', "We is goin' to see Papa Limba! We is goin' to see Papa Limba!" My grandpa go runnin' after my ma then, yellin' at her, "You come on in here, Eunice! Don't you know Papa Limba is the devil?" But after that my Ma find out that Papa Limba meant St. Peter and her pa was just foolin' her.[1]

Others have called this figure Liba, Laba, or Papa La-Bas (Papa Over-There). Not only did his name hearken back to the Haitian keeper of the crossroads, but so did one of his favorite songs:

> *St. Peter, St. Peter, open the door*
> *I'm callin' you, come to me!*
> *St. Peter, St. Peter, open the door*[2]

Compare this to the second verse of the *Priye Gineh,* the prayer that opens every Vodou fete:

St. Pierre, ouvrez la porte
St. Pierre, ouvrez la porte, la porte
St. Pierre, ouvrez la porte, la porte du paradis
(St. Peter, open the door
St. Peter, open the door, the door
St. Peter, open the door, the door to paradise)

While today Papa Legba is most frequently represented in Haiti by the lame beggar St. Lazarus, in the past he was more often represented by St. Peter. According to Christian mythology, Peter holds the "keys to the kingdom" and is charged with letting the righteous into heaven while keeping the less-than-virtuous out. The similarity between his role and Legba's seemed obvious to practitioners in both Port-au-Prince and New Orleans, so it is not surprising that they would use his image in serving the Old Man at the Crossroads.

But while St. Peter is generally seen as a stern but fair judge (except, perhaps, by those whose names do not appear on the celestial invite list), the Old Man at the Crossroads is famous for his sometimes brutal sense of humor. The African spirits of the crossroads are tricksters who love to sow chaos and strife, messengers who revel in misdirection and mistranslation. Papa La-Bas is by and large a kindly spirit who opens the gate for those who propitiate him. But he also has a mischievous streak and would happily lead astray the gullible, the pompous, and those who need to be taught a lesson.

A close study of St. Peter's life reveals many contradictions and interesting twists. He was "the rock" on which Jesus built his church—but he was also given to moments of wavering faith, nearly drowning when he doubted his ability to walk on water and denying Christ three times after his arrest. And while the Old Man at the Crossroads has sometimes been mistaken for the Devil, St. Peter has been symbolized by that image beloved of metalheads the world over—the inverted cross. (According to legend, he asked to be crucified head down because he was not worthy to die in the same manner as Jesus.) Like the spirit he represents in Haiti and New Orleans—and in Guatemala, where he is syncretized with the chthonic crossroads deity Maximón—St. Peter is a complex and ambiguous figure; it's not surprising that he wound up guarding heaven's doorway.

If you want to work with Papa La-Bas, you can start with an image of St. Peter. These are widely available in botanicas or Catholic supply stores. Images with Peter holding keys are preferred, since they represent his role as heaven's gatekeeper. When you are moving into a new house you can put a St. Peter image above your inside front door. A holy card will be sufficient, along with an old set of keys. Peter (and Papa La-Bas) will appreciate the attention and will see to it that good luck flows into your house while misfortune is kept outside.

As anyone in New Orleans will tell you, it's to your best advantage to be on good terms with the gatekeeper. Keeping his image in your house will catch his attention, but he'll work even harder for you if you provide him with lagniappe ("something extra" in Louisiana French, by way of the American Spanish *la ñapa,* by way of the Quechua *yapay*). Papa La-Bas will appreciate a yellow or a white candle burned in his honor on Mondays, and he is also fond of candy or spare change left by your doorstep or at a nearby crossroads. The more attention you give him, the more assistance he will provide for you—and when the time comes, he may even usher you to the front of the line and past the velvet rope outside the heavenly gates.

Tales of Papa La-Bas

As a child young Antoine Domino learned how to play piano from his older brother, and by the age of fourteen he had dropped out of school and was playing in clubs throughout New Orleans. When he hooked up with bandleader Dave Bartholomew, he scored his first hit—and got a new stage name, "Fats" Domino—with the 1949 boogie-blues tune "The Fat Man." Looking for a follow-up, Domino and Bartholomew tapped into the legend of Papa La-Bas with 1950's "Hey! La Bas Boogie."

"Eh La Bas" was a Cajun jazz standard popular throughout New Orleans and was frequently sung at Mardi Gras. In 1886 George

Washington Cable published a transcription of an early version of this in his *The Dance in the Place Congo*. Musicologists have noted the resemblance between this version and songs found in Guadeloupe, Martinique, Trinidad, and Santo Domingo.[3] The original chorus spoke to the narrator's "chere cousin" and discussed the joys to be had in a Cajun kitchen. While this would seem to be an appropriate subject for the portly Domino, he and Bartholomew took the song in a different direction. Drawing upon the African "call and response" tradition, they turned "Eh! La Bas" ("Hey, Over There!") into a greeting, encouraging the audience to shout it back. Scholar Henry Louis Gates has suggested that "eh là-bas" was actually a coded reference to the pan-African god of the crossroads. Gates said:

> Called Papa Legba as his Haitian honorific and invoked through the phrase "eh là-bas" in New Orleans jazz recordings of the 1920s and 1930s, Pa Pa La Bas is the Afro-American trickster figure from black sacred tradition. His surname, of course, is French for "down" or "over there," and his presence unites "over there" (Africa) with "right here." He is indeed the messenger of the gods, the divine Pan-African interpreter, pursuing, in the language of the text, "The Work," which is not only Vaudou but also the very work (and play) of art itself.[4]

Papa La-Bas appears to have appreciated the shout-out. While "Hey! La Bas Boogie" didn't chart, other Domino and Bartholomew efforts like "Ain't That a Shame" and "Blueberry Hill" went on to become classics, making both men wealthy. Today both Domino and Bartholomew remain active. Bartholomew still occasionally plays trumpet at the Preservation Hall jazz club, which is appropriately located at 726 St. Peter Street. Domino has stayed put in New Orleans since the 1980s (with a brief relocation during Katrina), claiming he couldn't get a decent meal outside the city.

Yet another take on Papa La-Bas comes from noted black American writer Ishmael Reed. In Reed's 1972 book *Mumbo Jumbo,* a Harlem houngan named Papa La-Bas goes on a Pynchonesque journey in an effort to understand the new viral dance craze sweeping 1920s America, Jes Grew. Along the way he encounters resistance from members of the Wallflower Order and the Knights Templar, sinister secret societies dedicated to stamping out dancing and keeping the black man down. But he also finds aid from the old Hoodoo magician Black Herman and from his daughter Earline, an avatar of the Haitian lwa Erzulie. Reed's rollicking tale incorporates historical black figures like millionairess C. J. Walker, Claude McKay, and Countee Cullen, as well as Warren G. Harding (who was rumored to have black ancestry and who winds up at a Harlem rent party in this story). As befits a story featuring Papa La-Bas, it combines various narratives in a metafiction that both tells a story and comments on the process of storytelling and mythmaking.

While most African diaspora practitioners identify as Christians and incorporate Christian imagery and prayers into their spiritual practices, *Mumbo Jumbo* presents the Christian influence as an infiltration perpetrated by the Atonists, monotheists who have been working for world domination since the days of the Egyptian pharaoh Akhenaton. Instead of a servant of Bondye, the one true god (Papa's role in Haitian Vodou), Papa La-Bas becomes a major player in the war against his forces and a crusader for a polytheistic worldview that recognizes the importance of African tradition and that favors direct experience and practice over rote memorization and imitation. This is not surprising, given that Reed is also the author of the poem "Neo-Hoodoo Manifesto" and has stated, "Neo-HooDoo believes that every man is an artist, and every artist a priest."[5]

Reed's take on Papa La-Bas may differ from others—but Papa has always defied easy description and reveled in ambiguity. And it seems that his Papa La-Bas resonated with many readers. *Mumbo Jumbo*, Reed's third novel, became his first major success and transformed him from a cult favorite into one of America's leading black writers and intellectuals. One might even say that the Old Man at the Crossroads had rewarded Reed and Domino for their devotion—and with that we come to one of the South's most enduring legends.

The Old Man at the Crossroads

It is one of the most well known of blues clichés: the talented musician who goes to a nearby intersection to make a deal with the Devil. Robert Johnson supposedly gained his legendary guitar skills after selling his soul to Ol' Scratch, and others have said that Charlie Parker gained fame after making a midnight trip to the crossroads. At first glance this may seem merely a retelling of the famous Faust legend, but closer analysis reveals a direct connection to central and southern Africa.

In the Kongo many oaths are taken on a cross scratched on the ground. The horizontal line represents this world and its position between the land of the gods and the land of the deceased ancestors. The vertical line is a pathway across that boundary, marking the relationship between the gods, man, and the dead. The oathtaker stands upon the cross, taking a place between life and death; in taking the oath, the person invokes the judgment and witness of both God and the ancestors.[6] (A similar tradition has survived in African American Hoodoo, in which many practitioners use powders to draw a circle with a cross inside, an X, or a "five-spot" dice pattern when working magic.)[7] The crossroads, where two paths meet, is a real-world representation of this important cosmology. Much as a large stone may be recognized in India as a *lingam,* or representative of Shiva, a crossroads became a sacred place where the spirit world could be contacted by those brave enough or foolish enough to seek it out.

In the Mississippi River Delta and along the Gulf Coast they claimed the crossroads was the home of "the Old Man," or "the Devil." While it is tempting to dismiss this identification as Christian brainwashing, it too has roots in African traditions. Along with great power the crossroads harbored danger. Bandits and highway robbers often lurked near the intersection, waiting for unwary travelers. A wrong turn might send you deep into the wilderness or unfriendly territory. Other cultures have noted a sinister side to the crossroads. In the Hellenic world, Hecate, patroness of sorcery, was saluted at the crossroads along with Hermes, the messenger. In Europe suicides and executed criminals were buried at the crossroads so their intranquil spirits would be unable to find their way back to haunt their neighbors and loved ones. The identification of the Old Man at the Crossroads with the Christian Devil may not be entirely accurate, but neither is it completely unjustified.

That being said, the Old Man at the Crossroads appears to have little interest in acquiring souls. And while some claim he brings his devotees easy money and fame, those who know better realize that he actually teaches marketable skills. Bluesman Tommy Johnson (whom many believe provided the prototype for the more famous story about Robert Johnson) described the ritual as he performed it.

> If you want to learn how to make songs yourself, you take your guitar and you go to where the road crosses that way, where a crossroads is. Get there, be sure to get there just a little 'fore 12 that night so you know you'll be there. You have your guitar and be playing a piece there by yourself. . . . A big black man will walk up there and take your guitar and he'll tune it. And then he'll play a piece and hand it back to you. That's the way I learned to play anything I want.[8]

Robert Johnson and Charlie Parker were not particularly promising musicians when they began their careers. Parker was laughed off the stage at Kansas City's High Hat when he first attempted jamming with a local band. Blues legend Son House, who knew Johnson, described Johnson's early attempts to play as "such a racket you never heard! It'd make the people mad, you know. They'd come out and say, 'Why don't y'all go in and get that guitar away from that boy! He's running people crazy with it!'"[9] And while both became famous for their technical wizardry, it didn't happen overnight. Parker's playing improved dramatically after years of practicing as much as fifteen hours a day, while Johnson spent time training with blues artists like Son House and Ike Zinnerman. So while the Old Man at the Crossroads may have given them a lesson, they did plenty of homework beforehand and afterward.

If you wish to improve your skills, you can visit the Old Man at the Crossroads yourself. While there are varying accounts of how this is accomplished, most agree that you need to be at the crossroads at midnight: he prefers a liminal time and a liminal space. Some say that you need to visit for nine consecutive midnights; others declare that one visit will do. Bring your chosen instrument—your laptop, your guitar, your dice, or whatever else you use when practicing your chosen skill. You can bring an offering for the spirit if you want to further encourage him to come. A silver "Mercury" dime is appropriate (even though it actually bears an image of the Goddess Liberty wearing a winged cap, it has come to be associated with Hermes the Messenger by Hoodoo and New Orleans Voodoo practitioners). Others have brought black chickens or even offered their music as entertainment. Sit by the crossroads and practice your craft, and in time you will be visited by a black man. He may take your instrument from you, or take hold of your hands, or just whisper advice into your ear. If you can resist the urge to run away screaming, you'll find your abilities greatly improved when he leaves. Throw in some dedication and practice, and you may even find people commenting on your uncanny mastery of your craft. How far you take the Old Man's lessons is entirely up to you.

12

THE DIVINE MOTHER

The Virgin Mary

For the Anglophone Protestants who came to New Orleans after the Louisiana Purchase—and for many Protestants today—veneration of Mary was a form of idolatry and diabolism. They claimed Catholics were not honoring the Virgin Mother of God but rather worshipping the Whore of Babylon condemned in the Bible's Book of Revelation as "Mother of Harlots and Abominations of the Earth" (Revelation 17:5). This did not discourage the devout and not-so-devout of New Orleans from continuing to honor her as patroness of their beloved city.

Although they have become popular in the Crescent City since the 1970s, the Haitian lwa Ezili Freda and Ezili Dantor were not traditionally served in New Orleans Voodoo. Instead, those seeking the aid of the divine feminine put their trust in Mary. Christ is King of Heaven, and many of the male saints were knights, royals, and wealthy warriors. Mary was a poor peasant girl who was chosen for her humility, piety, and loving nature. The righteous relied on her power as Queen of Angels, while sinners pled for her forgiveness and understanding. And while God might refuse your petition, he was certain to take it more seriously if his mother asked him for a favor. Even if you have been put off by the excesses committed in the name of Christ and his church, you will find his mother to be a sympathetic, powerful, and loving protector and friend.

Mariology

In 431 the First Council of Ephesus referred to Mary as *Theotokos,* or God-bearer. A homily from St. Proclus shows the regard in which she was held by many of the early Church Fathers.

> O man, run through all creation with your thought, and see if there exists anything comparable to or greater than the holy Virgin Mother of God. Circle the whole word, explore all the oceans, survey the air, question the skies, consider all the unseen powers, and see if there exists any similar wonder in the whole creation.[1]

Even at this early date there was controversy about Mary's role in Christian theology. Nestorius and many of his followers declared that she was not Theotokos, but *Christokos*—bearer of Christ and mother of his human form but not his divine nature. While the Council of Ephesus, and the 451 Council of Chalcedon, declared Nestorius and his followers heretics, he continued to be influential in the East and is still considered a Church Father by Syrian Rite Christians.

As Christianity grew and became the dominant religion of the former Roman Empire, so too did devotion to Mary. Shrines in her honor appeared throughout Europe and the Byzantine world. Legends spread that Mary had been assumed body and spirit into heaven upon her death and that she had been conceived without sin so as to be a fitting vessel for the Savior. And if she was honored by the Church hierarchy, she was loved by the faithful, who showered her with adulation and praise.

Marian devotion was always particularly strong in France. As early as 185 St. Iraneus of Lyons had said, "The knot of Eve's disobedience was loosed by the obedience of Mary. For what the virgin Eve had bound fast through unbelief, this did the virgin Mary set free through faith."[2] The country's greatest cathedral was devoted to Notre Dame du Paris (Our Lady of Paris). And Bernard de Clairvaux (later, St. Bernard), who declaimed at length on Mary's role as Mediatrix between God and Man, admonished his followers:

In dangers, in doubts, in difficulties, think of Mary, call upon Mary. Let not her name depart from your lips, never suffer it to leave your heart. And that you may more surely obtain the assistance of her prayer, neglect not to walk in her footsteps. With her for guide, you shall never go astray; while invoking her, you shall never lose heart; so long as she is in your mind, you are safe from deception; while she holds your hand, you cannot fall; under her protection you have nothing to fear; if she walks before you, you shall not grow weary; if she shows you favor, you shall reach the goal.[3]

Another movement that got its start in southern France and northern Italy was strongly devoted to the Virgin. The troubadours were enamored of the idea of courtly love—a chaste passion for a beautiful but inaccessible lover. Combining elements of Arab love poetry with Cathar imagery and popular music, troubadours traveled throughout France and Europe singing of the Virgin and inspiring others to follow their example. During their heyday (the eleventh through thirteenth centuries), Marian devotion reached a fever pitch.

But even after the troubadours faded from the scene, Mary remained an important part of religious life. Her statues were regularly decorated with flowers; while roses and lilies were particularly popular, other common offerings included violets (symbolizing Mary's modesty), marigold ("Mary's gold," offered in place of coins), snowdrops (for Mary's purity), and foxglove (also known as Our Lady's glove, or in France, *le gant de Notre Dame*). Paradise gardens, cloistered enclosed spaces filled with her favorite flowers, were dedicated to her in honor of her beauty and virginity.[4]

As the Middle Ages gave way to the Renaissance, Marian art became increasingly popular. Franco-Flemish composer Josquin des Prez, one of the most influential musicians of fifteenth- and early sixteenth-century Europe, produced Marian tributes like *Missa Ave Maris Stella, Missa de Beata Virgine,* and *Missa Mater Patris.* Nicholas Poussin painted *Holy Family on the Steps* in 1648 and *Assumption of Mary* in 1650, and Jacques Stella painted *The Nativity* in 1639. (Perhaps he was hoping to win favor from Louis XIII, who at the urging of Cardinal Richelieu dedicated the French throne to the Virgin in 1638.)

With the Renaissance came the Reformation and a move away from Marian devotions. Later the Enlightenment treated veneration of Mary as just another silly superstition. Intellectuals and worldly folk began neglecting the Virgin. But the common people retained their great love for her even in the face of persecution during the French Revolution. This devotion was carried over to the French colonies, including their riverfront city in the New World.

Our Lady of Prompt Succor

Our Lady of Prompt Succor, you are most powerful against the enemy of our salvation. Through your Divine Son you crushed the serpent's head; hasten, then, to our help and deliver us from the deceits of Satan. Intercede for us with Jesus that we may always accept God's graces and be found faithful to Him. As you once saved New Orleans from ravaging flames and our Country from an invading army, have pity on us and obtain for us protection from hurricanes and all other disasters. Assist us in the many trials that beset our path through life. Be to us truly Our Lady of Prompt Succor now and especially at the hour of our death, that we may gain everlasting life through the merits of Jesus Christ who lives and reigns with the Father and the Holy Spirit, one God world without end. Amen.

In 1727 twelve Sisters of St. Ursula arrived in the then-primitive settlement of New Orleans after an arduous journey from France. Some were less than impressed with their new surroundings—one young nun wrote home that "upon seeing New Orleans for the first time, I can only say it looks like a large cesspool."[5] But the sisters triumphed over adversity, establishing a convent and doing their best to preserve Catholic morals under adverse conditions.

But by 1803 the Ursuline Academy was facing a serious shortage of teachers and nuns. Mother André Madier wrote to France asking that more teachers be sent, but the bishop denied her request. The Church in France was under siege by the forces of the French Revolution, and he felt he had no nuns to spare. Mother André's only recourse was to appeal to Pope Pius VII, but that was a long shot indeed, since the Pope was a prisoner of Napoleon. Undeterred, her relative in France, Mother Saint Michel, sent a note to the Pontiff and petitioned the Virgin for aid, promising her, "O most Holy Virgin Mary, if you obtain for me a prompt and favorable answer to this letter, I promise to have you honored at New Orleans under the title of Our Lady of Prompt Succor."[6]

The prayer was granted. Within two weeks after the letter was posted, the Pope sent more nuns to the Ursuline Academy. Mother Saint Michel commissioned a statue in honor of Our Lady of Prompt Succor, and on December 31, 1810, they placed the image of the Madonna holding the Infant Jesus in the academy's chapel.

Soon after, Our Lady helped the nuns yet again during the great fire of 1812. As the Vieux Carré burned, the winds began driving the fire toward Jackson Square and the Ursuline convent. As evacuation began, a nun named Sister St. Anthony placed a small statue of Our Lady of Prompt Succor on a window seat, and Mother St. Michel began to pray aloud, "Our Lady of Prompt Succor, we are lost unless you hasten to our aid!"[7] As she prayed the wind shifted direction, blowing the flames back and allowing the fire to be extinguished. Amid the devastation the convent was one of the only buildings to be spared.

Three years later Our Lady of Prompt Succor came through for New Orleans yet again. On January 7, 1815, General Andrew Jackson and his six thousand troops were facing fifteen thousand British soldiers. All that night the nuns as well as many of the city's faithful gathered in the chapel in a prayer vigil, begging the Virgin for her aid. Mother Ste. Marie Olivier de Vezin, the convent's prioress, vowed that a Mass of Thanksgiving would be sung annually for Our Lady should the American forces win. On the morning of January 8, as the priest was offering communion, a messenger ran into the church and announced the British had been defeated.

General Jackson went to the convent himself to thank the nuns for their prayers: "By the blessing of heaven, directing the valor of the troops under my command, one of the most brilliant victories in the annals of war was obtained."[8]

Today the Our Lady of Prompt Succor shrine is still located at the Ursuline Academy, now on 2635 State Street. During hurricane season the congregation requests her help at every Mass, and when a hurricane threatens, the faithful gather before her statue to recite the rosary and recite the prayer "Our Lady of Prompt Succor, hasten to help us!" After Katrina, congregants gathered to ask her assistance in ensuring aid from state and federal agencies and in rebuilding their devastated city.

The Holy Rosary

In 1203 a Spanish priest named Father Dominic Guzman was sent to the Languedoc region of southern France to confront the Cathar heresy. But he had little success; while the Catholic clergy was largely worldly and had little interest in the poor, the Cathar prefects were noted for their piety, sanctity, asceticism, and approachability. Dominic realized that he would win the souls of the Cathari commoners only by setting a good example and by feeding their hunger for knowledge and righteousness. As he said to Papal legates in a later rebuke,

> It is not the display of power and pomp, cavalcades of retainers, and richly-houseled palfreys, or by gorgeous apparel, that the heretics win proselytes; it is by zealous preaching, by apostolic humility, by austerity, by seeming, it is true, but by seeming holiness. Zeal must be met by zeal, humility by humility, false sanctity by real sanctity, preaching falsehood by preaching truth.[9]

But despite his best efforts, he achieved little success in converting the people back to the True Faith. Then one day while he was in prayer, the Virgin appeared before him and said, "Wonder not that you have obtained so little fruit by your labors, you have spent them on barren soil, not yet watered with the dew of Divine grace. When God willed to renew the face of the earth, He began by sending down on it the fertilizing rain of the Angelic Salutation. Therefore preach my Psalter composed of 150 Angelic Salutations and 15 Our Fathers, and you will obtain an abundant harvest."[10]

For most of the Catholic Church's history, the laity was unfamiliar with the clergy's complex rituals. Few could read and write in their native tongue, let alone the Latin used by monks and priests. They knew the biblical stories and possibly even a few scattered verses, but were unable to read the Scriptures or to recite the long chants of the Breviary. But they knew the simple prayers, especially the Ave Maria (Hail Mary) and the Paternoster (Our Father). So when they wished to petition God, Jesus, and the saints they would recite 50 or 150 Hail Marys, and to keep an accurate count of their Aves they used a knotted cord. Dominic encouraged this among the people and began making some headway against the heresy. Ultimately the Church decided a crusade would accomplish the task more quickly and wiped out the Cathars with armies instead of prayer—but the tradition of the Rosary remained and became an important tool for contemplation among Catholics in France and throughout the world.

To pray the Rosary, you begin by making the sign of the cross and say the Apostles' Creed.

> *I believe in God, the Father Almighty, Creator of Heaven*
> *and earth;*
> *and in Jesus Christ, His only Son Our Lord,*
> *Who was conceived by the Holy Spirit, born of the Virgin*
> *Mary, suffered under Pontius Pilate, was crucified,*
> *died, and was buried.*
> *He descended into Hell; the third day He rose again from*
> *the dead;*
> *He ascended into Heaven, and sitteth at the right hand of*
> *God, the Father Almighty; from thence He shall come*
> *to judge the living and the dead.*
> *I believe in the Holy Spirit, the holy Catholic Church,*
> *the communion of saints, the forgiveness of sins, the*
> *resurrection of the body and life everlasting. Amen.*

After this you say one Our Father:

> *Our Father, who art in heaven*
> *Hallowed be thy name*
> *Thy Kingdom come, thy will be done*
> *on earth as it is in heaven*
> *Give us this day our daily bread*
> *and forgive us our trespasses*
> *as we forgive those who trespass against us*
> *and lead us not into temptation*
> *but deliver us from evil. Amen.*

Followed by one Hail Mary:

> *Hail Mary, full of grace, the Lord is with thee*
> *Blessed art thou amongst women*
> *and blessed is the fruit of thy womb Jesus*
> *Holy Mary, Mother of God*
> *Pray for us sinners*
> *Now and at the hour of our death. Amen.*

Continue with one Glory Be:

> *Glory be to the Father, and the Son and the Holy Spirit*
> *as it was in the beginning, is now and ever shall be*
> *world without end. Amen.*

You then announce the First Mystery and recite an Our Father. While meditating on that mystery, you say ten Hail Marys, followed by a Glory Be. Then you announce the Second Mystery, and repeat the process until all five mysteries are completed. The Mysteries are:

The Five Joyful Mysteries: The Annunciation of Gabriel to Mary that she was to conceive Jesus; Mary visits her cousin Elizabeth, who greets her with "Hail Mary, full of grace"; the birth of Jesus; the presentation of Jesus in the Temple; Jesus is found in the Temple preaching to the Rabbis.

The Five Sorrowful Mysteries: The agony of Jesus in the garden of Gethsameni; Jesus is scourged; Jesus is crowned with thorns; Jesus carries his cross; the crucifixion.

The Five Glorious Mysteries: The resurrection; Jesus ascends into heaven; the Holy Spirit descends at Pentecost; Mary is assumed body and soul into heaven; Mary is crowned Queen of Heaven and Earth.

The Five Luminous Mysteries: The baptism of Christ in the River Jordan; the wedding at Cana, where Jesus turns water into wine; the proclamation of the Kingdom of God; the transfiguration of Jesus; the Last Supper.

The Joyful Mysteries are said on Mondays, Saturdays, Sundays of Advent, and Sundays from Epiphany until Lent; the Sorrowful Mysteries are said on Mondays, Saturdays, Sundays of Advent, and Sundays from Epiphany until Lent; the Glorious Mysteries are said on Wednesdays and Sundays; and the Luminous Mysteries (a recent addition by Pope John Paul II) are said on Thursdays.

You can also say a novena, a series of nine Rosaries on nine separate days. At the beginning of each Rosary, you offer your petition or request. You then say the Rosary while meditating on the mystery appropriate for that day. When your prayer is answered, you say another nine Rosaries for nine more days, but instead of a petition, you begin with a prayer of thanksgiving to the Virgin Mary for her intercessions on your behalf.

All this Catholic prayer and imagery may seem out of place in a book about Voodoo. But New Orleans folk spirituality has been strongly influenced by Roman Catholicism. This has a great deal to do with the Crescent City's history and culture. But perhaps more important is the fact that the Virgin and the Saints respond to prayers and intercede on behalf of those who ask for their aid. New Orleans Voodoo has always been a practical tradition, and its followers will happily call on any spirit who will answer their petitions.

13

THE GREAT SERPENT

Li Grand Zombi

In Christian mythology, snakes are associated with Satan, thanks largely to the Garden of Eden legend. According to that story sin and death came into the world when Ol' Splitfoot, in the guise of a serpent, tempted Eve to partake of the forbidden fruit. Many icons of the Virgin Mary picture her standing atop a globe and stomping on the head of a snake (since her son Jesus conquered sin, death, and the Devil, who messed things up in the first place). Still other stories discuss the "flaming serpent" who tormented the Israelites during their sojourn in the desert and the proverbial ungrateful child who brings more pain than a serpent's tooth.

In Africa snakes were viewed differently. Serpent veneration was found throughout much of the continent. A 1705 report shows how one English crew who made land at the African port of Whydah learned this the hard way:

An English Captain having landed some of his men and part of his cargo, they found a snake in their house, which they immediately killed without the least scruple, and not doubting but they had done a good work, threw out the dead snake at their door, where being found by the Negroes in the morning, the English preventing the question who had done the fact, ascribed the honour to themselves;

126

which so incensed the natives, that they furiously fell on the English, killed them all and burned their house and goods.[1]

The Fon-speaking peoples of Dahomey honored the great serpent Ayida, who stretched across the sky as a rainbow by day and shimmered among the stars as the Milky Way by night. The Tumbuka of central Malawi paid homage to the sky-dwelling python Chikangombe. The Bantu of central and southern Africa had Monyoha, the great water snake who ensured that the rivers and lakes would never dry up for those who honored him. And during the Middle Passage and the horrors of slavery, this snake veneration was carried to the New World, particularly New Orleans.

The Snake Dances of New Orleans

Writing in 1895, New Orleans journalist Henry C. Castellanos described a Voodoo ritual.

> The King and Queen take their positions at one end of the room, near a species of altar, on which is placed a box, wherein the serpent is imprisoned, and where the affiliated can view it outside the bars. As soon as a strict inspection assures them that no intruder is within hearing or sight, the ceremony begins by the adoration of his Snakeship, by protestations of fidelity to his cult, and of submission to his behests. . . .
>
> [The Voudou King] suddenly seizes the precious box, lays it upon the floor, and places the Queen upon the lid. No sooner has her foot touched the sacred receptacle than she becomes possessed, like a new Pythoness. Her frame quivers, her whole body is convulsed, and the oracle pronounces its edicts through her inspired lips. On some she bestows flattery and promises of success, at others she thunders forth bitter invectives. . . .
>
> As soon as the oracle has answered every question propounded, a circle is formed and the serpent is put back upon the unholy fane.

Then each one presents his offering, and places it in a hat impervious to prying curiosity.[2]

Snakes became an integral part of Voodoo rituals in New Orleans and throughout the Mississippi River Delta. Numerous titillating reports described how the entrance of the serpent was prelude to wild orgies of drumming, sexual abandon, and race-mixing. An 1894 report in the *New York Times* described a Mobile, Alabama, ceremony in which

> As the strokes of the tom-tom and the banjo quicken, a bacchanalian abandon takes the place of the usually decorous demeanor of the negro. A vigor unknown to polite society characterizes his steps and contortions of body. . . . The women tear off their clothing and re-enter the furious revel almost nude, shouting aloud with the rest of the company. . . . A naked white girl acted as a voodoo priestess wrought up to frenzy by dances and incantations that followed the sacrifice of a white and black hen. A serpent, trained to its part, and acted on by the music, coiled around the limbs of the girl, its motions studied by the votaries dancing around or standing to watch its contortions. The spectator fled at last in horror when the poor girl fell writhing in an epileptic fit.[3]

In New Orleans some conjure folk and rootworkers kept one or more snakes around their house. This served to establish their credibility as powerful magicians. They might explain this by quoting Scripture, more specifically Mark 16:18, wherein it is said that those who believe shall "take up serpents." Or they might use their scaly pets for sinister effect. Since most of their neighbors were terrified of snakes, their nonchalance might be read as a sign that they had made a pact with evil. Like the black cats of European witch legends, their reptiles were seen by outsiders as familiar spirits masquerading in the guise of animals. This helped cement the rootworker's reputation as a powerful sorcerer who could work miracles for clients.

But there is evidence that a fair bit of this snake veneration, as has

often been the case in New Orleans, was done for the benefit of a paying audience. The ritual nudity described in the Alabama ceremony (and
frequently mentioned in other descriptions of New Orleans Voodoo) is
not found in African or Afro-Caribbean religious practices. And the lurid
descriptions of snake handling were often not taken directly from eyewit-
nesses but from second-hand or even third-hand sources. (The Castellanos
account referenced above was plagiarized almost word for word from a
1797 account of a Saint-Domingue ceremony by French lawyer and historian Moreau de Saint-Méry!)

Haiti had a reputation as a savage place filled with witchcraft and
Satanic rituals. Even a century later, the bloody tales of the uprising and
the revenge of the slaves still resonated in a city where ruling whites tried
to maintain control over the black population. The rumors of primi-
tive Voodoo rituals in the bayous simultaneously terrified and titillated
wealthy New Orleanians, especially when combined with accounts of
overheated Negro sexuality in action. Since snake veneration was one of
the most well-known and controversial aspects of Haitian spirituality, a
serpent added that air of authenticity to a "religious ceremony" that was
essentially a nudie show to the tourists.

This is not to say that snakes played no part in actual New Orleans
Voodoo rituals. Marie Laveau (chapter 14), who was no stranger to the
city's entertainment industry, drew upon the teachings and practices of
Saint-Domingue and Africa for her work. In naming her famous snake "Li
Grand Zombi," Laveau paid homage not to shambling animated corpses
but to a powerful spirit—the Kongo creator Nzambi.

Nzambi, Simbi, and Li Grand Zombi

According to Kongo legend, Nzambi created the heavens, the earth, and
the animals. Then, after creating man and woman, he taught them how to
survive in his world and how to harness the magical power of his creation.
By using those teachings they could break the blazing droughts and bring
down the summer rain; they could heal sickness and ensure fertile crops.
They could also communicate with the *mpungas,* deceased ancestors and

nature spirits who assisted Nzambi in maintaining his creation. Today Nzambi is still honored in Cuba by practitioners of Las Reglas de Congo (also known as Palo Mayombe), who say *"Nsambi primero,"* or "Nsambi is first."

Kongo cosmology envisioned the cosmos as two worlds—*nza yayi* (this world) and the *nsi a bafwa* (the land of spirits). Between these two worlds lay the *kalunga,* a vast ocean that served as threshold between the living and the dead. Because snakes were frequently seen climbing trees, burrowing beneath the ground, and resting in or near rivers or bodies of water, they were considered travelers between the realms. Since Kongo religious practices were concerned largely with commerce between the various worlds, it is not surprising that snakes play a major role in Kongo religions.

In Haiti, Vodouisants honor the Simbi family of lwa. Like the basimbi, snake spirits living in the rivers and streams of southern Africa, the Simbis are known to be shy but powerful magicians. Those who approach them with due patience and respect and gain their trust find they are powerful allies who can act as intermediaries between the worlds of flesh and spirit and life and death. Haitian houngan and author Milo Rigaud said of them:

> The voodoo Mercury has the name of Simbi, a loa of many forms. He is the conductor of souls, who leads the souls of the dead in all directions bordered by the four magical orients of the cross. He is the Messiah of Legba, the messenger of the sun. Simbi corresponds to the hermetic Mercury of the cabalistic alchemy of the ritual sacrifice.[4]

The lwa Simbi Makaya is one of the great sorcerers of Haitian Vodou. As patron of the secret Sanpwel society, he teaches his chosen followers powerful *wangas* (magical spells) that can be used for healing or destruction. Those who are not members regularly accuse the Sanpwel of human sacrifice, corpse desecration, and all sorts of related misdeeds. Within New Orleans, Li Grand Zombi had a similarly mixed reputation. Believers and practitioners considered the great serpent a benevolent protector and wise teacher. Those who were not so affiliated generally associated Grand Zombi with orgies and devil worship. As with Simbi Makaya, one's attitude toward Grand Zombi marked your status within the group.

In New Orleans the snake served simultaneously to advertise to one's clientele and to set them apart as outsiders. This is similar to Simbi's liminal position in Haiti. As a traveler between worlds, Simbi is tough to pin down. One of the most popular Simbis, Simbi Andezo, literally resides "in two waters" (*an de zo*), occupying the space where freshwater meets the salty ocean. Li Grand Zombi is similarly placed between public Voodoo rituals for tourists and private devotions, between religion and entertainment, between African roots and American money-making spectacles. In this, he is a fitting patron for the city of New Orleans and its religion.

The best way to honor Li Grand Zombi is with a live snake. This is not a commitment to be undertaken lightly. Taking responsibility for a pet is no small matter, especially when that pet is also a spirit animal! While snakes are relatively low-maintenance companions, they have certain needs that must be met. If not provided with appropriate temperatures and humidity, they are likely to become ill and die. A suitably large cage must be procured, along with a supply of the proper food.

A snake that is going to be handled in public ritual also needs to have a suitably tractable disposition—and when stressed, even the most docile snake may respond by biting, musking, or defecating on the nearest available target. That large python you are dancing with may be less impressive when you are soaked with runny snake dung or nursing a bloody open wound. Providing guidelines for the care of your personal Grand Zombi is beyond the scope of this book. As with any other pet, do your research before making your purchase, and make sure you are able to live up to your commitment.

Should you be unable to do so at this time, there is no shame in admitting this. Snake sheds can also be used as offerings for Grand Zombi, as well as snake statues or imagery. I do not recommend using snake skins, since they are harvested by killing the animals. (You want to honor the great serpent, not present him with the corpse of one of his siblings!)

These can be placed on an altar along with offerings of eggs, candles, or if you are rhythmically talented, drumming. All these will show your devotion and help you to establish a link with Li Grand Zombi.

St. Michael the Archangel— or Mr. Daniel Blanc

Daniel Blanc, mighty against wickedness, defend us against the snares and schemes of the evil one and his minions. You who are sovereign over all the angelic hosts, you who command the powers and principalities and hate that impiety and evil should triumph, hear my prayer. Cast down my enemies from their high places and help us to be worthy to sit in the thrones of the righteous.

With the re-creation of New Orleans Voodoo (chapter 4), many began to identify Marie Laveau's snake with the great white serpent Damballah. This is incorrect. Li Grand Zombi's roots are in the Kongo and Bantu religions of central and southern Africa, not in the West African cultures that honor the rainbow serpent Da. This is not to say that Damballah is not served by the root doctors and Voodoo queens of New Orleans. He is, although not in a way one might expect. In Haiti Damballah is one of the leading spirits honored in public Vodou ceremonies, while Simbi is a patron of the secret societies. Their positions are reversed in New Orleans Voodoo: Li Grand Zombi plays a public role, while Damballah is served largely by insiders and is little known to those who are not of the faith.

St. Michael the Archangel has a worldwide reputation as a powerful defender against evil. According to Christian legend, it was he who gave Lucifer his heavenly eviction notice. His icons frequently show him trampling on a demonic figure with his shield in one hand and his fiery sword in the other. But in New Orleans there is a belief that he will work for you faster and more effectively if you address him by his real name: Mr. Daniel Blanc. (Others say his name is really Danny or Blanc Dani.)

While this may seem to be a rather silly superstition, those who are familiar with Haitian Vodou will recognize a common praise name for

Damballah: *Blan Dani*, or White Dani. He did not come to New Orleans as a serpent—perhaps because Simbi/Grand Zombi had already filled that role—but as a warrior and ruler over the angelic armies.

Writing in 1904, journalist and author Helen Pitkin described a Voodoo ritual that called on Archangel Michael with this song:

> *Blanc Dani,*
> *Dans tous pays blanc*
> *L'a commandé*
> *Blanc Dani, dans tous pays blanc*
> *L'a commandé*[5]
> *(Blanc Dani,*
> *In all white countries*
> *He has command*
> *Blanc Dani, in all white countries*
> *He has command)*

While Damballah is generally seen as a peaceful and even-tempered spirit, he can wreak a terrible vengeance on evildoers. Those who think snakes are slow have never seen one strike at a threat or a prey item. Damballah's great love of purity and righteousness is matched by his loathing for injustice. Those who find themselves facing powerful enemies can count on him for assistance, so long as they are in the right. One does not trouble Damballah with trivial matters or ask for his help in wrongdoing.

To call on Daniel Blanc, use an image or statue of St. Michael the Archangel. Like Damballah, he is served with clean white cloths and white candles, and like Damballah, he is a fastidious spirit who prefers being served in a tidy home. Put his shrine atop a high shelf or in an elevated place to honor his position in heaven alongside the Most High. Make him offerings of sweet white foods like coconut or rice pudding.

14

THE VOODOO QUEEN

Marie Laveau

She was a skilled Voodoo priestess who led a huge coven of worshippers and used her magical abilities to amass great wealth and power. She was a charlatan whose primary expertise was in the arts of blackmail, pandering, and showmanship. She was a symbol of feminine power and triumph over the forces of racism and sexism—or a con artist preying on the vulnerable. There are innumerable myths about Marie Laveau; her story has been reinterpreted by various sources to support their cause or sell their products. Finding the facts about her life is considerably more challenging. If we are to learn more about the Crescent City's most famous native, we will need to deconstruct the legends to get at the kernels of truth contained therein.

Today most images of Laveau are based on an 1835 painting by portraitist George Catlin. It depicts an attractive copper-skinned woman of color with penetrating eyes and an enigmatic expression. She wears a lacy shawl and a yellow and red plaid *tignon* (an elaborate headwrap worn by New Orleans women of color). A copy of the 1835 painting still hangs at the Cabildo, a historic building in New Orleans, and is labeled "Marie Laveau, legendary African American Voodoo Queen during the early nineteenth century." But when Louisiana Writers' Project interviewers asked elderly blacks who remembered Laveau if the image resembled her, they all said it did not.[1] Some of those interviewed said that Laveau was a dark-skinned black woman; others said she could have passed for white.

Although we cannot be sure what Marie Laveau looked like, the interviewees were unanimous in saying that she was a tall, strikingly beautiful woman with a magnetic presence and a regal manner befitting her later title as "Voodoo Queen of New Orleans." And the mystery that surrounds her appearance is matched only by the uncertainty surrounding many of the particulars of her life.

Birth and First Marriage

Some stories claim that Marie Laveau was born in Saint-Domingue; others say that she was the daughter of a white plantation owner and a slave. But according to a baptismal record in St. Louis Cathedral, Père Antonio de Sedella (better known as Père Antoine) baptized a six-day-old Marie Laveau on September 16, 1801. Her mother, Marguerite d'Arcantel, was a freed mulatto slave. Her father, Charles Laveau, was a prosperous free man of color who had made his fortune as a real estate speculator, money lender, and slave trader. She grew up in her grandmother's modest cottage on St. Ann Street, in the Creole neighborhood of Faubourg Tremé (in English, the Tremé suburb).[2]

On August 4, 1819, Marie married a quadroon carpenter from Saint-Domingue named Jacques Paris. As a Saint-Domingue refugee, Paris would have been much sought after for his woodworking and construction skills. Saint-Domingue *gens du couleur* (people of color) were generally better trained and more skillful than those from still-rustic New Orleans. The newly married couple settled into what promised to be a comfortable but unexceptional middle-class life in a house on the 1900 block of North Rampart Street in another Creole neighborhood, Faubourg Marigny.

But tragedy soon struck, and Jacques Paris disappeared from the lives of Laveau and their two children. Perhaps he died in one of the yellow fever epidemics that regularly descended on New Orleans during the humid summers. Perhaps he deserted his wife and returned to the Free Black Republic of Haiti to seek his fortune. Perhaps, some would whisper darkly after Laveau became famous, he had been sacrificed to the African devils his wife served. Whatever the reason for his disappearance, by 1825 Laveau was calling herself the "Widow Paris," and a death certificate was filed with the authorities.

In his nonfiction book *Voodoo in New Orleans* and his novel *The Voodoo Queen,* Robert Tallant claimed that Laveau supported herself after Paris's disappearance by working as a hairdresser. Although evidence for this claim is murky, it is not unreasonable. At that time many New Orleans *femmes du couleur* (women of color) supported themselves by styling the locks of the city's wealthy and well-dressed white and mulatto women. Before one of the Crescent City's many social functions, women would hire a hairdresser to make sure their tresses were as lovely as their fine outfits. Hairdressing required both skill and artistic sense: a good stylist would work to emphasize the client's strongest features while drawing attention away from her weak points. She might take special pains to minimize any sign of kinky hair in a woman from a supposedly "white" family and dye any traces of gray for a belle whose youth was beginning to fade.

As a hairdresser, Laveau could certainly have gained the confidence of her clients and learned their secrets. She also may have provided them with Voodoo remedies, potions, and charms to win back a straying lover or attract a new one. But it seems that Laveau's tenure as a hairdresser was a relatively brief one. While one woman said that she "called herself a hairdresser, and that's how she got in the good graces of the fine people," another said she was "some kind of a hairdresser and seamster, but she did all that in her early days. Shucks, she soon cut that stuff out."[3] It could be that she was beginning to focus on her trade in Voodoo, or it could be that she preferred to concentrate on the new man who had come into her life.

Christophe Glapion

In 1820s New Orleans, young white men frequently took free women of color as mistresses, set them up in houses, and fathered children with them, a practice known as *plaçage.* The women of these relationships were called *placées*. In 1840 *femmes du couleur libre* (free women of color) owned about 40 percent of the property in the Faubourgs Marigny and Tremé. Many of these homes were provided by white lovers who wanted to ensure the security of their placées. Often they would build a double Creole cottage, ensuring a home for their families and a steady means of support from rents paid on the other side.[4] (Alternately, the second side could be used as a vacation home for the visiting man when he wished to spend time with his Creole lover.)

The only thing that made Christophe Glapion's arrangement with Marie Laveau unusual was her relatively advanced age (twenty-five) and her status as a widow who had already born children. Even for one of the young beauties who debuted at the city's quadroon balls, Glapion would have been a fine catch. Scion of an aristocratic French family with roots in Normandy, he had also served with distinction in the Battle of New Orleans. It is a tribute to Laveau's charisma and beauty that she was able to capture his heart. While many white New Orleanian men abandoned their placées after marrying a white bride, Glapion stayed with Laveau until his death in 1855.

Glapion's devotion to Laveau has inspired a number of legends. Some claimed that he was actually a free man of color, while others said that he had chosen to present himself as such so that he could live freely with Laveau and their two daughters. While some reports claim that Laveau bore fifteen children with Glapion, records indicate they had seven children, only two of whom survived to adulthood. Infant mortality in New Orleans was very high in those days. Laveau's two children by Paris both died young of yellow fever or one of the other epidemic diseases that frequently swept the city during the hot summers. Even his contemporaries were sometimes confused by his unseemly devotion to his colored mistress. An 1850 census listed all of the occupants of Laveau's home on 911 St. Ann Street, including the white Glapion, as "mulatto."

But while Glapion was a devoted husband, father, and grandfather, he was no great businessman. At the time of his death in 1855, he was heavily in debt, having mortgaged the family house and other properties in a desperate attempt to raise cash. The Citizens Bank of Louisiana foreclosed on the property and auctioned it off at a sheriff's sale on July 17, 1855. (Pierre Crocker, a prosperous free man of color and father of several of Laveau's grandchildren, purchased the house for $1,880 and gave the Laveau family a life estate on the premises.) Marie was now fifty-four years old, her longtime companion was dead, and she had few prospects for continued income. To support herself, she threw herself into the trade that would make her famous.

The Voodoo Queen

On July 2, 1850, Marie Laveau and another free woman of color, Rosine Dominique, filed a complaint before Recorder John Seuzenau seeking the return of a statue that had been confiscated during a June 27 raid on an illegal Voodoo gathering. The statue, described by a contemporary newspaper as "a quaintly carved figure resembling something between a centaur and an Egyptian mummy," was valued by Laveau at fifty dollars. Ultimately the court decided that it would be returned upon payment of $8.50 in court costs; the records show, however, that the fine was paid and statue taken not by Laveau but by an unknown "young quadroon."[5]

This is the first mention of Laveau in connection with Voodoo. The priestess who presided over the gathering in question was a woman named Betsy Tolenado, who later charged the police with illegally breaking up a religious ceremony. (The court found that the arrest was valid, since it involved a gathering of mixed free people and slaves—a serious concern in those days of militant abolitionism.) But it seems she was already a personage of some importance in the Voodoo community, since she was willing to present herself before the court and claim ownership of some of the paraphernalia used at the ceremony.

In the summer of 1859 Marie Laveau's name appeared in the local newspapers. The *Crescent* unflatteringly referred to her as "the notorious hag who reigns over the ignorant and superstitious as the Queen of the Voodoos." They went on to report that her neighbor had complained that Laveau and her followers were "disturbing his peace and that of the neighborhood with their fighting and obscenity and infernal signing and yelling" during their "hellish observance of the mysterious rites of Voudou."[6] No record exists as to the disposition of this complaint. It could be that Laveau used her Voodoo skills to woo the judge, or she may have made out-of-court arrangements with her neighbor to keep the noise down after dark. What we can surmise from these reports is that she was by this time holding ceremonies in her home and was recognized (by some journalists, at least) as a Voodoo Queen.

Around this time Laveau began officiating at the weekly public dances at Congo Square. These events, where blacks gathered together to perform African-inspired dances and drumming, were popular with citizens throughout the city's various racial and social strata. Laveau used these events to sell charms and services to observers, including wealthy white patrons. (She may have been inspired by Doctor John, chapter 10, who had become rich through catering to a white clientele.) Those who showed special interest might be allowed to attend services in Laveau's home, which was filled with statues, candles, and images of various saints. Or they might be invited to the annual St. John's Eve (June 23) ceremonies at Lake Pontchartrain. Once semisecret gatherings of devoted Voodoo practitioners, during Laveau's era they became far more popular with the "smart set." (Those who did not receive invites would frequently wander through the woods in search of the ceremony, but only rarely found it.)

In her later years Laveau became increasingly frail and was unable to attend many public functions. By 1869 Malvina Latour had taken her place as presiding officer at the St. John's Eve ceremonies. Laveau remained a figure of legend and terror in her neighborhood, with children running from the once-beautiful woman who now resembled classic portrayals of the "wicked witch." In the summer of 1881 Marie Laveau died. Writer Lafcadio Hearn penned a glowing eulogy for her. Although he had little sympathy for Voodoo, referring to it as "impious ceremonies of worshipping the prince of evil," he called Laveau "one of the kindest women who ever lived" and suggested she had been called a Voodoo Queen only because of her skill in herbal medicines.[7]

Later, rumors would spread that Marie Laveau's daughter had taken her mother's place as Voodoo Queen. Robert Tallant and other writers would speak of "Marie Laveau I" and "Marie Laveau II." There is no evidence to suggest that any of Laveau's daughters followed in their mother's footsteps. It is possible that Tallant took the claims of interviewees who were too young to have known Laveau as evidence that her daughter continued the family trade, rather than proof his subjects were fabricating their stories. It is also possible that other rootworkers and Hoodoo women used Laveau's name or spread the rumor that they were related to her.

But whatever the case, Laveau's death did not end her fame or her notoriety. Her relative poverty at the time of her death was explained by claims that she had given away all her money to the poor. Legends and half-truths were repeated as facts, then repeated again. A widow who supported her extended family through Voodoo became one of the wealthiest and most feared citizens of New Orleans and founder of a dynasty that lasted through generations. And her grave became a site where many pilgrims came to offer their respects and to seek her otherworldly assistance.

The Tomb of Marie Laveau(s)

Perhaps the most famous grave in New Orleans is the Glapion Family Crypt in St. Louis Cemetery No. 1. One inscription on the tomb reads, *"Marie Philome Glapion, décédé le 11 Juin 1897, âgée de Soixante-deux ans"* ("Marie Philome Glapion, deceased June 11, 1897, aged sixty-two years"). Another inscription on the tomb reads, *"Famille Vve. Paris / née Laveau"* (Family of the Widow Paris, born Laveau), while a bronze tablet announces, under the heading "Marie Laveau," that "This Greek Revival Tomb Is Reputed Burial Place of This Notorious 'Voodoo Queen.'"

Some have claimed that Marie Laveau was buried elsewhere, as was her daughter. Several other tombs have been credited as the resting place of each. But Laveau I's 1881 obituary claimed that she had been buried in her family tomb in St. Louis Cemetery No. 1, and most believers consider the Glapion crypt to be where both Laveaus are interred. As a result, it has gained widespread attention from the curious, the lovelorn, and the tourists seeking an "authentic" New Orleans Voodoo experience.

Visitors seeking the favor of the Voodoo queen have long left small gifts at her tomb. Coins, Mardi Gras beads, flowers, rum, and candles are often left at the site. Robert Tallant described the rituals that took place at the "Marie Laveau tomb" at St. Louis Cemetery No. 2:

> Its slab is always covered with literally hundreds of crosses made with red brick. Until recently there was a crack in the slab, and into this devotees would drop coins and make a wish. There was a particular belief here that any girl wishing a husband could be certain of having her desire fulfilled. The rite consists of rapping on the slab three times, saying the wish out loud, then making a cross with red brick, a piece of which always reposes on top of the row of crypts. This place is also known as the "Wishing Vault" and the "Voodoo Vault," and probably more Voodoos will accept it as the burial place of Marie Laveau than they will the tomb in St. Louis Cemetery No. 1.
>
> However, others will tell you that this is a mistake, and that another Voodoo queen, Marie Comtesse, is buried here, that in some way the two became confused. The sexton will tell you that "there ain't nothing in that oven but some old bones of people what died of Yellow Fever. I don't know how this started, but they keep coming—white and colored—and making their crosses. It's a damned nuisance."[8]

Today it has become customary to draw three Xs on the tomb while making a wish. This is generally done using a piece of crumbling brick, although some use charcoal and others use permanent markers or other graffiti tools. Along with the inevitable Xs, the Glapion tomb is now decorated with hearts, pentagrams, poetry, and initials. Sextons regularly clean the crypt, but to no avail: the Laveau legend has ensured that as fast as old markings are removed, new ones take their place.

But while popular, this tradition is scorned by Voodoo practitioners as destructive and disrespectful. Many of the people making these brick Xs use chunks of brick they have pulled from other tombs, and many of the monuments around the Glapion crypt have sustained considerable damage from the demands of well-meaning wishmakers. One professional guide has claimed that the tradition of drawing Xs at St. Louis Cemetery No. 1 began with an early cemetery guide who wished to explain away some graffiti on the tomb. Thinking quickly, he described a "Voodoo custom," which then became part of the ever-growing Marie Laveau legend.

There is a long tradition that those who desecrate a gravesite can incur the wrath of the deceased spirit. Many New Orleans locals say that those who anger Marie Laveau will be haunted by the ghost of Li Grand Zombi, who was buried with her and who still protects his beloved mistress. Grand Zombi's zombie has been described as a massive coal-black snake who slithers between the tombs. Irreverent tourists who disrespected Laveau's tomb have reportedly awakened to find Grand Zombi beside them. Others have reported seeing a massive black cat with fiery eyes, or even the ghost of Marie Laveau herself, wandering through the cemetery in her finery and trademark red turban and muttering curses at evildoers. And if that isn't enough to keep you away from the nearby bricks, you may want to avoid the New Orleans police department. Marking graves or otherwise desecrating cemeteries can land you a stiff fine or a stay in one of the city's infamous jails. Don't take the chance. This is one tradition that deserves a decent burial.

15
THE WARRIORS
Joe Féraille, St. Marron, and Yon Sue

Throughout its long history, New Orleans has seen more than its share of violence. It's not surprising, then, that a number of warrior spirits are honored in New Orleans Voodoo. These hard-boiled fighters can assist you when you need a helping hand—but like all soldiers, they should be approached with caution. It's good to have them on your side—but it's even better not to have them working against you!

Joe Féraille

Laughing soldier, wily enemy, I call on your aid, Joe Féraille. Lend your strength to my cause and give me the courage I need to triumph. Do not lead me into danger, and do not tempt me into folly. Give me your cunning but not your madness. Let me stand firm as your anvil against the blows of my enemies and let your blade cut through the bonds that entangle me.

In West Africa the mighty spirit Gu was honored as the patron of blacksmiths, metalworkers, and soldiers. The Yoruba peoples honored him as Ogun, a mighty warrior, while the Fon of Dahomey placed him third in their pantheon, behind only the creators Mawu and Lisa. All considered him a great intercessor who could hack through all barriers and push aside any obstacle. During the dark days of the Middle Passage, he came to the New World, where he is still honored today. In Cuba people pay tribute to him as Ogun, master of iron, Brazilians honor him as Ogum, while Haitians call him Ogou. And in New Orleans he has become a well-known part of local folklore as "Iron Joe" or "Joe Féraille."

Haitian Vodou has many Ogous: Ogou Badagris is a cagey *neg politik* ("political guy" or diplomat), while Ogou Balindjo is a naval captain who answers to the ocean emperor Met Agwe, and Ogou San Jak is a cavalry knight represented by images of Saint James the Greater (in French, St. Jacques Majeur) on horseback. But while Ogou Feray is a general known for his short temper but also his loyalty to his family, Joe Féraille is a freebooter and smuggler. He may fight for your interests or your opponent's interests—but you can always be sure he is fighting for his own.

One traditional Cajun song (recorded by Edier Segura in 1934) tells the story of Joe Féraille trading his wife for a bucket of pecans. The pecan salesman may have thought he got the best of the bargain—until Mrs. Féraille ran away and returned to her husband! As the song goes on, Féraille acquires barrels of corn, peanuts, and other prizes in exchange for his lady. Each time he comes out of the trade wealthier than before, while the seller is left with nothing.

As is often the case with folk songs, one can find multiple layers of meaning behind the deceptively simple lyrics. Is Joe Féraille a populist hero who uses his wits to get the better of more prosperous businessmen? Is he a pimp making a tidy living with the aid of his woman? Is he a con artist taking advantage of hard-working farmers? However you may interpret Joe's actions, one thing is clear: if you trust him too much, you may find yourself poorer for your gullibility. Those who would work with Joe Féraille are advised to take that lesson to heart.

A darker take on Joe comes from contemporary Cajun singer Zachary Richard. His "Joe Férraille" begins with the narrator in prison. As he awaits execution he sings to his mother, who awaits outside the gates, and to the girl who loved him but who has forgotten him. He also lays special blame on Joe, that "goddamn canaille" (rabble, blackguard) who sold him whiskey, then loaned him a pistol. The sad tale ends with the narrator awaiting the dawn, when he will be dancing on the gallows.[1]

Richard captures an important truth about Iron Joe and about the various faces of Gu. He is an ambivalent figure who can get you in a great deal of trouble if you aren't careful. Yoruba legends tell of Ogou swimming in rivers of blood and slaying friend and foe alike when he flies into a berserk rage. Joe Féraille will happily sell you his whiskey, then loan you his weapons when you're in a fighting mood. But once you sober up, you may find yourself paying a terrible price for your actions. When you go drinking with Joe, you had best be sure you can hold your liquor.

If you wish to work with Joe Féraille, you may do best to treat him as a mercenary for hire. If he respects you, he will do his best to honor your requests—provided, of course, that you pay him a fitting salary for his efforts. As with any mercenary, you will need to keep an eye on him and make sure that you are getting your money's worth. A small payment beforehand with the promise of a larger one after you see results is a good approach. Make absolutely sure that you carry through with your end of the bargain if Joe carries through with his, and you'll find that he is a quick and powerful worker.

You can serve Joe with red candles and booze; like all his African and Caribbean brothers, Joe is a prodigious drinker. An image of a pirate or a mercenary soldier can be used to represent him. A cutlass or scimitar would be a worthy offering, as would bullets or a pistol. (But be sure to take appropriate gun safety precautions if you do. Remember that Joe doesn't mind lending out his weapon to people who might not be in a state of mind to use it!) And always be on your guard when you're dealing with him. Like many New Orleans locals, Joe isn't afraid of taking advantage of those who are naïve or careless.

St. Marron

Oh, St. Marron, I seek your aid in my hour of need. As you were able to break your chains and find your freedom, help me to avoid the snares of those who would capture me. In my hour of darkness and fear I call upon you. Pray for me that I may go about my business untroubled and that my enemies may be caught up in their own pitfalls.

Those slaves who escaped from captivity often made their way to the cypress swamps. There they established colonies of *maroons* (from the Spanish *cimarrón,* or fugitive) or, in French, *marrons.* Joining forces with other escaped slaves and indentured servants, outlaws, pirates, and Indians fleeing colonial genocide, they created tight-knit communities protected by their inaccessibility.

Some sought a settled existence in which they could build farms and raise their families in freedom. Others supported themselves by raids on outlying farms. Maneuvering through the canebrakes and sloughs of the wild regions between plantations and towns, they established trade and smuggling networks with slaves and free persons of color. Scorned by the white establishment as savages and criminals, many became folk heroes to the black population.

The most famous of these marron bandits was an escaped slave named Squier. Squier was one of Congo Square's most brilliant dancers, known especially for his performance of the bamboula. His master, General William de Buys, had given him a gun and encouraged him to hunt on his own. Squier became not only a talented hunter but an expert marksman who taught himself how to shoot with both hands because of a premonition that he might one day lose his arm.

Squier's time in the wilderness gave him a taste of freedom. He tried to escape several times but each time was caught by slave hunters and returned to de Buys. In 1834 he was shot by patrollers; his injured right arm became infected and was ultimately amputated. As soon as his wound healed, Squier made yet another escape. This time he was able to make it to the swamps, where he joined a marron community and became infamous as the bandit Bras Coupé (Cut Arm).

For several years Bras Coupé and his marrons led a campaign of robbery and pillage against the settlers. The whites considered him the most dangerous bandit in the Louisiana swamps, spreading tales of his atrocities in whispers and offering ever-increasing rewards for his capture. But the slaves and free blacks told very different stories. Among them, Bras Coupé's exploits became legendary. Some claimed that he had superhuman powers and that he was immune to fire and bullets.

On July 18, 1837, Bras Coupé's luck ran out when he was killed by a Spanish fisherman named Francisco Garcia. Garcia claimed that he had been attacked while at work on his boat. Garcia grabbed an iron bar and beat the escaped slave to death in self-defense. (Skeptics suggested that Garcia was actually one of Coupé's henchmen and murdered him in his sleep for the bounty.) Whatever the circumstances of Bras Coupé's demise, his body was brought back to New Orleans, where it was displayed in Jackson Square as a warning to any other slave who might wish to escape bondage.

But though Bras Coupé was dead, he was still honored by many blacks as St. Marron. The stories of Squier's exploits were now told about this legendary escapee who led many other slaves to freedom and who avenged the wrongs committed against his people. In the best tradition of folk Catholicism and ancestor veneration, he became in death an honored protector of those who labored under the yoke of oppression and racism.

Even after slavery ended, black people in Louisiana still had plenty to fear from the wealthy and powerful whites. Where once they had enforced their will with slave hunters and overseers, they now used the police force to make sure black people "knew their place"—which was, of course, beneath respectable white citizens. Efforts to better one's lot through numbers-running, moonshine-distilling, or other profitable but illegal means were often met with beatings, arrests, and long sentences in Louisiana's notorious prisons. St. Marron was now called on to avoid confrontations with the police or to secure freedom for prisoners.

In death as in life, St. Marron is a secretive fellow. Those who work with him in New Orleans are generally loath to provide specific details of how he is served. Suitable offerings might consist of cornmeal, okra, and corned beef or other salted or cured meats—all foods that a marron might have eaten in the swamps. His shrine might include broken chains (to symbolize his escape from slavery) and an image of an escaped slave. You might burn a red candle to petition him. But ultimately you will have to go out into the wild and make contact with St. Marron yourself. He will let you know what he wants from you. Keep in mind that he may want to be left alone.

Yon Sue

Yon Sue, mighty warrior and king, hear my plea. Always you have been the champion of your people. You raise up the weak and bring low the mighty. King Agassou, panther who stalks in the night, strike down those who would do evil against me. As you led your people to their promised land, guide me through the darkness and protect me from the schemes of those who would hold me back.

Since the days of Marie Laveau, many in New Orleans have petitioned Saint Anthony of Padua by another name. When addressed as "Yon Sue," the benevolent old monk could become a powerful guardian. Indeed, some said that he was the special protector of those who followed the old African traditions. A few of his wealthy Creole followers claimed he was actually a mighty king. They wore red neckerchiefs in honor of their royal patron, whom they addressed as "Monsieur Agassou."

A bit of research will soon verify M. Agassou's regal bona fides. According to an African legend, a young princess named Aligbonon of Tado met a leopard in the jungle and fell in love with it. Their union produced a son named Agassou. When the king of Tado died, Agassou tried to ascend the throne. Alas, his claim was denied; while his mother's royal lineage was not in question, no one could determine whether his feline father was of the right social set.

Undeterred, Agassou and his followers left the kingdom and moved to the Abomey plateau (in modern-day Benin). There he proved his leadership credentials by setting up and ruling a small colony. The chief of one small nearby village, Da, complained that these new migrants were taking up so much room that they would soon be building a palace on his belly. Agassou responded by taking up arms against Da's village. After killing him, they threw him into a pit and proceeded to place their new palace atop his body. Its name, Dahomey, can be translated as "On the Belly of Da."[2] To honor his divine ancestor, the new king chose the leopard as the heraldic symbol of his dynasty.

While skeptics may question tales of Agassou's divine parentage, none can dispute the success of his kingdom. Dahomey became famous for the discipline of its armies, including thousands of female soldiers, who were known to European observers as the Amazons of Dahomey. This military might allowed them to expand throughout the Abomey plateau and on toward the coast. In 1645 King Houegbadja declared that each Dahomean king should leave his successor more land than he inherited. His successors took his suggestion to heart, and by 1724 Dahomey had conquered the important port of Allada and had become an important slave-trading kingdom.

The slave trade brought great wealth to Dahomey's monarchy and to the artisans and weavers who worked to decorate its palaces and temples. But although Dahomey was flush with gold, it lacked in basic human freedoms. Each citizen of Dahomey owed absolute allegiance to the king, who was honored as *Dada* (father of the whole community), *Dokounnon* (holder and distributor of wealth), *Sèmèdo* (master of the world), and *Aïnon* (master of the earth), among other titles. The slightest disobedience could be punished by death. A court official who fell into royal disfavor, or a relative who might pose a challenge to the throne, could be sold into slavery.

But even in the New World those slaves who carried Agassou's blood continued to pay tribute to their half-divine ancestor. In New Orleans Yon Sue was known as the guardian of the old ways, the one who kept trouble away from the Voodoo queens and ensured they could continue their devotions to the African spirits. When the chips were down and legal or social pressures threatened the community, Yon Sue would make sure that his people survived to perform the traditional rituals. Police, crusading evangelists, and muckraking journalists regularly launched crusades against Voodoo and its believers, but Yon Sue saw to it that all their efforts came to naught.

To serve Yon Sue, you can get a small statue of Saint Anthony of

Padua or a leopard or spotted panther figurine. Tie a red ribbon about the statue; as you do, welcome Yon Sue into his new home and offer him your respects. You can serve him with red candles, rare steak, and high-proof alcohol. Yon Sue is not one to be petitioned lightly: you don't trouble the king for trivial matters. But if you approach him with the appropriate reverence and respect, he will help you to triumph and prosper in the face of adversity.

If you are being harassed for your interest in Voodoo, you can ask Yon Sue for his aid—but make sure you are prepared for his response! Your tormentors may very well wind up dead or horribly injured. As a Dahomean king, Yon Sue has little patience for blasphemy and disrespect; he also knows the value of fear in maintaining order and discouraging wrongdoers. You may do better to call on him for advice in leading your group, or ask him to bless your rituals so that the spirits look upon them with favor.

16

THE MIRACLE WORKERS

St. Expidité, St. Jude, and St. Roch

When you're poor and disenfranchised, you need quick and powerful protectors. Many New Orleans natives know that all too well. In the ragged crime-ridden neighborhoods outside the tourist sections, lots of people are in need of miracles. While many saints and spirits will help out, some are known for being especially prompt and powerful. These miracle workers have become particularly popular in the Big Easy. If you are in need, you will find they are ready to lend you a hand.

St. Expedité

Oh, St. Expeditus, in you I place my hope that my petitions may be granted if they are for my own good. Please ask our Lord through the intercession of the Blessed Virgin for the forgiveness of my sins and the grace to change my life particularly (here mention the particular grace desired), and I promise to follow your examples and will propagate your devotion. Amen.

It has become one of the most popular fables of New Orleans folk Catholicism. The chapel of St. Anthony of Padua (a "mortuary chapel" built to perform funeral masses for victims of the city's frequent yellow fever epidemics) received several saint statues. One of the boxes lacked a label identifying the saint whose statue appeared therein. It did, however, have an *Expedité* (rush shipping) sticker attached. The uneducated New Orleans locals assumed this was the saint's name and began making prayers to "Saint Expedité." As befits his name, St. Expedité soon acquired a reputation for performing quick and frequent miracles. Before long he was one of New Orleans' most popular and frequently propitiated saints.

The story, while amusing, is an urban legend that has several variants. According to the original version, a packing case containing a martyr's relics was sent to a community of Parisian nuns in or around 1798. The nuns allegedly misread the Expedité sticker and began asking St. Expedité to intervene on their behalf. When he did, his veneration spread rapidly throughout France and other Catholic countries. And Reunion, a French-speaking island in the Indian Ocean near Mauritius, claims St. Expedit as their patron. According to their story, the colonials requested religious relics from the Vatican and received a box labeled Expedit (dispatched). Historical evidence suggests that the cult of St. Expedité began in seventeenth-century Italy and spread to Germany. In 1781 the Sicilian town of Acirale declared Expeditus their patron saint.

Once we get past the legends, we know very little about the original St. Expeditus. He was apparently a Roman centurion stationed in Armenia, one of the early strongholds of Christianity. When he decided to become a Christian, the Devil sent a crow to tempt him with its cries of "Cras! Cras!"—Latin for "Tomorrow! Tomorrow!" But Saint Expeditus was not to be deterred. He grabbed the crow, threw it to the ground, and stomped on it, declaring, "I shall become a Christian today!" Later he achieved the crown of martyrdom when he was killed during Emperor Diocletian's Great Persecution of 303.

Expeditus is typically shown as a young Roman centurion. In his hands he holds a cross inscribed with the Latin word *hodie,* meaning "today." Beneath his foot is a dying crow, which is sometimes declaring "cras, cras" with its dying breath. As a result, he is frequently called upon to discourage procrastination or in situations where quick action is required. He has also gained a following among computer programmers and hackers. As Kathy Dupon, a freelance computer consultant living in New Orleans, says,

> I'm not a big believer in the saints, but St. Expedité is another whole story—he's so good he's scary. My clients were forever paying me late until I taped a card with the saint's picture behind my mailbox as a joke last year. Now my checks almost always arrive on time.[1]

St. Expedité is most commonly served with red candles and a glass of water on his left-hand side. After he intercedes on your behalf, you should give him a gift of flowers and a slice of pound cake as a reward. (If you do not give him his due, it is said that he will take back everything he has done on your behalf.) You should also let others know about his assistance. In New Orleans his name frequently appears in classified ads as grateful patrons offer their public thanks for his private favors.

Should you develop a personal relationship with St. Expedité, you may consider setting up an altar on his behalf. His statues, images, holy cards, and candles are readily available in most botanicas or online. Given his propensity for working quickly, he has acquired a large following. By providing him with regular offerings of water, candles, and pound cake, you will establish a relationship with a powerful and speedy protector. And if you want to make a pilgrimage to New Orleans, you'll find his statue can still be found at 411 North Rampart Street, in what is now the Our Lady of Guadalupe Chapel and International Shrine of St. Jude.

St. Jude

Holy St. Jude, apostle and martyr, great in virtue and rich in miracles, near kinsman of Jesus Christ, faithful intercessor of all who invoke your special patronage in time of need. To you I have recourse from the depths of my heart and humbly beg whomever God has given such great power to come to my assistance. Help me in my present and urgent petition. In return I promise to make your name

*known and cause you to be invoked. St. Jude, pray for me and all
those who invoke your aid. Amen.*

When you're talking about miracle workers, few saints are more prominent than St. Jude. He has become famous as the "Saint of the Impossible" and "Helper in Desperate Cases." His devotees regularly publish classified advertisements thanking him for his intercessions, and it is said that no situation is hopeless once St. Jude is involved. The shrine on Rampart Street became popular in the 1930s with parishioners who had their petitions to St. Jude answered favorably. Soon regular novenas were offered at the parish in St. Jude's honor and at a shrine erected on his behalf. Later, when St. Jude Memorial Hospital in Kenner was sold to the city and became Kenner Memorial, the hospital donated its statue to the church.

To distinguish him from Judas Iscariot the Traitor, this apostle became known as Judas Thaddeus (Judas the Loving). Because he was present at Pentecost, when tongues of fire descended on the heads of the believers, his images traditionally feature a flame above his head. They also include a picture of Christ's face, which Jude is said to wear on his breast. This pays tribute to the miraculous healing of Abgar, king of Edessa. According to legend, King Abgar was cured of leprosy when St. Jude brought him a cloth impressed with an image of the face of Jesus. Thanks to this, and to Jude's eloquent preaching, Abgar and his household converted to Christianity.

St. Jude wrote one letter, the Epistle of Jude, which has become part of the New Testament. A brief note consisting of one chapter and twenty-five verses, Jude is primarily a condemnation of various false teachers who were spreading dissent and discord among the early Christians. But it has become most famous for this exhortation to the faithful, found in Jude 1:20–21.

But you, my beloved, building yourselves upon your most holy faith, praying in the Holy Ghost, keep yourselves in the love of God, waiting for the mercy of our Lord Jesus Christ, unto life everlasting.

Because he told the confused and persecuted Christians to remain steadfast and promised them an eternal reward, Jude became known as "the optimistic apostle." He also became famous as the saint who would help his devotees in the most dire circumstances, and ultimately was declared the patron saint of desperate cases.

As is often the case with early Christian saints, the history of St. Jude is cloudy at best. Legend has it that after leaving King Abgar's castle, he went out through Mesopotamia and Persia preaching the Gospel and attracting many followers. But his success—and his penchant for undoing the sorceries of the magi and their idols—incurred the wrath of the Zoroastrians who ruled the region. Ultimately he, like St. Expidité, was allegedly martyred in present-day Armenia. Alas, little evidence exists to confirm this, and no record of St. Jude is found in any contemporary reports from the region.

But while separating the truth from legend may prove challenging, there is no question that St. Jude remains popular as a powerful intercessor. The primary gift he demands in exchange for his service is recognition. Those who benefit from St. Jude's aid are expected to testify publicly of his help and his power. Many will take out advertisements thanking him for his miracles. These classified ads are often found in newspapers in New Orleans and around the world.

Perhaps the most famous modern devotee of St. Jude is a comedian named Muzyad Yakhoob (or Amos Jacobs). Like many performers, this son of Lebanese Catholic immigrants started out small: one of his first roles was making the sound of horses' hooves on a Lone Ranger radio program by beating his chest with two toilet plungers. And as with many actors, that big break proved elusive. Jacobs's wife urged him to give up show business and find steady work. At wit's end, the aspiring comedian prayed to St. Jude, promising Jude that if he would intercede on his behalf, Jacobs would build a shrine for him.

"I never prayed for fame and fortune," Jacobs explains. "I wasn't trying to do anything but make a living. I was hoping that the radio producers would have more faith in my ability to play character roles. All I wanted was to get a house in the country, buy a station wagon, raise my kids."[2] But St. Jude had other ideas. Jacobs—under his stage name, Danny Thomas—became a popular nightclub act and later starred in his own TV show, *Make Room for Daddy*. After this, he joined forces with Sheldon Leonard and Aaron Spelling to produce programs like *The Andy Griffith Show* and *The Mod Squad*. A grateful Thomas kept his end of the bargain, helping to found the shrine that would become the famous St. Jude's Children's Research Hospital in Memphis, Tennessee.[3]

St. Roch

Oh, blessed St. Roch, patron of the sick, have pity on those who lie upon a bed of suffering. Your power was so great when you were in this world, that by the sign of the cross many were healed of their diseases. Now that you are in heaven, your power is not less. Offer, then, to God our sighs and tears and obtain for us that health we seek. St. Roch, pray for us, that we may be preserved from all diseases of body and soul through Christ our Lord. Amen.

Like many notable figures in New Orleans history, St. Roch came from the French aristocracy. His father was the governor of the city of Montpellier. But unlike the Crescent City's notorious rogues and wastrels, Roch would become famous for his lifelong piety. Born with a cross-shaped birthmark on his breast, the infant Roch abstained from nursing on days when his devout mother was fasting. In his twentieth year (approximately 1315) Roch's parents died, leaving him a sizeable legacy. Instead of squandering it on wine, women, and song, the young nobleman distributed his wealth among the poor and set out on the road as a beggar.

On his way to Rome, Roch stopped at the plague-stricken city of Aquapendente. Contemporary doctors were powerless against this disease—but Roch healed the sick simply by making the sign of the cross over them. Those he could not heal he nursed as best he could. Traveling from city to city, he ministered to the ill and unfortunate until finally, at Piacenza, he came down with the pestilence himself. Unwilling to burden others with his suffering, the ailing Roch went out to a hut in the woods and lay down to die.

But in his hour of need the holy man who had worked so many miracles was now aided by God. A dog from a nearby hovel found the ailing Roch and tended to him by bringing him bread and licking his sores. Cured of the plague, Roch set back out on his pilgrimage with his canine friend until he heard rumors of civil war in his home. Still wearing the rags of a mendicant holy man, he returned to the city where his uncle had governed since his father's death. Living on the streets he might have ruled, he preached the Gospel and worked miracles for the poorest of Montpellier's poor.

Alas, the city was on high alert for spies—and the charismatic beggar soon attracted the attention of his uncle's military forces. Arrested by the army, Roch humbly refused to reveal his identity, and none of the courtiers and politicians recognized the ragged, plague-scarred preacher who wandered about the city with his faithful hound. Roch and his dog were cast into the city's dungeons. There Roch ministered to fellow prisoners for five years until he died. When his corpse was prepared for burial, the cross-shaped birthmark was discovered, along with a document proving Roch was the former governor's son. Where once the citizens of Montpellier had locked him up as a spy, they now hailed him as a saint—especially after many who called on the now-deceased Roch reported miraculous healing

While New Orleans was safe from bubonic plague, it suffered regular outbreaks of malaria and yellow fever. During a particularly virulent outbreak in 1867, German priest Peter Leonard Thevis called on St. Roch to protect his congregation at Holy Trinity Catholic Church. Father Thevis promised to erect a chapel in St. Roch's honor if no one in the parish should die from the fever. St. Roch answered the priest's prayer: not one member of Holy Trinity died from yellow fever in the 1867 outbreak or a later epidemic in 1878.

Today Father Thevis's chapel and its accompanying *campo santo* (resting place of the holy) give their name to the St. Roch neighborhood, a vibrant largely African American neighborhood that was the birthplace of noted jazz pianist Jelly Roll Morton and other musical luminaries. St. Roch's Gothic shrine is filled with testimonies to Roch's healing intercession. Cast-off crutches and braces lie next to crucifixes and cockroach carcasses; artificial eyes, feet, and other commemorative votives hang on the walls alongside thank-you notes.

If you are suffering from a disease or injury, you should definitely seek appropriate medical attention. But even doctors can use some assistance—and St. Roch has a long history of alleviating suffering. A red candle and an offering of bread and table scraps for his faithful dog can help to attract his attention. After you recover, hang a *retablo* (an image of a bodily part, available online or in many Mexican stores) of the area that Roch cured in his shrine—be that shrine in your home or in a church dedicated to St. Roch (also known as St. Rocco, St. Roque, and St. Rochus).

Unfortunately, St. Roch's New Orleans shrine has seen better days. After Interstate 10 was run through the neighborhood in the 1960s, property values declined and crime soared. Then in 2005 Katrina did major damage to the area's homes and businesses. Years later little has been done to repair the blight or encourage the repopulation and revitalization of this once-thriving region. We can only hope that St. Roch sees fit to work his healing magic on the place that bears his name.

17

THE BRINGERS OF GOOD FORTUNE

St. Joseph, Assonquer, and John the Conqueror

New Orleans has become famous for its relaxed way of life—but relaxation requires funds, and while Spanish moss may grow thick on the city's live oaks, money does not. Those who practice New Orleans Voodoo can rely on the assistance of many spirits who understand their situation. Prosperity means more than a fat bank account; it means having what you need to enjoy your life. With the aid of some of the city's favorite saints, you too may be able to keep yourself in a style that allows time for both business and pleasure.

St. Joseph

Oh, St. Joseph, you worked as a humble carpenter, earning your wages by the sweat of your brow. Assist me in obtaining my wages that I may be able to support myself and my loved ones as you supported Jesus and Mary. Oh, St. Joseph, whose protection is so great, so strong, so prompt before the throne of God, assist me by your powerful intercession, and obtain for me from your divine son all spiritual blessings, so that I may offer my thanksgiving and homage to the most loving of fathers.

After the Civil War New Orleans became a favorite destination for Italians traveling to the New World. Between 1850 and 1870 the city had more Italian immigrants than any other city in America, and the French Quarter became known as "Little Palermo" and "Little Sicily," thanks to its large Italian population. These new residents brought with them their cuisine (which is still enjoyed today in po' boys and muffaletta sandwiches) and their work ethic. They also brought with them an undying devotion to a saint who has become a New Orleans favorite—St. Joseph, the foster father of Jesus.

In Italy, as in New Orleans, one celebrates a holiday by feasting. St. Joseph is typically honored on his day (March 19) with groaning tables of food put out in his honor. This tradition has been carried over to the Crescent City. A table put out in the 1920s by Mrs. Messina, a New Orleans Italian, gives you some idea of how big these repasts can be:

> I have five hundred different kinds of food. Besides the three sorts of St. Joseph's bread, I have stuffed artichokes, stuffed crabs, stuffed peppers, stuffed celery, stuffed eggs and stuffed tomatoes. I have lobsters, red snapper fish, shrimps, crayfish, spaghettis, macaronis, spinach, peanuts, layer cakes, pies, pineapples. . . . My God! I have everything![1]

In addition to food, these tables are also decorated with flowers, candles, electric lights, and statues of saints, with a large statue of St. Joseph occupying the place of honor. Whatever else they may contain, they always have St. Joseph's Bread (a braided egg bread that is almost identical to the challah bread served on the Sabbath in Jewish homes). They also have a large bowl of fava beans. At the end of the feast, the leftover food is given to the poor. Participants take with them a bean and a small piece of bread. The bread is kept in the house until next year; it is said that in return, St. Joseph will keep the household from going hungry. The beans are said to bring good luck. While it is traditional to leave a coin on the altar in exchange for this gift, gamblers will sometimes leave large sums of money in exchange for a lucky bean.

If you want to win St. Joseph's favor, you can make a special St. Joseph's potpourri for him. Place in a white bowl the following: Balm of Gilead buds, juniper berries, tonka beans (also known as wishing beans), fava beans, and star anise. If you can find them, add fishberries, also known as Levant berries. Fishberries were part of the original mixture catalogued by Zora Neale Hurston but can be difficult to find, as they are quite toxic and no longer widely used in conventional or alternative medicine. Basil (also known as St. Joseph's Wort) is an acceptable substitute. Put this bowl before your St. Joseph statue or image and add fresh potpourri regularly. Not only will it be a great offering, but it will fill your space with a subtle fresh scent that will draw positive energy and good fortune.

To make a powerful St. Joseph's Oil, pour this mixture into the bottom of an oil lamp and fill the lamp with high-quality olive oil. Place the lamp before your St. Joseph image, then light it and leave it burning while you say a Rosary in St. Joseph's name. When you are finished, snuff out the lamp. Repeat this for nine days (a novena). After you have said these prayers, strain out the potpourri and save the oil. You can then use the oil to anoint the doorway of your business or your workplace. You can also put a few drops on your wallet or bankbook if you are looking for a raise. As the patron saint of workers, St. Joseph will be happy to offer his assistance if you're willing to do your share and earn your money.

And while St. Joseph is typically called upon to help out in money matters, he is also a sympathetic defender of lovelorn men. New Orleanians who suspect their wives of infidelity will often come to St. Joseph for his help. They reason that since his wife had someone else's baby, he will understand their plight and come to their aid. This may seem disrespectful, but it has a long history. In medieval mystery plays, St. Joseph was often played for comic relief as a cuckolded husband. Among Eastern Christians, he was frequently presented in Nativity scenes as despondent and downhearted, unable to comprehend the great mystery of the Incarnation and filled with doubt at his wife's purity. Yet he was able to overcome those doubts, become a loving husband to Mary, and support the young Jesus as his own child. It is not surprising that he would take pity on others who find themselves in a similar situation and offer them his help.

Assonquer

Assonquer, you appreciate the finer things of this world and take joy in the pleasure of others. Grant me good fortune and bless me with your generosity. Let me live not only righteously but joyously, and let me share your benevolence with those who are in need so that we may celebrate together and sing your praises. For it is not your will that we should suffer but rather that we should rejoice and partake of the blessings that God has created for us in this life and in the next.

Many African spirits have been forgotten in the New World or never made it here. With Assonquer we find a different situation—a spirit who appears to have been forgotten on his home continent, and throughout most of the African diaspora, but who is remembered and served in New Orleans. Frequently mentioned in nineteenth- and early twentieth-century accounts of Voodoo in New Orleans and the Mississippi Valley, Assonquer (also spelled Onzoncaire) receives much less attention today. But though outsiders may have forgotten him, some still remember his power and benefit from his friendship. If you have financial problems that need solving, you may find Assonquer to be a benevolent protector and helper.

In his 1880 novel *The Grandissimes,* New Orleans writer George Washington Cable describes a ritual that calls on Assonquer:

The articles brought in by the servant were simply a little pound-cake and cordial, a tumbler half-filled with the sirop naturelle of the sugar-cane, and a small piece of candle of the kind made from the fragrant green wax of the candleberry myrtle. These were set upon the small table, the bit of candle standing, lighted, in the tumbler of sirup, the cake on a plate, the cordial in a wine-glass. This feeble child's play was all; except that as Palmyre closed out all daylight from the room and received the offering of silver that "paid the floor" and averted guillons (interferences of outside imps), Aurora,—alas! alas!—went down upon her knees with her gaze fixed upon the candle's flame, and silently called on Assonquer (the imp of good fortune) to cast his snare in her behalf around the mind and heart of—she knew not whom.

By and by her lips, which had moved at first, were still and she only watched the burning wax. When the flame rose clear and long it was a sign that Assonquer was engaged in the coveted endeavor. When the wick sputtered, the devotee trembled in fear of failure. Its charred end curled down and twisted away from her and her heart sank; but the tall figure of Palmyre for a moment came between, the wick was snuffed, the flame tapered up again and for a long time burned a bright, tremulous cone. Again the wick turned down, but this time toward her,—a propitious omen,—and suddenly fell through the expended wax and went out in the sirup.[2]

Mambo Samantha Corfield, a New Orleans Voodoo priestess currently residing in Albuquerque, New Mexico, refers to Assonquer as "the Spiritual principle of propinquity."[3] For her, Assonquer is the spirit who ensures that you are in the right place at the right time—or at the right times. Behavioral psychologists have described a propinquity effect. After extensive studies, they have determined that we are most likely to become friends, lovers, and business partners with the people with whom we interact most frequently. (Any New Orleanian, even those without advanced degrees, can tell you that success is not just about what you know but whom you know!) Assonquer can help to bring you acquaintances who are not only entertaining but also profitable.

If you want to stay on the good side of your boss—or to convince him or her that you are indispensable—Assonquer can help. Give said boss a lamb's head if you can find it (if not, a nice lamb roast, cooked rare, will suffice) and a quart of whiskey. Add a drop of your blood to some black ink, which you will then use to write your boss's name on a piece of paper nine times. Take this, and your offerings, to a nearby oak tree. After you have asked Assonquer for his assistance, leave them behind and return home. Your boss should warm up to you in a big way soon after this. Assonquer is famous for the speed with which he grants even the most difficult petitions.

In New Orleans Assonquer is frequently represented with images of St. Louis IX. This could be a tribute to Louis' royal wealth or to Père Dagobert, the former pastor of St. Louis Cathedral in New Orleans. Père Dagobert never allowed his vows of poverty to stand in the way of his love of good food, fine clothing, and beautiful women. Although his bishop accused him of "gluttony, drunkenness and a fondness for brown women," his congregation rallied to his support, and the charges came to nothing.[4] Some say that the Père still haunts the cathedral, wearing his beloved satin breeches and flowing lace cuffs and dipping from his bejeweled snuff box. He was certainly the sort of spiritual leader Assonquer would look favorably upon—a priest who realized that one could enjoy the pleasures of this world while preparing parishioners for the next. Green bayberry candles, cane syrup, and fine cordial liqueurs will make fine gifts for Assonquer and will help you to establish a working relationship with this well-beloved bringer of prosperity.

John the Conqueror

John the Conqueror, your kingdom was stolen from you, and you were sold as a humble slave. But you did not allow the vicissitudes of fortune to grind you down. With only your wits and your charm, you made the best of your situation and were able to get the best of those who would abuse you and take advantage of you. Look upon me with favor and grant me your silver tongue and keen mind so that I too may better myself and gain what should rightfully and justly be mine.

Blacks living under slavery, and later under the Jim Crow laws, were well accustomed to the slings and arrows wielded by the mighty against the powerless. If they were fortunate they might find work as mammies, maids, cooks, or porters, where they were expected to be properly obsequious to their white betters. Others might work as farmhands under the supervision of white overseers or as day laborers alongside whites who received higher wages for the same work. If they dared question the status quo or became too "uppity," they were liable to find themselves in jail or swinging from the nearest convenient tree.

In this milieu, "conquest" took on a very different meaning. Stories of grand heroes who emerged victorious against overwhelming odds were all well and good—but those who regularly faced overwhelming odds knew that those fights generally ended not with triumph but with tragedy. Their resistance often took the form of subverting the system and making it work for them. Overthrowing their white bosses was out of the question; getting one over on them was a more readily attainable goal.

According to African American folk tales, John the Conqueror (also known as High John or High John the Conqueror) had been a prince in Africa before he was captured by slavers and brought to America. There he was put to work on a plantation under the watchful eye of "Ole Massa." But though his circumstances were reduced, his intelligence was not. By using his wits he was able to make the most of his situation, playing practical jokes on Ole Massa and talking his way out of trouble whenever he was caught.

In one story Ole Massa came into John's cabin while he was cooking a stolen piglet. When asked what was on the fire, John told Ole Massa it was a stringy old possum. Ole Massa demanded a taste. John tried to dissuade him but Massa was insistent. Realizing he was caught, John served his Massa a big bowl of pork, telling him, "Massa, when I put this in here it was a possum, but if it came out a pig don't blame me!" Amused by John's answer, Ole Massa let him get away with his theft.

In another story, John so impressed Ole Massa with his intelligence and gift for precognition that he bet his plantation that John could guess what was hidden under a kettle. Alas, John's gift for prophecy was due largely to his talent for eavesdropping. As John walked around the kettle, he knew that Ole Massa was about to lose his bet and his plantation and that he was about to be hanged for his failure. He thought and thought about what might be hidden there, but couldn't figure it out. Finally, he threw up his hands in despair and said, "Well, you got the old coon this time." At that, Ole Massa turned the kettle over and a fat raccoon ran out. Massa won a new plantation and John won his freedom.

John's stories were told with many variants. In the Carolinas Low Country his antics combined with Cherokee folk legends and African trickster tales to become the Br'er Rabbit cycle. (In New Orleans these yarns starred Confrére Lapin.) In these stories, the smallest and most powerless of creatures managed to defeat powerful enemies like Bear, Wolf, and Fox through his superior wits. For disenfranchised, oppressed people surrounded by hostile white folks who had all the advantages over them, these myths offered hope and suggested ways by which they too could better their lot.

Today these stories make many people uncomfortable. Disney's 1946 retelling of the Br'er Rabbit legends, *Song of the South,* has never been released on home video in the United States because of controversy about its vision of happy black servants catering to rich whites. Lincoln Theodore Monroe Andrew Perry, who captured the "shiftless" wiliness of John the Conqueror with his Stepin Fetchit character, has been relegated to obscurity. Contemporary black Americans can express their anger openly and call public attention to the injustices that they have suffered and continue to suffer. Exploring the High John stories can give us an idea of what life was like before such open rebellion was possible—and teach us coping strategies for situations where it still is not an option.

African and Native American custom combined once again in the magical use of High John the Conqueror root (*Ipomoea* spp.). Named after this folk hero, this root was an integral part of a powerful mojo hand (chapter 23) used to bring personal mastery over others and to draw luck. John was able to rely on his luck and charisma to persevere despite his troubles, and by calling on his blessings through this root, you will find that your situation improves as well. You can also call on his aid with regular offerings of pork, chicken, or other barbecued meat and with generous helpings of whiskey. If you treat John right, he will treat you right, but be sure you honor your end of the bargain. If you are stingy or forget to reward him for services rendered, he'll happily make you the butt of one of his notorious jokes.

18

THE INDIANS
Black Hawk and the Black Hawk Spiritual Churches

I am now an obscure member of a nation that formerly honored and respected my opinions. The pathway to glory is rough, and many gloomy hours obscure it. May the Great Spirit shed light on yours, and that you may never experience the humility that the power of the American government has reduced me to, is the wish of him, who, in his native forests, was once as proud and bold as yourself.

BLACK HAWK[1]

In 1832 a Sauk war chief named Makataimeshekiakiak (Black Hawk) launched a campaign to reclaim Sauk lands that had been taken by American troops. Throughout the Midwest settlers trembled at tales of thousands of "bloodthirsty savages" who were scalping corpses. In reality, Black Hawk led a group of 1,500 Sauk, 1,000 of whom were old people and children. His Black Hawk war was doomed from the beginning. Ultimately, at the Battle of Bad Axe, hundreds of unarmed Indian civilians were massacred and Black Hawk and other war leaders captured.

Dispirited, defeated, and imprisoned by the Americans who had stolen the lands of his people, Black Hawk dictated his life story to a U.S. government interpreter. The resulting 1833 book, *The Autobiography of Black Hawk,* helped to transform his reputation. Once feared as the brute who led a war against white settlers in Illinois and Wisconsin, he was now seen as a tragic hero and noble savage. After his 1838 death, his skeleton was stolen and placed on exhibition until the governor of Iowa Territory intervened on behalf of Black Hawk's sons. He would give his name to roads, sports teams, and U.S. military regiments. And within a few decades he would inspire a Chicago Spiritualist to found a number of churches in the Crescent City.

Leafy Anderson and Black Hawk

Black and white Spiritualist churches in the United States ultimately trace their modern ancestry to Kate and Margaret Fox and their 1847 encounter with a spirit named "Mr. Splitfoot." Communicating by knockings and rappings, Mr. Splitfoot attracted wonder and notoriety throughout the small village of Hydesville, New York. He—and the Fox sisters—became an international sensation. Forty years later the ailing, alcoholic sisters claimed the whole thing had been a juvenile prank and the "rappings" produced by knuckle-cracking—but by then Spiritualism had become a major American religious movement that attracted both black and white adherents.

While little is known of Alethea "Leafy" Anderson, she appears to have been born around 1887 in Wisconsin. She was of black and Native American ancestry, and claimed to be half Mohawk. After moving to Chicago, she became known as a medium and Spiritualist among the blacks who had come northward as part of the Great Migration. In 1913 she established the Eternal Life Christian Spiritualist Church in the city. In homage to her heritage, one of her primary spirit guides was the war chief Black Hawk.

Within a few years Black Hawk gave Anderson some unusual advice. At a time when most blacks were heading out of the segregated South, Black Hawk told Anderson to set up shop in New Orleans. (He explained that he was the "saint of the south," while another Indian, White Hawk, ruled over the northern United States.) On October 25, 1920, Anderson received a Louisiana state charter for her organization, which eventually occupied Eternal Life Christian Spiritualist Church Number 12 on Amelia Street.

Plate 1. The famous Brennan's at 417 Royal Street—home of Bananas Foster and considered one of the city's finest restaurants.

Plate 2. Guests can choose to be seated outdoors in Brennan's lush courtyard.

Plate 3. Votive candles (right) honor St. Mary at the St. Louis Cathedral (above), the oldest church in Louisiana, located in Jackson Square.

Plate 4. Reverend Zombie's Voodoo Shop (top) at 725 St. Peter Street is worth visiting for the enormous collection of statues and other voodoo-related accessories (left). Detail of sign above.

Plate 5. The work of this street-side artisan captures the voodoo flavor of the city's culture. Detail at right.

Plate 6. Festive Mardi Gras colors and decorations festoon a wrought-iron balcony. The balconies are a common style found in the city after Governor Esteban Rodriguez Miro introduced a Spanish influence when rebuilding the city after a March 21, 1788, fire destroyed 856 buildings.

Plate 7. The New Orleans Historic Voodoo Museum: "taking all the mysteries, the secrets, the history and folklore of rituals, zombies, of gris-gris, of Voodoo Queens and all that jazz, and putting it all in one place in the heart of the New Orleans French Quarter" (from www.voodoomuseum.com).

Plate 8. A fertility statue.

Plate 9. Simple voodoo dolls come in all shapes and colors.

Plate 10. A skull in a top hat with a cigar is a "dead" giveaway that this shrine is dedicated to Ghede, the god of the dead.

Plate 11. An example of a "Main Altar," which represents many spirits and can be changed depending on which spirit the worshipper wants to honor or propitiate. The center pole is believed to be a channel through which the spirits can come down.

Plate 12. Traditional voodoo dolls.

Plate 13. In New Orleans Voodoo, the primary, most important spirit is called "Li Grand Zombi," whose image and altar are shown here. Worship in New Orleans Voodoo is centered around this spirit.

Plate 14. Altar dedicated to Papa La-Bas, the god who guards the entrance to the spirit world and the god of the crossroads. He enjoys offerings of rum, toys, cigars, and money. Detail at left.

Plate 15. Placard for the Voodoo Spiritual Temple founded by Osman and Miriam Chamani at 828 North Rampart Street. Offering African bone readings, oils, baths, and other healing services, it soon became a major center for New Orleans natives and tourists interested in the more spiritual side of Voodoo.

Plate 16. Traditional 7-day ritual candles surround an image of Marie Laveau at the New Orleans Historic Voodoo Museum, located at 724 Dumaine Street.

Plate 17. An image of Mami Wata, the "serpent priestess"; she is often depicted as a mermaidlike figure with a woman's upper body and the hindquarters of a fish or serpent. Devotees appeal to this spirit in matters of health, sex, children, and fertility.

Plate 18. Shrine to Mami Waters (also known as Mami Wata), an aspect of Yemaya, goddess of the sea. Worshipped throughout Central West Africa, she is invoked for love, peace in the home, and protection of mothers and children.

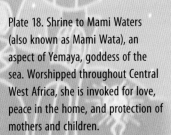

Plate 19. Shown is an example of a passport mask. These masks were carried during the annual migration of families as signs of tribal identification when crossing foreign regions. Smaller masks were carried for less extensive travel.

Plate 20. Kefabe mask, from Zaire.

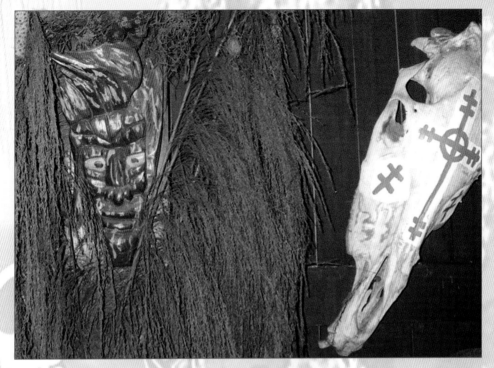

Plate 21. The horse skull on the right served as a warning to keep people away from certain areas. It indicated the presence of rampant disease and visitors should go no farther.

Plate 22. A display of voodoo dolls for purchase at the New Orleans Historic Voodoo Museum.

Plate 23. Flowers and mementos mark individual grave markers along a cemetery wall. The area's high water table makes belowground burial an impossibility, thus the standing crypts and memorial walls. Detail at right.

Plate 24. A particularly colorful memorial.

Plate 25. The tomb of Marie Laveau in St. Louis Cemetery No. 1., at the intersection of Basin Street and St. Louis Street in New Orleans.

Plate 26. A colorful array of offerings lay at the foot of Marie Laveau's tomb.

Plate 27. A voodoo doll rests next to a traditional 7-day candle as offerings to the Voodoo Queen. The tradition of marking three Xs while making a wish in hopes of having it granted by the spirit of Marie Laveau is still popular, despite discouragement from local law enforcement and warnings from traditional practitioners that desecrating tombs is frowned on by the voodoo spirits.

Anderson's church developed a large congregation, with both blacks and whites visiting her for readings and consultations. It was also a largely matriarchal organization. At a time when most orthodox churches expected women to remain silent in church, or at the very least to leave the running of affairs to men, the leaders of Anderson's church were mostly female. This was in keeping with black and white Spiritualist churches of the time, where female mediums and leaders commonly occupied positions of power and privilege. It has also remained the case to this day. Many women who have converted to Spiritual churches from Pentecostal movements have stated they felt stifled by the gender roles forced upon them by their former organizations and sought greater avenues of expression and authority.[2]

Anderson encountered prejudice and suspicion from the white establishment of New Orleans. Harassed by police as a con artist and fraud, she called on Black Hawk to protect her. His intervention helped her to win her court case and to secure protection for her church against further police harassment. After overcoming these obstacles, she was able to earn a tidy income through readings, classes, and jazz parties. A typical week saw Mother Anderson presiding over five services: a training class for future leaders on Tuesdays, two services on Sunday, and meetings on Thursday and Friday. At those services readings from the Bible and hymns alternated with members and leaders "getting the spirit" and becoming possessed by Black Hawk or other spirit guides like "Queen Esther" and "Father John."

In the best New Orleans tradition, Anderson dressed the part of a spiritual leader. According to Mother Doris, one of her students: "Sometimes she wore all white wit' a purple veil, but other times she wore a gold gown wit' a Black Hawk mantle over her shoulders: it had a picture of Black Hawk sewed on it. Once in a while she wore a man's full dress suit, but that was only for special occasions."[3]

On December 17, 1927, Mother Leafy Anderson died of complications from a cold. Although she was only forty years old, she had laid the foundations for a major spiritual movement. The women who had taken her classes were now church matriarchs—and they shared her veneration of the mighty Black Hawk and other Indian spirits. Today New Orleans Spiritual churches combine Roman Catholic icons and priestly vestments with spirited Pentecostal preaching, "laying on of hands," and speaking in tongues. Herbs, sacred oils, and incense are used as spiritual tools, while "bishops" and "mothers" prophesy and experience spirit possession by their guides, including Indians.

Those who are not part of the Spiritual Church frequently look upon Indian spirits with some ambivalence. They are derided by some as "Voodoo saints" even though many Spiritual Church members identify as Christians and take pains to separate their own activities from "sinful" Voodoo. Still others believe Indian spirits are dangerous warriors used for vengeance magic. Many Spiritual Church members will deny that they work with Black Hawk, although they will vouch for his power. But Black Hawk's presence on many altars and in many churches testifies to his enduring popularity and power.

> *He came to my aunt in Chicago . . . he told her to go and heal the people. . . . She healed through Black Hawk. I have healed through Black Hawk. . . . But you have to use him right. You can't ask him to harm [anybody]. He'll help you, as a guide and protection. People going to jail, he'll help you. But I've never known him to do [any] dirty work. Only good things come to me [through him]. He will give you a blessing . . . through God. You can't do anything without God.*
>
> BISHOP EDMONIA CALDWELL,
> NIECE OF MOTHER LEAFY ANDERSON[4]

Working with Indian Spirits

You fought mightily for your people, Black Hawk. You protected the weak and the powerless against overwhelming odds and kept your dignity even in defeat. In the name of the Great Spirit from whom we all come, I call on you. Give me your strength and your wisdom that I might stand firm against tribulation and that I might have the courage to defend those who cannot defend themselves. Help me to walk with honor as you walked with honor, and keep watch for me that no enemy may catch me unawares.

Indian spirits come from the frontier, from the wild world beyond the boundaries of the home. They are seen by the Spiritual churches as protectors who can keep out the dangers of the outside—including the dangers of the urban environment. Accordingly, they are traditionally kept near the doorway to ward off unwanted attention from potential enemies. In Hoodoo those who wish to avoid conflicts with the law may protect their brothels or speakeasies by placing Indian head pennies over their doors. (It's not unheard of to find hundreds of Indian head pennies lined up on the walls of New Orleans houses of ill repute.) And one of the most popular hymns to Black Hawk proclaims, "He'll fight your battles, he's on the wall. He's a mighty good watchman, he's a mighty good leader . . . he's on the wall."[5]

Black Hawk is typically honored with red, black, or white candles, and he is given offerings of fruit, roasted corn, or tobacco. His altars can be enormous, elaborate affairs featuring massive "cigar store" Indians or discreet shrines placed beside a doorway. He is also served with a bucket or coffee can filled with white sand or dirt. His statue or bust is placed atop this, as are his offerings. (This may be a nod to the Kongo tradition of pots containing various spiritually active items like roots, bones, and dirt from certain sacred places.) He stays "on the wall" and watches for breaches in the defenses of those who honor him, and protects them from those who would do evil.

Black Hawk is a no-nonsense spirit with a keen sense of justice. He will seek vengeance for those who have been wronged, but he is not to be called on trivial matters. If you want him to take action against your enemies, be certain that you are in the right, and make sure you have exhausted every chance to make peace. Black Hawk was a fierce fighter when he was forced into battle, but he was always a reluctant warrior who preferred peace to war and who was gracious in defeat as well as in victory. He may help you to triumph against your adversaries, but he may also teach you how to maintain your dignity and honor after the battle is lost.

Yellow Jacket and Money Magic

Because the wild frontier is a place where riches can be discovered, the Indian spirits can be called upon for financial assistance. Given their passion for justice, they are especially helpful in situations where you are not getting money that is owed to you or when you are being victimized by those who are wealthier and more powerful than you. St. Daniel's Spiritual Church calls on the assistance of an Indian spirit named Yellow Jacket. As Archbishop Jackson explains,

> [Yellow Jacket] would steal from the rich, and give to the poorest Indians. And he didn't steal their cattle . . . but their money, their jewelry. He's good for financial blessings. So whenever you call on that spirit, that means money, big money coming from somewhere. . . . Every now and then we give him a yellow light. And sometimes one of my members will say "Bishop! The spirit of Yellow Jacket is in [our] midst" and pretty soon everybody's on the floor claiming they're blessed with money![6]

Among Yellow Jacket's favorite tools are salt and ammonia. These are both powerful spiritual cleansers that can help to remove unclean spirits, bad luck, and barriers that are keeping you from receiving what you deserve. If you're having a run of financial misfortune, clean your house with ammonia and take a saltwater bath. You can then light a yellow candle for Yellow Jacket and make an offering of roasted corn, black coffee, and pipe tobacco. This double-pronged attack will address any negativity that may be holding you back while providing a positive business stimulus.

Yellow Jacket is an example of an Indian spirit with a smaller following. Many Spiritual ministers have personal Indians who look after them and protect them. Uncle Bucket, Sitting Bull, and other Indians receive homage from Spiritualists around New Orleans. This veneration is also found outside the Crescent City: throughout South and Central America, practitioners of Espiritismo (Spanish for "spiritualism") honor "Los Indios," and Indian statues are commonly found in American botanicas. Other Spiritualists have called on Indian guides. The noted magician and artist Austin Osman Spare, for instance, claimed inspiration from the Indian spirit Black Eagle. If you begin honoring Indian spirits, you may find that you have a hitherto unknown warrior watching over you. Let your conscience be your guide and trust your instincts; ask your spirit what he wants and honor his requests.

Archetypes and Stereotypes

When dealing with Indian spirits, we run into the embarrassing issue of stereotyping. The Indian spirits often play into old images of Indians as doughty warriors who are happy to assist the white people who call the shots for them. (Where would the Lone Ranger be without Tonto?) Warwhoops, face paint, feather headdresses, tomahawks, and "Ugh. Me think-um heap big trouble ahead" pidgin English can all be found in Indian possessions. Skeptics may note that these "Indians" behave not like Native Americans, but rather like extras from old Westerns. Like Shylock, Amos 'n' Andy, and other negative cultural images, we may wish to forget about these reminders of our unsavory past.

Broad roles are often found in Spiritualism. In Cuba and Guyana, where Chinese immigrants often worked as wandering merchants, we find spiritual possessions by "Chinamen" who speak with thick accents and who can bring prosperity. In Brazil *Gitano* (Gypsy) spirits are known for their lascivious behavior and penchant for thievery—all accusations that have often been raised, to tragic effect, against Romany people. The line between archetype and stereotype can often be very thin.

Archbishop E. J. Johnson of the Israelite Divine Spiritual Church (3000 Frenchman Street), one of the oldest and most influential of the Spiritual churches currently active in New Orleans, offers an interesting if politically incorrect view on the question.

People ask us why we got an Indian in our church. Well, children, you should remember that when Jesus left his people for the second time . . . He told his apostles he was going away, but he would send them his divine spirit which was the Holy Ghost. And when he sent that spirit they began to preach and heal and speak in tongues . . . and there was all kinds of people in that room . . . there was Dagoes there, and Chinese, Japanese and all kinds of people. And everybody received the spirit. So it's not so unusual that we should have an Indian guide . . . an Indian Spirit in our church.[7]

Perhaps the best offering we can make to the Indian spirits is awareness of the tragedy they and their people have suffered and continue to suffer. One way to do this is to learn about the various ethnic groups that have been lumped in under the label "Indian." Another is to understand that some Native American religious ceremonies and offices are open only to those of Indian ancestry. It's easy to sniff at Spiritual Churches and their "Red Indian" guides. Are we ready to acknowledge the racism and appropriation of claiming oneself a "medicine man" or "medicine woman" after attending a weekend seminar? And are we ready to do something to address the injustices upon which our culture was built? These questions have no easy answers—but for those who will work with these entities, they must be addressed.

19

THE ROOTS

The Dead

American culture tends to focus on the person as an individual. Our prevailing mythology honors the "self-made person" and promises us that we can become whatever we want to be no matter where we started out. The African worldview sees the person not as a discrete unit but as part of an ongoing process. You are defined not only by your achievements, but also by the ancestors who came before you and the descendants who remain after your death. You can redeem your family's sins, you can add to your family's accomplishments, or you can besmirch your family's reputation—but you cannot escape being part of your family.

While we may wish that our dead will "rest in peace," in the Kongo the deceased ancestors play a vital and continuing role in the lives of their descendents. They occupy the space between the gods and the living, and they can be called upon to offer counsel, protection, or assistance. This veneration is an important part of their religious and magical practices—and it is an integral part of New Orleans Voodoo.

The Cemeteries of New Orleans

Because most of New Orleans is below sea level, the water table is very high. A sexton who tries to dig a classic six-foot-deep grave will soon be faced with a floating coffin. When it rains the table rises even higher—and so do the deceased! A good storm will pop the caskets out of the ground and send them floating into the churchyard. Early settlers tried to avoid these premature resurrections by weighting the coffins, placing stones atop them, or even boring holes in them—all to no avail.

In 1789, during the Spanish rule, a wall vault system was placed in the new St. Louis Cemetery No. 1. Frequently used in Spain, these vaults were less prone to giving up their contents during the rainy season. After a series of 1830s epidemics were blamed on vapors from flood-disinterred corpses, the city council passed an ordinance requiring all further burials at existing cemeteries to take place in above-ground structures. In most of the United States, above-ground interment is only for those wealthy enough to afford it. The cemeteries of New Orleans are true "cities of the dead," housing the remains of the rich and the poor alike.

But as with most cities, the rich dead have more luxurious surroundings. The barrel-vaulted tombs of wealthy families, which date from the early nineteenth century, often have ornate facades and decorations. Great stone sarcophagi house those who preferred to rest in peace alone and who could afford the cost of a single tomb. Multilayered "society tombs" house those who shared common interests in life. The Orleans Battalion of Artillery Tomb of St. Louis Cemetery No. 1 contains the remains of veterans of the Battle of New Orleans, while many departed Chinese New Orleanians rest in the Soon On Tong Tomb in Cypress Grove Cemetery (120 City Park Avenue). Other society tombs house firefighters, police officers, and other working-class locals who might not have been able to afford such lavish afterlife accommodations on their own.

Offerings decorate many of these tombs. While the tomb of a famous Hoodoo queen like Marie Laveau may be covered with candles and other offerings, family members may leave toys on the grave of a deceased child, football memorabilia on the grave of a Saints fan, or bottles of beer on the grave of a departed relative who liked a drink in life. Real and artificial flowers are found in abundance in simple or elaborate vases. Clocks are found on many graves, and many graves are also decorated with shards of glass or upside-down soda bottles. This is a New World survival of the African practice of using these objects to trap or cut evil spirits.

But while these resting places are grand, they are not necessarily final.

Many of the vaults are leased rather than purchased. Should no rent be forthcoming, the remains are removed. The old casket is burned and the bones deposited in a communal depository at the bottom of the structure to make way for the latest tenant. One New Orleans cemetery offered the vain but impoverished dead "three-day burials." The deceased could be interred in a fancy vault to impress his grieving friends and relatives. Three days later the remains could be cremated or disposed of in some other less expensive manner.[1]

Even if you are not in the Big Easy, you can practice one of their most beloved customs. Each year the neighbors gather in their local cemetery for a picnic and maintenance. Tombs are whitewashed, weeds are pulled, flowers are planted or replaced, and trash is taken away. Then, after the work is completed, people sit down to share food, conversation, and memories of their dearly departed. Like the city's famous "jazz funerals," these working picnics bring together the living to celebrate the lives and accomplishments of the dead. It's a tradition that could stand to be exported—and a great way for you to make a connection with the spirits residing in your local graveyard while doing something good for your community.

Haunted New Orleans

New Orleans is a city of ghosts, with many homes and establishments boasting proudly of their spiritual stowaways. But some locations have become especially (in)famous for their paranormal activity.

Josie Arlington's Tomb

In Metairie Cemetery (which, despite the name, is located not in Metairie, a nearby suburb, but at 5100 Pontchartrain Boulevard in New Orleans) stands the tomb of infamous madam Josie Arlington. As her health failed, Arlington decided to invest her considerable earnings in a memorial. She purchased a plot in Metairie Cemetery (then the city's most prestigious graveyard) and had an enormous red granite tomb built there. Society matrons were outraged at the thought of their loved ones sharing a final resting place with Josie Arlington—especially since many of their men had already shared her bed! But there was little they could do, and when Arlington passed away in 1914, she was interred in a grand style.

Soon thereafter rumors began to spread. Reports claimed that the Arlington tomb glowed with an unearthly night during the evening, as if the flames of hell were licking at it. At the front door of Arlington's tomb stood a statue of a young girl. Some said it represented an innocent being turned away from Arlington's establishment, since Josie had always boasted proudly that no virgin had ever been despoiled in her bordello. Others said it represented the young Josie turned away from her father's house and forced into her life of vice. But the most sensational stories claimed that this statue would move at night and walk around the tombs.

Before long the Arlington mausoleum became a tourist attraction, with people visiting the Metairie Cemetery to see if the marble urns would glow with unearthly light or if Josie's statue would move for them. Her horrified family ultimately moved Arlington's remains to an anonymous grave within the cemetery. Today her former tomb is occupied by the Morales family, but it still remains a popular destination for ghost hunters and paranormal buffs. In her new, more discreet location, Josie remains in good company. Among the fellow residents of Metairie Cemetery are Confederate General P. G. T. Beauregard, jazz legends Al Hirt and Louis Prima, and Ruth Fertel, founder of the Ruth's Chris Steak House chain.

The Lalaurie House

In the early 1800s, the parties at Delphine Lalaurie's mansion were the talk of New Orleans high society. The city's finest families came to 1140 Royal Street for fine dining and sparkling conversation amid gilded furnishings. But there were whispers that the charming hostess was a cruel and sadistic woman who abused her slaves. In 1833 the streets of the Vieux Carré were buzzing with a terrible story: Mme. Lalaurie was responsible for the death of a young slave girl. The girl had supposedly run upstairs in an attempt to escape her whip-wielding mistress, but fell to her death from the balcony. Before the horrified eyes of her neighbors, Lalaurie had the girl's body buried in the courtyard. (Modern versions of the story claim Lalaurie was fined for the murder of her servant, and her slaves were sold at auction, but that her relatives purchased them and returned them to her. No corroborating historical records or newspaper accounts have been found.)

Then, on April 11, 1834, a fire ripped through the Lalaurie Mansion. When firefighters made their way into the house, they discovered several slaves chained to the wall. One old woman had been kept on her knees for so long that she was unable to stand, and a man had a gaping, worm-infested wound on his head. (The stories have become more colorful with the passage of time. Today one hears that Lalaurie disemboweled slaves and nailed them to the floor by their intestines, stuffed their mouths with excrement and sewed their lips shut, performed impromptu sex-change operations on them, and drilled holes in their head so she could insert a stick and "stir their brains.")

Whatever happened, it led to an outraged crowd milling about the mansion's doors. Fearing for her life, Mme. Lalaurie rode off in her carriage, never to return. Some say she died in Paris, while others say she remained with relatives on the north shore of Lake Pontchartrain. And many others say that she not only returned to the city after her death, but resumed residence at her 1140 Royal Street home. Visitors have reported hearing agonized cries in the night or told tales of menacing manacled ghosts wandering the hallways along with their spectral mistress. The house is rumored to bring misfortune to those who live there. It certainly did no favors for its latest inhabitant, actor Nicolas Cage. He acquired the property in 2007, only to lose it to foreclosure less than two years later.

The Sultan's Ghost

When Jean-Baptiste La Prete found himself short on funds, he was happy to lease his winter home on 716 Dauphine Street to a turbaned gentleman who claimed to be the sultan of Turkey. The lease was signed and the sultan moved in along with his entourage. There he redecorated his new lodgings in the finest Ottoman style, with heavy carpets and draperies that protected him from the prying eyes of the rabble. (The eunuch guards who marched over the balconies and galleries with drawn scimitars served to further discourage the curious.) But the smells of opium and incense wafting from the home, as well as the rumors of wild orgies attended by the Crescent City's finest citizens, served to fuel speculation of the sultan's debaucheries.

Then, one morning, neighbors noticed rivulets of blood running out from the iron gates. Police were called. When no one answered their summons, they forced the doors and entered the home. There they found body parts scattered throughout the house; the servants, guards, harem girls, and slave boys had all literally been hacked to bits. In the garden they found a hand sticking out from the dirt; the sultan had been buried alive and suffocated before he was able to claw his way out of his shallow grave. The crime was never solved. Some claimed the culprits were pirates who wanted the sultan's treasure. Others said the sultan was really the sultan's brother, who had escaped to New Orleans after stealing gold and slaves only to find that an ocean was no shield against the Ottoman emperor's wrath.

Today the details of this story are sketchy. Some versions of the legend claim the atrocity took place in 1792, even though the La Prete House was not built until 1836. And an earlier story (compiled by historian Charles Gayarré in 1866) suggests that in 1727 a Turkish fugitive was killed in New Orleans in his cottage at the corner of Orleans and Dauphine Street—the spot on which Jean-Baptiste La Prete later built his house![2] But whatever the facts behind this legend, 716 Dauphine retains a reputation as one of the most haunted houses in New Orleans. People have reported hearing the tinkle of Oriental music, the smell of incense, and bloodcurdling screams, and apparitions of a light-haired man in Turkish garb have also been spotted.

Safer Ghost Hunting

Today "ghost hunting" has become a popular hobby. People flock to graveyards, abandoned houses, crime scenes, and other sites that are purportedly "haunted" in an attempt to contact the dead. Most deceased spirits are harmless and have little interest in the affairs of random living folks.

A few are willing to play games with electrical equipment, make knocking and rapping noises, or otherwise entertain paranormal researchers. And a few are ill-disposed toward anyone who remains above the dirt. Haitians call these bad-tempered ghosts *mo,* from the French *mort.* Practitioners of Espiritismo call them "intranquil spirits"; the Japanese call them *yurei;* and English folk tales speak of "unsettled ghosts." All agree that they can be exceedingly dangerous.

If an intranquil spirit attaches itself to you, it can leech off your energy, leaving you weak and ill. It can cause horrible nightmares in which you find yourself reliving its death over and over. It can produce the symptoms of the disease that killed it—symptoms that no medical treatment will touch. It can try to take over your life and your body, leading to fugues or radical personality changes. If left untreated, this infestation can literally destroy you in body and soul. If you are seeking to commune with the dead, you had best be sure that you have adequate protection. A little bit of caution and common sense now can save you a whole lot of trouble down the road.

When going into places where there are active dead spirits, you should make sure you have a holy symbol on you, preferably one connected to your ancestral faith. Even if you're a lapsed Catholic or a secular Jew, a blessed crucifix or a Chai will help keep away negative spirits. Do not open yourself up to contact with any random entity who wishes to speak with you. You wouldn't lend your car keys to a stranger, so why would you let an unknown spirit into your head? A holy symbol serves the same purpose as a locked door on your vehicle. While it won't stop a truly powerful or determined spirit from getting in, it provides a layer of protection and will keep out most miscreants.

For added protection, you can carry a sprig of rue (*Ruta graveolans*) in your pocket. Rue strengthens your connection to elevated spirits while protecting you from intranquil or troubled ghosts. It's a very powerful and useful herb for those who wish to work with the dead. You can also use it to make a very effective floor wash: add a few drops of holy water (available in Catholic churches) and a pinch of salt, and you've got a mixture that will dissuade most unwanted ghosts from sticking around the premises. Rue is available in most botanicas and is fairly easy to grow for those who might want to add it to their indoor or outdoor garden.

In spiritual as in mundane matters, the best offense is a good defense. Don't try to send spirits "into the light" unless you know what you are doing and are prepared to have them say, "I don't want to go into the light, and you can't send me there." Exorcism is advanced work. Those who are qualified do it only with the greatest reluctance. It is grueling and hazardous labor. Don't put yourself in the line of fire without careful consideration of potential consequences. Avoid "ghost hunting" in sites where atrocities have taken place or where malevolent ghosts reputedly reside. If you don't have a good reason to speak to a killer or a murder victim, don't disturb them. They won't appreciate the intrusion, and they're likely to make their displeasure known in a painful way.

Above all else, treat communication with the dead as a sacred and a serious endeavor. To stand between here and the hereafter and speak to those on the other side is a great blessing. It is not a diversion for bored tourists engaged in spiritual slumming; neither is it a game to impress your friends. The dead carry powerful magic and can be strong allies for those who approach them with reverence and respect. They can also be fearsome enemies for those who would treat them as carnival tricks or workhouse slaves. Understand this and act accordingly and you will be fine. Ignore it at your own peril.

PART FOUR

PRACTICES

Now that you've learned something about the history of New Orleans and the spirits served there, it's time to take a closer look at the city's magical traditions. The cultural forces that created the Big Easy's unique cuisine and music have also shaped its spirituality. Catholicism, African, and black American folk customs and the economic influence of the tourist trade, among others, have all helped to create New Orleans Voodoo.

20

CANDLES

When it comes to setting a mood, there are few items as useful as the humble candle. They can turn a meal into a seductive adventure or a college bedroom into a romantic boudoir. Not surprisingly, candles can also be used to craft potent magic. Many magical folks use candles to create a "witchy" or "spiritual" atmosphere—but for practitioners in New Orleans, that's just the tip of the iceberg. Candle burning is an important part of their practice. Their candle rituals involve elaborate codes and symbols that can be used to send messages to the spirits or to effect changes in the real world.

Candles are inexpensive and versatile tools that come in a variety of shapes and sizes. Learning some of the secrets of candle magic can help you become a more competent and successful magician without spending an inordinate sum on magical items. New Orleans Voodoo practitioners have always been good at making do with available items and spellcasting on a tight budget—and if you follow their lead, you can too!

Candle Colors

Writing in 1935, Zora Neale Hurston gave the following meanings for candle colors used in New Orleans Voodoo:

White: For peace and to "uncross" and for weddings

Red: For victory

Pink: For love (some say for drawing success)

Green: To drive off (some say for success)

Blue: For success and protection (for causing death also)

Yellow: For money

Brown: For drawing money and people

Lavender: To cause harm (to bring triumph also)

Black: Always for evil or death[1]

But in the 1940s another author, using the pseudonym Henri Gamache, combined old-fashioned Hoodoo with the Rosicrucian teachings of Pascal Beverly Randolph, an African American medical doctor and Spiritualist. (Randolph's teachings on sex magic inspired yet another prolific writer, Aleister Crowley.) While Gamache's real name remains a mystery to this day, his influence on New Orleans Voodoo and Southern Hoodoo is undeniable. Today most New Orleans Voodoo practitioners use the color scheme given in his 1942 *Master Book of Candle-Burning*.

White: Spiritual blessings, purity, healing, rest

Blue: Peace, harmony, joy, kindly intentions, healing

Green: Money spells, gambling luck, business, a good job, good crops

Yellow: Devotion, prayer, money (gold), cheerfulness, attraction

Red: Love spells, affection, passion, bodily vigour

Pink: Attraction, romance, clean living

Purple: Mastery, power, ambition, control, command

Orange: Change of plans, opening the way, prophetic dreams

Brown: Court case spells, neutrality

Black: Repulsion, dark thoughts, sorrow, freedom from evil

Red and Black (Double Action): Remove a love-jinxing spell

White and Black (Double Action): To return evil to the sender

Green and Black (Double Action): Remove money-jinxing[2]

Most botanicas stock a wide range of seven-day candles in these colors. When they have something they need to accomplish, Voodoo Queens and conjurers start out by burning one or more candles in the appropriate color or colors. A spell to sexually dominate a prospective partner, for example, might use a red (passion) and a purple (control, command) candle. A spell to bring business to your spa, by contrast, could combine white and green candles to produce a peaceful, relaxing aura that encourages your patrons to spend money.

Double-action candles in Gamache's chosen colors are widely used to remove "crossed conditions." These hexes can be set deliberately or can be the result of jealous neighbors whose evil intent alone causes harm to the target. (Italians have long recognized the power of the *malocchio*, evil eye, and so do practitioners of New Orleans Voodoo.) If you have had an unexplainable run of bad luck or poor health, you may be suffering from a vengeful person's evil eye. To use a double-action candle, cut off the tip and carve a new tip on the black half so it will burn first. Carve the name of your enemy on the black half and your name on the other half. This can help you send their ill wishes back to them and free you from the hex their envy and hatred has laid upon you.

After Fidel Castro's rise to power, many practitioners of Santeria made their way to America as refugees. This led to a new interest in Afro-Cuban practices, an interest that has had a great impact on New Orleans Voodoo. One popular candle is made with seven different colors of wax and calls upon the Seven African Powers—the Orishas Ellegua, Yemaya, Oshun, Obatala, Ochosi, Oya, and Ogun—to intercede on behalf of the petitioner, and can be used in times of great need. While initiates in Lukumi focus on their crowning Orisha, those who are not initiated find it most efficacious to call on several of the most well-known Orishas at once, in the hopes that one will answer their prayer.

Candle Sizes

Today the most commonly used candles are seven-day candles, also known as vigil candles. These burn inside a glass jar, making them a bit safer to use. (That being said, lit candles should never be left unattended or in a place where a child, pet, or careless roommate could knock them over.)

Frequently the glass will be decorated with an appropriate saint image or figure describing the candle's intended purpose. Brown seven-day candles marked "Court Case" can be found beside green "Money Drawing," black "Breakup," and white "Uncrossing" candles. Most are made by pouring wax into the jar. Slightly more expensive "pull outs" can, as the name suggests, be pulled out of the chimney for purposes of carving, anointing, and otherwise preparing them for magical purposes. (More on this below.)

Taper candles (the kind typically used in candelabras) are used in many spells. If you can't leave a seven-day candle burning continuously, you can light a taper candle for a brief period of time while you pray and make petitions to your spirit. You can then snuff it out and repeat as necessary. Taper candles can be customized like seven-day candles with anointing oils, herbs, or markings scratched into the wax. They generally offer a short and intense burst of spiritual energy, where the seven-day candle gives a more gradual and sustained release. For situations that need a quick push, you may find a taper candle to be ideal.

Sabbath candles, sometimes called utility candles, are smaller but no less useful. These small white candles are burned by observant Jews on Friday evening to celebrate the Shabbat. They are also good to have in the house when the electricity goes out—a not-uncommon occurrence in storm-prone Louisiana. A popular Voodoo spell uses a utility candle and a jar of honey to "sweeten up" a person and make him or her more favorably disposed to you. Write the person's name on a piece of brown paper, and then write your name over that name at a 90° angle. Place the name in the honey and close the jar. Now run a match over the bottom of the utility candle until the wax is softened and stand it atop the lid. Light the candle and let it burn down. Whenever you'd like to make the person feel sweet again, repeat the purpose. In time your honey jar will come to resemble a large ball of candle-drippings, but it will grow more powerful with each use.

And if you want to petition a saint for a favor, you can use the traditional votive candle. These small candles generally come in glass holders (which can be in varying colors). They are lit before a crucifix or a statue or image of the saint. As Father Colin Donovan explains: "A Catholic who lights a votive candle, makes an offering and places an intention before the Lord. The candle symbolizes their intention, it can also stand for their presence in prayer before God, and their union, as a Christian, with Christ the light of the world. The votive element is the exchange of the offering for God's answer to their prayer."[3]

Even if you are not Catholic, you can light these small candles in honor of your saints, your spirits, or your ancestors. Votive candles are also used in the Eastern Orthodox, Anglican, and United Methodist churches (among others), while observant Ashkenazic Jews will light a votive *yahrzeit* (a year's time) candle on the anniversary of a loved one's death.

Preparing Candles

Lighting a candle is only one part of a New Orleans Voodoo candle ritual. If you have a standard seven-day candle that cannot be pulled out of the chimney, you could scratch your intention into the top of the candle. If you have a pull-out, you could put it down the candle's side. If you have a specific target in mind for your working, you might carve his or her name in the wax. (If you wanted to control that person, you could carve your name atop that carving, so as to establish your dominant position over that individual.) Or you could simply write the name of the saint or spirit you are calling on, with a message like "Papa La-Bas open the door for me" or "St. Joseph please help me find a job."

Candles are also frequently anointed with oils (chapter 21). If you are trying to draw in positive energy—for example, if you are lighting a candle to bring a new lover or improve your business—you start anointing at the bottom of the candle and draw the oil toward the wick. While doing that, feel the energy that you are seeking pouring through the candle and up toward the wick, where it will become a bright beacon to draw your desires. If you wish to drive something away, as with a candle for uncrossing or for warding off an unpleasant neighbor, you would start at the top of the candle and pull the oil down toward the bottom. As you do, imagine the condition you want removed burning away as the wax burns, simultaneously going up into smoke and melting.

After you are done, you can roll the oiled candle in herbs or some other appropriate substance. You could roll a love candle in sugar or rose petals to make your target more sweetly disposed toward you, or in magnetic sand to draw them in your direction. If you wanted to discourage an overly enthusiastic suitor, by contrast, you might roll the candle in red pepper, black pepper, and crushed fire ants—a combination known as Hot Foot Powder, which is said to make the target irresistibly restless and unable to stay near you. A candle to High John the Conqueror (chapter 17) might be anointed in High John Oil and then rolled in pieces of crushed High John the Conqueror root. A candle to the ancestors might be anointed with myrrh oil (since myrrh was used for embalming in ancient times) and rolled in rue to attract the benevolent dead.

While you are doing this, you can recite an appropriate prayer or petition. Psalms are used frequently in New Orleans Voodoo. With 150 to choose from, you are likely to find one that fits your specific need. If you are calling on a saint, you call on them using a prayer in their honor. (I have included some in this book, and you can find others on holy cards, at Catholic websites, or in spiritual supply stores that cater to a Catholic clientele.) If you serve spirits or deities from other pantheons, you can pray to them as you are preparing your candle. New Orleans Voodoo has always been inclusive rather than exclusive. Practitioners are open to working with any well-disposed spirit who gets them results.

You can also decorate the candle in a manner befitting your petition. Using a glue stick, you can put a saint image or holy card on the chimney. You can then decorate with glitter, glass paint, or a Sharpie or other permanent marker. With the appropriate heat-safe glue, you may even be able to add small rhinestones or crystals to the finished product. This has both an aesthetic and a spiritual purpose: the flashes of light from sparkly items serves to draw good spirits and drive away entities that are more comfortable in darkness. You can also decorate the chimney with colored ribbons. Like glitter, these are both pretty and practical: as you tie the ribbon you are "tying" spiritual energy to the candle so that it can work for your desired ends.

If you are going to burn candles, you need to be concerned about safety issues. One good technique is placing the candle in a large bowl of clean water. This will help to attract positive spirits and keep away bad ones, and it will also help prevent fires should your candle tip over. You can also fill a baking dish with sand, mixed with items befitting your cause, like herbs or charms. (Make sure the items you are using aren't flammable. If you have any doubts, put them at the edge of the dish where they aren't likely to get overheated.) You can write your petition or your target's name in the sand as well as on the candle, thereby grounding your spell in earth as well as lighting it in fire and sending it into the air.

Figural Candles

Many popular New Orleans spells use candles that are molded into a variety of shapes and images. These are particularly effective when you wish to do magic for or against a particular individual. The figural candle combines the force of the poppet or "Voodoo doll" (chapter 22) with the magical power of fire—and practitioners often add to the mix by anointing with oils! If you want to attract someone's attention or drive someone away, you can use figural candles in a number of ways.

Penis Candles

When you want to get back at a cheating or abusive ex-boyfriend, you can use a black penis candle to "mojo his nature." Carve his name on the black penis candle and light it on a night when the moon is waning (the new moon is ideal for this). As it burns down, imagine his member falling limp and going soft, despite his best efforts to make it stand at attention again. This spell will be more effective if you have some of his personal items. Anything that contains his semen will create an intense magical bond with the candle: unwashed underwear, a stained bed sheet, or a used condom can be used to forge the link. Lacking these, you can use his signature (especially if it comes from a love letter to you or someone else!), a lock of his hair (pubic hair is especially good), a photo, or some other personal effect.

　　If you'd rather raise the tower than tear it down, you can use a red penis candle. Carve this with the name of your target (which can be yourself) and light it during a waxing or full moon. When the flame rises on the candle, imagine the flame rising through the penis that you are blessing so that it stands straight and tall and ready to serve. As before, you can use personal items to create a magical link between the candle and the desired recipient. You can anoint the candle with your own semen or, if you feel too self-conscious for that, some appropriate oil, like Attraction Oil, Compelling Oil, Fast Luck Oil, or whatever else best fits your plans for the weekend.

Adam and Eve Candles

These images of naked men or women can be used for all kinds of beneficial and baneful magic. If you want to bring two people together, you can set up an altar with a red Adam and a red Eve on opposite sides of the table. Scratch the target names into the candles. Burn them for a few minutes while you read the first chapter of the Song of Solomon, then put them out. Repeat this each night with another chapter until you finish with the eighth chapter; as you do, move the figures a little closer to each other until they are touching on the eighth night. (You can also do this with Adam and Adam or Eve and Eve candles. God thinks that it is good that two people should love each other and is less particular about gender than some of His followers.)

If you want to use these images for a breakup, use black Adam and Eve figurines and start the spell with the candles touching each other. Light them and read Psalm 7, then snuff the candles out. Each night move the candles a bit farther apart until they are consumed completely. Before doing this make sure you have a good reason for breaking these people apart. Psalm 7:4–5 offers a warning:

4. if I have done evil to him who is at peace with me or without cause have robbed my foe—
5. then let my enemy pursue and overtake me; let him trample my life to the ground and make me sleep in the dust.

Appropriate oils that could be used in these spells would be Come to Me, Follow Me Boy (or Follow Me Girl), or Marriage, if you want to make a commitment-adverse lover settle down. To accomplish a breakup you might use Crossing Oil or Break Up Oil.

Devil Candles

Devil candles may seem a bit off-putting at first. You may worry that burning a representation of Ol' Scratch will invite his Infernal Majesty into your home. But these devils aren't the bloodthirsty soul-stealers of Christian legend. These devils are not figures of evil so much as spirits of the material world. Like the Devil Tarot trump, they are connected with earthly and carnal concerns. When you have physical needs that aren't being met, you can burn a devil candle and get some assistance from those spirits who are such an intimate part of the material world with all its treasures and temptations.

Those in need of money will often rely on a green devil candle. By rubbing this fellow with Lodestone Oil or sprinkling magnetic sand on him, they hope that he will draw good fortune to them. (This is often used to get a recalcitrant debtor to pay up. By carving his or her name on the back of a green devil, conjurers hope that their deadbeat client will be tormented until such time as the bill is paid in full.) Those who are looking for some sexual fun and games (as opposed to love) may burn a red devil candle, anointed with Commanding Oil or Fast Luck Oil. And those who seek revenge may rub Crossing or Black Arts Oil on a black devil candle and ask that their enemy receive a suitably painful and memorable punishment for wrongs committed against them.

Reading Your Candle Working

The best outcome generally comes when the candle burns clean, leaving no marks on the glass chimney and little or no residue if a free-standing candle. A candle that "burns dirty," leaving a lot of soot on the glass, suggests that there are forces working against the client, and that additional work may be in order. If the flame hisses and sizzles, a smart worker will listen carefully; this may be the voice of spirits trying to communicate. And a candle that burns unusually fast may foretell quick but not lasting success in your work.

The patterns made by the melting wax from a free-standing candle can also provide information. A luck candle that melted in the shape of a four-leafed clover would be an excellent sign, as would a love candle that melted into a heart. A candle that breaks or goes out prematurely may mean the spell has failed and the worker needs to set another light. And should the candle tip over and become a fire hazard, you may need to do an uncrossing and cleansing for yourself and your client, since you are facing a powerful and malicious enemy.

21

OILS

Throughout the southeastern United States, rootworkers and Hoodoo practitioners swear by the efficacy of various magical oils. With colorful names like Follow Me Boy, I Will Fear No Evil, and Fiery Wall of Protection, these sweet-smelling anointing unguents are used for all sorts of magical operations. History suggests there is something to their claims; throughout the world spiritual and temporal leaders have been anointed with oil as a way of connecting them with divine power. (Indeed, *Jesus Christos* means, literally, "Jesus who is anointed by oil," and the Hebrew *Moshiach,* or *Messiah,* also means "anointed one.")

Oils can be used in several different ways. You can dress an appropriately colored candle (chapter 20) with an oil designed for your intended purpose, or use it to moisten or anoint your mojo hand (chapter 23). You can also use it to anoint yourself and use the scent and magical properties of the oil in a combination of spellwork and aromatherapy. All these uses are regularly found in New Orleans Voodoo, and several of New Orleans' most traditional recipes have become an integral part of Hoodoo practice throughout America.

Van Van Oil

When folks in Algiers were having a run of bad luck or wanted to make sure their enemies didn't cast Hoodoo (a spell) on them, they would run down to the drugstore or their Hoodoo doctor for a bottle of Van Van Oil. This cologne (which was also available as soap, incense, bath crystals, and hair tonic) was alleged to ward off evil and offer protection. It was also believed to help charge amulets and mojo bags and was frequently added to rabbit foot charms or lodestones for luck magic.

Van Van gets its name from the Creole French pronunciation of vervaine, also known as lemon verbena. When crushed, the leaves of lemon verbena give off a distinctive sweet, complex, lemony scent with hints of licorice and mint. Lemon verbena is commonly used in herbal teas or for flavoring desserts, but it can also be used as a substitute for oregano when cooking fish and poultry. In aromatherapy lemon verbena is prized for its relaxing and sedative properties, and it is used to quell anxiety and insomnia. Folk magicians also use lemon verbena to exorcise evil, remove blocks, and eliminate negative conditions.

Lemon verbena essential oil is quite expensive and was until recently very difficult to acquire. As a substitute, perfumers used the cheaper oil of lemongrass, which smells quite similar. Since lemongrass also has very similar magical and aromatherapeutic uses, it is a very effective substitute and has become the main traditional ingredient in Hoodoo formulations of Van Van Oil. Many Hoodoo pharmacists and root doctors put flecks of iron pyrite (also known as fool's gold because of its color) in the bottle to emphasize its luck and money-drawing properties. Others add citronella and palmarosa oils to add complexity and strength to the scent. If you wish to make your own Van Van Oil, you can come up with your own formulation, using lemongrass or lemon verbena oils and going from there. (Be sure to cut them sufficiently with a neutral base like almond or olive oil, as pure essential oils can irritate the skin!)

If you need to cleanse your house, you can add Van Van Oil to a bucket of water and warm natural soap. For extra spiritual and mundane cleansing strength, add a tiny bit of ammonia. Place a few broom straws (you can get them from a used broom) in the bucket. Now wash out your domicile from back to front, sending all the dirt and spiritual bad stuff out the front door. This is known as a Chinese wash. Many rootworkers and Voodoo practitioners swear by it as an effective way to improve your luck. It's also a very effective way to wash that so-and-so out of your life after a messy breakup. Before going into a tense or dangerous situation, you may want to put on a little Van Van Oil. Of course, you should take all necessary mundane precautions too! And if you want to put a little more money in your wallet, try anointing a $2 bill with some Van Van Oil and carrying it about with you so that it can attract some company.

Follow Me Boy Oil

As any sex worker can tell you, the world's oldest profession is also one of the world's toughest. The competition is fierce, the customers may be difficult and are frequently dangerous, and the forces of law and order are more interested in protecting decent, respectable citizens from you than vice versa. A working girl needs all the help she can get—and the working girls in New Orleans have traditionally gotten their help from liberally applied doses of Follow Me Boy Oil. This sweet-smelling fragrance didn't just attract the attention of prospective clients; it ensured that they would behave and pay well for the privilege.

There are innumerable formulas for Follow Me Boy Oil because every oil maker of the past had a particular combination of floral notes that he or she swore by. Most used rose geranium oil because true rose essential oil, also known as rose otto or attar of roses, is prohibitively expensive. Other florals that were frequently added include jasmine, tuberose, honeysuckle, gardenia, and carnation. (The latter three were invariably synthetic formulations, since the flowers in question yield no essential oil.) These were supposed to make the wearer smell appropriately sweet and feminine, like any fine perfume. To this base was added a bit of Van Van Oil. This added a lemony scent to the oil and helped to keep the heavy flowery notes from becoming too oppressive. It also took advantage of Van Van's power to drive away evil, draw luck, and strengthen the efficacy of other magical operations. Adding Van Van to a standard perfume formulation helped to amp up both the olfactory appeal and its magical power to draw male attention.

And then the final touch was added to the mix: a tiny bit of calamus root (*Acorus calamus*). Found in marshy areas around the world, calamus root has an unusual but pleasant fragrance that many find evocative of baby powder. Calamus was an important ingredient in the anointing oil used in the Temple of Jerusalem and by Egyptian priests. In perfumes it acts as a fixative, ensuring that the scent does not fade away too quickly, and many herbalists say it also has psychoactive and aphrodisiac qualities. But practitioners of Hoodoo and New Orleans Voodoo use it for its power to command and dominate. Calamus is a sweet, soft scent but one that subtly inspires others to do your will. Once the sweet florals attract a man's attention, the calamus, combined with the amplifying powers of the Van Van Oil, helps incline him to do the wearer's bidding.

You don't have to be a prostitute to use Follow Me Boy Oil. There are many situations where you might wish to use your feminine wiles to persuade a man. And while Follow Me Boy has most often been used by the ladies, gay men have used it to make their partners suitably pliant. Follow Me Boy may not be politically correct; all this talk of controlling men through sexual attraction may cause consternation in some feminist circles. But it is a very effective blend and one that can be used to good effect by those who wish to take advantage of its powers. It can be worn or used as an anointing oil for a mojo bag, and it can also be rubbed on a picture or other artifact of your target to gain a magical link and thereby control him in a fashion that will prove beneficial to both of you.

Red Fast Luck Oil

New Orleans is generally known as a place where things happen at a leisurely pace. But sometimes you need to get things moving, and moving fast. When folks in the Crescent City need to get their situation turned around, they use liberal doses of Red Fast Luck Oil. While some oils are meant to improve your financial situation and others are used to make you irresistible to potential lovers, Red Fast Luck Oil is an all-purpose ointment that is intended to bring you good fortune in both love and money—and quickly!

Red Fast Luck Oil begins with cinnamon oil. Cinnamon has long been used in magical and spiritual operations. Cinnamon was one of the ingredients of the holy anointing oil of the ancient Hebrews, while the Egyptians used it in mummification. Its uses as an antibiotic and a culinary supplement made it a particularly treasured spice in medieval and Renaissance Europe, and demand for cinnamon was one of the major factors behind the explorations that led to the Colonial era. In Hoodoo cinnamon is believed to heat up magical operations and is said to draw wealth and inspire lust.

Wintergreen oil is also an important component of Red Fast Luck Oil. This must be added in very small quantities, as its active ingredient (methyl salicylate) is a powerful dermal and mucous membrane irritant. But only a little bit of this sweet, sharp, balsamic-smelling oil is required. Wintergreen is said to be a powerful money-drawing oil, and it is also said to "heat up one's nature" and improve both desire and performance in the bedroom arts. (That being said, do NOT put Red Fast Luck Oil on or near your genitals. The ensuing redness will happen fast, but you won't feel at all lucky about it!)

These two hot oils are counterbalanced by a third ingredient, oil of vanilla. Vanilla acts as a cooling and mellowing agent. A drop or two of vanilla can tame the bite of an overly spicy chili or an overly acidic tomato sauce. It is also believed to be an aphrodisiac. In 1762 German physician Bezaar Zimmerman wrote that "no fewer than 342 impotent men, by drinking vanilla decoctions, had changed into astonishing lovers of at least as many women," while Dr. Alan Hirsch of the Smell and Taste Treatment and Research Foundation in Chicago found that the scent of vanilla was highly effective in increasing penile blood flow.[1]

The red coloring is often created by synthetic dyes, but according to Hoodoo expert Catherine Yronwode, the traditional coloring agent was alkanet root. Alkanet root is also known as dyer's bugloss and is used to redden textiles, makeup, and food. (It was once used to darken the color of inferior wines and to give wine corks an aged appearance.)[2] It was also magically employed in drawing luck and protecting money, so, as Yronwode says, "It is a better colourant for Fast Luck than any synthetic dye could ever be."[3] But it is also a tricky dying agent: too little and you get Pink Fast Luck, while too much will turn your oil a muddy crimson brown. If you are going to make your own, you are advised to add a few flecks of alkanet root per every half ounce of oil and let it steep for a day or so until you get the desired shade of red. While it may bring you fast luck, its creation requires patience.

It also requires caution: both wintergreen and cinnamon oils can be corrosive on sensitive skin, so make sure you use enough carrier oil and test with a tiny amount to see if you find it irritating before putting on more. You would probably be better advised to use your Red Fast Luck Oil for anointing a mojo bag (chapter 23) or using it in a floor wash to bring in a quick run of success to your business or your bedroom.

Algiers Triple Strength Oil

During the early part of the twentieth century, Algiers attracted many black Americans looking for a good time—or a good Hoodoo worker. Like the French Quarter today, the Algiers district had a thriving business catering to tourists in search of spiritual aid. Blues musicians sang of the Seven Sisters of Algiers (chapter 10) and their magical talents, while thirsty black travelers could wet their whistle at any of Algiers' thirty-nine taverns after picking up a mojo hand or a love potion. (Indeed, many black New Orleanians took the ferry across the river when they needed spiritual work or wanted to party without worrying about color lines.)

Today Algiers has become a quieter place. The Huey P. Long Bridge ended the twenty-four-hour ferry service that connected the district with the French Quarter, while the closing of the Algiers railroad terminal in the 1970s and the oil bust in the 1980s led to unemployment and an exodus of many once-prosperous black Algerines. But Algiers still retains its reputation as a Hoodoo and Voodoo capital in many quarters, and many rootworkers still swear by the efficacy of Algiers Triple Strength Oil in their magical operations.

There are many variations in the recipes for Algiers Triple Strength Oil, but most begin with the three oils used in Red Fast Luck Oil—vanilla, wintergreen, and cinnamon. To this is added patchouli. While the smell of patchouli may evoke images of headshops and hippies in your mind, it has a long history of magical use. Its earthy fragrance is said to draw money and attract sexual passion, and to increase the magical power of other substances. Patchouli is also a fixative that extends the life of other scents and spiritual operations. It turns Red Fast Luck Oil's powerful but short-lived magical blast into a longer-lasting, mellower run of good fortune.

But Algiers Triple Strength Oil also calls on the power of numerology—more specifically, the magical number three. Three is the number of the Holy Trinity; the Three Wise Men who came bearing gifts; the three virtues of faith, hope, and charity; and the triplicity of body, mind, and spirit that is humanity. Algiers Triple Strength Oil includes three ingredients that are known for their powers in drawing money, love, and luck. Some combine magnetic lodestones with bits of High John the Conqueror root (chapters 17 and 23) and devil's shoestring (long roots said to "trip up" the Devil while drawing money and luck to the bearer). Others include flecks of iron pyrite (fool's gold), magnetic sand, or a pinch of nutmeg (which is said to bring good fortune and is used in whole form in a powerful gambling mojo). Just about any love or money-drawing ingredients can be used in Algiers Triple Strength Oil, so long as you include three of them.

Depending on what you wish to accomplish, you can use Algiers Triple Strength Oil in a number of ways. If you are tired of sleeping alone, you can sprinkle a few drops in each corner of your bedroom and anoint your bedposts. This will work nearly as quickly as Red Fast Luck Oil but will tend to attract a longer-lasting relationship instead of a one-night stand. If you are heading out to a job interview, a dab of Algiers Triple Strength Oil behind your ears will make you magnetically attractive to prospective bosses and leave them thinking about you after you have departed. If you need to close a deal that will require extended negotiations, Algiers Triple Strength will stay with you through those all-night debate sessions. Add it to your spiritual tool kit and you'll soon find many other situations where it can give you that extra edge over your competitors.

Has No Hanna

When you first hear of Has No Hanna Lotion, you might assume it was used primarily for love spells, especially when you get a whiff of its sweet floral scent. But in the Big Easy, Has No Hanna is mainly used not by lovelorn women but by gamblers hoping to make that lucky break. When you are playing poker with an old-time New Orleans cardsharp, you might note the smell of jasmine lingering about him—and about your money after he wins it from you! Among those who know their Hoodoo, jasmine is a scent that can help you to become lucky in both cards and love.

The name *Has No Hanna* comes from the Bengali word for night-blooming jessamine (*Cestrum nocturnum*), *hasnuhana*. As per its name, night-blooming jessamine releases its perfume only after sundown. Its small greenish white tubular flowers are not particularly showy; gardeners typically plant more showy flowers at the base of jessamine bushes. But though their flowers are modest, they are overwhelmingly fragrant. Some find the aroma overpowering, but most find it heavenly. Although it originates in South Asia, hasnuhana has become naturalized in many tropical and subtropical climes, where it is treasured for its powerful, intoxicating scent. It is found throughout Louisiana and perfumes many a moonlit New Orleans garden.

Night-blooming jessamine is not related to the jasmine family (*Jasminum* spp.). It is more closely related to deadly nightshade and datura (angel's trumpet). But its scent strongly resembles that of the jasmines, as does its penchant for releasing its fragrance after dark. And while night-blooming jessamine's essential oil is almost impossible to come by and extremely expensive when you do find it, jasmine has long been cultivated for use in perfumery. As a result, Has No Hanna is scented not with *Cestrum* but with *Jasminum* flowers. Much as lemongrass has taken the place of lemon verbena in Van Van Oil, so jasmine has become the standard scent for hasnuhana's namesake lotion.

The same qualities that make jasmine so popular with romantics are also useful to professional gamblers. Jasmine promotes feelings of well-being and intimacy. Those who smell it are more inclined to let down their guard, thereby giving a smart player the advantage in a game of strategy. Jasmine relaxes the wearer while simultaneously clearing the mind, and some aromatherapists claim that jasmine promotes alertness and increases the memory. Those who make their living by knowing what the cards hold can use all the help they can get in these areas, and hence many New Orleans gamblers have scented their hair or rubbed their skin with Has No Hanna Lotion before an evening at the tables.

Unfortunately, many modern formulations of Has No Hanna are made without jasmine. Gardenia and rose are often combined with citrus scents like orange or tangerine. The resulting product smells lovely but is no substitute for the traditional formulation. Those wishing to make their own Has No Hanna Lotion can add some jasmine essential oil to an unscented hand cream and rub it sparingly on the hair and hands. (While you should always check for sensitivity, you will probably have no problems. Jasmine is generally considered to be good for the skin and is sometimes used for dermatitis and dry skin conditions.) You can also anoint your wallet with your homemade Has No Hanna and watch it fill with money. And if you are already in a relationship, some say that regular use of Has No Hanna will keep your lover close by you—especially if your beloved is fond of jasmine!

22

SPIRIT DOLLS

We all know the common cliché: the gnarled old witch doctor stabs a doll by the light of a flickering bonfire; the camera cuts to the target writhing in the throes of shrieking agony. You have probably seen "Voodoo Doll" kits, complete with pins and instructions for use on your enemy, and you may even have purchased one! Dolls are an important part of Hollywood's horror show vision of Voodoo; whether they are seen as spooky props or entertaining toys, they are certainly not something one needs to take seriously.

The Voodoo dolls beloved of New Orleans tourists are typically sticks or spoons wrapped with brightly colored yarn, then decorated with feathers and appliqués. It would be easy enough to write them off as gewgaws for the tourists, based on myths. But like many New Orleans myths, these legends have a basis in truth. Most casual observers will be satisfied with their souvenirs. Those who wish to tap in to their power will need to explore a bit deeper.

Feitiços, Fetishes, and Minkisi

An Nkisi called Kikokoo, which appears also in other records, was a man's image of black wood standing in the village of Kinga on the coast of Loango. It kept the sea calm and brought much trade and many fish to Loango. Stolen one night by two young men from a Portuguese boat, it was damaged. Therefore the young men drove nails into its head and arm in order to attach them again to the body, and, in the night, returned the statuette to the village. A story was immediately diffused by the nganga saying that Kikokoo had been to Portugal and brought back with him a boat full of merchandise. Shortly after this, a Portuguese boat was wrecked on the Loango coast.

ZDENKA VOLAVKOVA[1]

In the Kongo, *ngangas* (medicine men) make a handsome living constructing magical statues (*nkisi,* plural *minkisi*) for their clients and community. The Portuguese sailors who first encountered these magical objects in the fifteenth century called them *feitiços,* a word they used to describe charms and amulets. Today they are commonly called fetishes. Some fetishes have the heads or stomachs hollowed out to hold special substances like earth, blood, or magical herbs. Others are decorated with horns, shells, nails, feathers, metal, twine, paint, cloth, or beads. Some of these fetish figures combine male and female attributes to hearken back to the original androgynous ancestor of all humanity. Others have two faces, so they can guard their owners from attacks in any direction. The eyes and "medicine pack" (cover for the hole that contains the secret herbs and substances that empowered the statue's spirit) are generally covered with reflective mirrors. These are intended to dazzle and frighten evil ghosts, and they can also be used for divination. By gazing into these, the ngangas are able to enter a trance state and go into the spirit world (chapter 24).

The *nkondi* (meaning "hunter," plural *minkondi*) fetish is used to hunt down thieves, evil sorcerers, and other threats to the community. To inspire the indwelling spirits to action, gunpowder was exploded before them and nails driven into their wooden bodies while gory invocations urged them to take bloody revenge against these enemies. An nkondi could also serve as witness to oaths. The parties would make their promises and seal the deal by driving a nail or spike into the nkondi. It was believed that should either violate the terms of their agreement, the nkondi would punish them by illness or death. An old and powerful nkondi might have so many nails and blades driven into it that it resembles a porcupine: each nail was said to have "awakened" the spirit to perform a specific task.

Someone who believed he or she had been cursed with illness might drive a nail into an nkondi to send the illness back to the spellcaster. Or the cursed individual might seek the services of an *mbula,* a statue covered with small gunpowder-filled tubes representing rifles. These the mbula could use to kill evil spirits afflicting an individual or a village. People might also call on a *na mgonga* statue, a benevolent image that was believed to bring healing and good fortune to those who propitiated it. A pregnant woman might surround a nkisi with a *bilongo,* offerings of clay, herbs, and other substances that were placed in cloth and then wrapped around the statue to ensure safe childbirth and a healthy infant. And while most villages have several communal minkisi, many individuals and families also had their own nkisi for protection and prosperity.

There is evidence that at least some New Orleans Voodoo Queens of the past had minkisi of their own. The statue confiscated from Marie Laveau (chapter 14) supposedly resembled a centaur. Many minkisi statues combined human and animal elements, and Voodoo Queen Betsy Toledano claimed their society "was a religious African institution, which had been transmitted to her, through her grandmother, from the ancient Congo Queens."[2]

While the contemporary Voodoo dolls sold in New Orleans shops are generally made in China, their design shows a Kongo influence as well. Spoons or sticks wrapped in colored cloth are regularly used as fetishes in Kongo and Bantu practices. The wrappings most commonly conceal herbs or other sacred materials that are intended to draw the spirit into the item and thereby ensoul it, something that is lacking in the tourist dolls. The feathers that decorate the top of the doll can be seen as a symbol of the lightning flash of spirit descending into the item. They can also serve the practical purpose of "giving the spirit wings": by adding artifacts from a bird, the spirit is believed to gain the power of flight.

The creators of the tourist Voodoo dolls may not have done much research into the African roots of New Orleans practices. But they (or the

Chinese companies that filled their orders) reproduced Kongolese fetishes with surprising fidelity. In turn, many of the black and Creole Voodoo practitioners incorporated a common European practice into their work—the making of poppets. In time they would become so famous for these items that they would come to be identified not with European witchcraft but with African spiritual practice.

Poppets

Perhaps the most familiar application of the principle that like produces like is the attempt which has been made by many peoples in many ages to injure or destroy an enemy by injuring or destroying an image of him, in the belief that, just as the image suffers, so does the man, and that when it perishes he must die.

JAMES G. FRAZER[3]

Many magical spells are based on what James G. Frazer (author of *The Golden Bough*) called the Law of Similarity. If Item A resembles Item B, it can be used to influence Item B for good or for ill. In creating an image or simulacrum of your target, you build a link by which you can work magic. This concept began in the mists of prehistory. Sixteen thousand years ago Paleolithic shamans painted stags and bulls on the walls of their Lascaux cave to ensure a good hunt. During the reign of Rameses III (1187–1156 BCE), a group of priests, courtiers, and harem ladies were sentenced to death for using wax figurines to work baneful sorcery against the king and his bodyguards. Over 2,600 years later, in 1591, several people of North Berwick, a seaside town in Scotland, were executed after they were accused of making and then melting a wax image of King James VI of Scotland.

To make these images especially powerful, witches would often add to it what Frazer called the Law of Contact, or Law of Contagion. While an image could be used effectively, something directly connected with the individual would provide an especially powerful link. A lock of hair or fingernail clippings are among the items commonly used. Menstrual blood or semen are often used for sexual or love magic, and in a pinch you can even use a person's signature. (One particularly African touch common in New Orleans is using the dust from your target's footprints. It is believed that the footprint contains some of the person's essence and that an individual can be attacked through the feet with lameness, paralysis, madness, and even death.)

Poppets can be made out of many substances. You can construct a poppet using wax, clay, or even gingerbread. The poppets used in New Orleans magic are generally constructed of fabric that has been sewn into a human shape and stuffed with Spanish moss or cotton ticking along with appropriate herbs and personal effects. For example, a poppet to make an obnoxious neighbor move away might combine dust from that neighbor's footprints with dried cat manure, red pepper, and sulfur—the sort of stuff that would make you leave the area if you stepped in it! A poppet designed to kill your target may mix some of that person's hair with dirt gathered in a graveyard. A poppet to win your target's affection might be stuffed with rose petals and sugar. (Contrary to Hollywood myth, you can do much more with poppets than stick pins in them!)

Once you have constructed your poppet by whatever means you choose, you should then name it after your chosen target. The traditional Catholic way of doing this is the rite of baptism. While the full solemn rite can be performed only by an ordained priest, there is a shorter private rite that can be done by anyone. To do this you should first dress your poppet in white clothing, ideally a white gown. You will also need a white candle, preferably blessed by a priest, and some holy water (available in any Catholic church). Light the candle and say some prayers; a Rosary (chapter 12) would be ideal. Then sprinkle your poppet with holy water and say "[target's name], I baptize you in the name of the Father, and of the Son, and of the Holy Spirit." Breathe on the poppet, and as you do, feel it being filled with the breath of life and becoming a living being with an intimate connection to your target.

Now that your poppet is properly charged, you can do for it, or to it, what you want to have happen to your target. If you wish to use your poppet in a love spell, you might surround it with candy and sweet things. Talk to it each day, telling it how much you love it and how much you want your love reciprocated. You could rub honey or cane syrup oil over its heart to make your target feel sweet toward you, and you could anoint it with Follow Me Boy Oil (chapter 21) to encourage your target's attention. If you wish to make your supervisor more inclined to give you a raise, you might put a rope around the poppet's neck and tie it so that it is on its knees in an appropriately submissive position. You might also insert five-finger grass and masterwort (both used to gain command over a person) in the doll along with brown sugar to make your boss feel more kindly toward you. For a spell to do harm, you could use the time-honored tradition of sticking the doll with pins. You could also put the doll in a tiny coffin and bury it in the graveyard, hoping that your target dies as the doll rots away. A poppet for healing might involve regular laying on of hands and praying (or even Reiki treatments!) along with herbs intended to treat the target's condition. Your usage of poppets is limited only by your imagination.

Religious Statues and Images

Veneration of statues and images has long been controversial. In 726 Byzantine Emperor Leo III issued edicts banning the veneration of statues and icons. The ensuing outcry plunged the empire into over fifty years of religious conflict. In Europe Protestant reformers defaced many historic artworks, and today some Protestants still accuse Catholics of idolatry. And in 2001 the Taliban destroyed two enormous sixth-century Buddha statues in Bamiyan, Afghanistan, claiming they were un-Islamic graven idols. But the very existence of these arguments only proves the importance of religious and spiritual imagery.

Critics may claim that statues and lithographs lead us to worship the creation rather than the creator. Practitioners counter by saying that these images help us to move closer to that which is beyond our grasp. Images of Jesus remind us that he was simultaneously true God and true man. They make him a tangible reality to his followers, not just an arid symbol. Images help us with visualization and concentration; they help us to experience our gods on a visceral rather than a purely intellectual level. In cultures where much of the population is illiterate, images can be used to transmit ethical and spiritual teachings. The signifier helps us to reach the signified. It can serve both as a means of transmitting the artist's ideas and as a communications device allowing us to reach out toward the divine.

Statues and images were very important to the Christians of central and southern Africa. In 1491 Nzinga Nkuwu was baptized as João I, king of the Kongo. With the help of many Portuguese clergy and lay people, he and later his son, Afonso I, established a syncretic religion that combined Roman Catholicism with many traditional Kongo beliefs. As Scottish observer William Winwood Reade (a devout secular humanist and atheist with little sympathy for religion in general and Catholicism in particular) observed in 1864: "In matters of ceremonial religion the negroes are not fanatics. As long as operations were confined to baptism, to exhibiting images of the Virgin and saints, and to distributing beads, and relics, and Agnus Dei's, the people were amused and delighted by becoming Christians."[4]

During the era of the Middle Passage, most of slaveholding America was Protestant. The slave owners and overseers would have seen veneration of Christian imagery as no less idolatrous than honor given to an nkisi or African fetish. As a result, Hoodoo in most of the United States had comparatively little usage of statues or religious images. Instead, the Protestant emphasis on studying Scripture led to a tradition of "psalms magic," which used the holy Book of Psalms and other biblical verses to work spells.

But Louisiana had a sizeable Catholic population. The high-society families who traced their roots to France and Saint-Domingue were Catholic by birth if not necessarily by devout observance. Later, immigrants from Italy and Ireland came to New Orleans. At one point the French Quarter was largely Sicilian, while the area between Magazine Street and the river became known as the Irish Channel. These believers had no qualms about showing their devotion through artworks. Early

New Orleans Voodoo temples were traditionally filled with statues of saints, virgins, and angels alongside African and other images. (One of Doctor John's most prized possessions was an elaborately carved elephant tusk, while Marie Laveau reportedly kept statues of a lion and tiger on her altar for "bad work" or combat magic.)

The saints sometimes stood in for African spirits, as in the case of St. Michael the Archangel becoming Daniel Blanc (chapter 13) or St. Anthony of Padua becoming Yon Sue (chapter 15). But they were also honored in their own right as powerful protectors and wonder-workers. This is not surprising, given the Kongo emphasis on honored ancestors and spirits as intercessors between God and man. But whether they were seen as African spirits or saints, the treatment accorded their images was much the same. They were feted with flowers, food, drink, and candles by devotees who spoke to them as if they were alive—because those devotees believed they were!

From a magical standpoint, this makes perfect sense. Many psychics have noted that a child's well-beloved toy can take on a life of its own. (Bill Watterson was on to something when he chronicled the adventures of Calvin and his stuffed tiger Hobbes.) By giving energy to an image, you create a thoughtform that grows stronger with repeated feedings of attention and offerings. This process becomes far stronger when this image has already been fed by millions of worshippers before you. The many images of the Virgin, for example, have been fed for centuries and have been credited with numerous miracles. By setting up a saint image in your home or temple, you simultaneously tap in to and further empower a well-established *egregore*—a thoughtform that has been fed by generations of spiritual workers and worshippers.

If you don't want to put up a holy statue in your house, you can use a doll. These are commonly used by Spiritualists as receptacles for spiritual energy and homes for their noncorporeal friends. You can write the name of the spirit or saint on the doll's body in appropriately colored ink. Black might be used for a death deity, red for a war spirit, green for a fertility goddess, blue for an ocean or water god. You could also use the colors most commonly associated with that spirit. (Silver or gold ink is almost always acceptable.) Dress the doll in appropriate clothing, and place it in a position of honor. Feed it regularly with offerings and conversation, and listen for any words of wisdom it may wish to share with you.

This technique can be applied to spirits besides those commonly served in New Orleans Voodoo. The Voodoo Queens were always open to working with any entity that was well disposed toward them and that could produce results. If you have already established contact with a spirit guide, you can give it a home in an appropriate image. This can help you to develop a more concrete and personal relationship and improve your communications. By providing offerings to your spirits, you strengthen them and ensure greater success in your petitions. Reciprocity applies in the spirit world as well as in this one. Those who give generous gifts are far more likely to receive abundant rewards.

23

MOJO HANDS AND GRIS-GRIS BAGS

In 1999 swinging spy Austin Powers lost his mojo and had to travel through time to get it back—and get it up—in *The Spy Who Shagged Me*. ("First, he fought for the Crown," the posters read. "Now he's fighting for the Family Jewels.") Rock star and legendary lothario Jim Morrison used an anagram of his name, Mr. Mojo Risin', in the Doors' 1971 hit "L.A. Woman." And of course many a bluesman has sung about the potency of his mojo and how he's got it working overtime. From this it would be easy to conclude that a "mojo hand" was the spiritual equivalent of Viagra, something men use for purely sexual purposes.

Indeed, many mojo hands are prepared to help men or women "get their nature back." But that is only one of the many uses for these little magical bundles. A mojo hand (also known as a conjure hand, a gris-gris bag, a toby, and a conjure sack) can be used for healing, for love, for good luck, for financial success, and for protection against evil, among other purposes. Mojo hands are found throughout the southeastern United States and just about anywhere with a large African American population. But the mojo hands that can be purchased in New Orleans and surrounding areas have always had a reputation for being particularly efficacious.

Gris-gris in Africa and America

[The natives of Senegal] place implicit faith in the efficacy of a talisman, which they call gris-gris: they wear it round

*their neck, at their waist, and on their legs and arms. Each
has its particular virtue: one preserves them from bullets;
another from poison; and when a man has been killed,
burnt, or drowned, they say, that his gris-gris was not so
efficacious as that of his enemy. . . .*

*These talismans are made of goat skins, with the hair
on, or of morocco leather; and they are of different sizes,
from one to three inches; they are filled with a kind of
powder, and with scraps of certain sentences of the alkoran
[Qur'an] in the Arabic. The priests, or marabous, have the
exclusive privilege of preparing and selling them.*

JEAN BAPTISTE LÉONARD DURAND, 1806[1]

Wherever they went in western and central Africa, colonists and slavers
noted the African devotion to charms, amulets, and phylacteries. In areas
with a strong Islamic influence, Qur'anic verses were used for protection;
in Christian areas a holy medal or small cross might serve the same purpose. These were then combined with other substances that were reputed
to have power. Among the most popular were bits of human bone and
dust from graves, which were believed to call upon the protection and
wisdom of the dead. Items from an animal—lion claws, snakeskin, bird
feathers—were also frequently added to the charm, along with herbs,
leaves, roots, or other plant matter. Although uprooted from their native
land, Africans in the New World retained their amulets. Writing in 1758,
French historian Le Page du Pratz (who had left the New World in 1734)
said of the Louisiana slaves, "They are very superstitious and attached to
their prejudices and to charms which they call *gris-gris*."[2]

The precise etymology of this word, which literally means "gray-
gray" in French, is unknown. Scholars have suggested a number of possible antecedents from various African languages: perhaps the most
reasonable guess is that it comes from the Mande word for these amulets,
gerregerys. In a similar vein, the term *mojo* may come from the Fulani
language, where *moco'o* means medicine man. The amulets themselves are
found throughout the African diaspora. In Brazil they are called *bolsas de*

mandinga (Mandingo purses). An 1840s report of African slaves disembarking in Trinidad noted that most of the 441 men, women, and children "had amulets very neatly sewn up in leather, suspended either round their necks or loins."[3] But they are particularly common in the American South, largely because of Louisiana's rice farms.

When the Mississippi Delta region was being colonized during the early part of the eighteenth century, the country's rice industry was in its infancy. French slavers brought in a large number of Mande slaves from the region between the Senegal and Niger rivers. Their experience in cultivating rice was so invaluable that the overseers were willing to overlook their unwillingness to part with their amulets and fetish charms. As a result, gris-gris was established in Louisiana at an early date. The Mande were also famous for their *griots,* singer-historians whose music would later become the Delta blues (chapter 7). (Another colony where the Mande were imported en masse to develop the rice industry, South Carolina, produced the unique Creole-African Gullah culture of the South Carolina and Georgia lowlands.)

Later, as Louisiana fell under American control, authorities became less tolerant of this "African witchcraft." Where once gris-gris were worn openly, they were now kept hidden. In time many African Americans came to believe that your gris-gris bag would lose its power if you let someone else touch it, or even see it. Instead of being worn as necklaces or pinned to a cloak as they were in Africa, they were now commonly kept hidden in underwear or in one's pocket. Today most Hoodoo workers advise clients that their gris-gris bag is to be kept hidden. You may tell people that you have a mojo hand (as many blues musicians did), but you are to keep it hidden from their view. Should someone see or touch it, you will need to start over with a new bag.

In Africa and the United States, constructing the gris-gris is only the first part of the process. After the appropriate ingredients are selected and placed in the bag, it must then be "fed." There are many ways in which this can be done. Some rootworkers breathe on the bag to "bring it to life." This may show the influence of Jewish folk magic, in which a rabbi breathes into the golem's nostrils to bring it to life much as G-d breathed life and spirit (*ruach*) into Adam. Jewish spiritual merchants have played a large but little-studied role in the development of African-American folk magic. See Carolyn Morrow Long's *Spiritual Merchants* or Cat Yronwode's Lucky Mojo (www.luckymojo.com) for further details. The bag can also be passed through the flame of an appropriately colored candle or through incense smoke to charge it.

But the most common way of bringing the item to life is through anointing it. Typically a few drops of oil are sprinkled on the bag. The specific oil used will depend on the purpose of the bag. Whiskey or rum can also be used, as can certain perfumes (Hoyt's Cologne is particularly loved by gamblers, as are Red Fast Luck Oil and Has No Hanna [chapter 21]). The owner of a gris-gris bag will continue to "work" the item by regularly anointing it and reminding it of its purpose. With this continued feeding of offerings and energy, the bag will grow increasingly powerful over time.

Creating Your Own Mojo Hand

To understand the ingredients that go into a gris-gris bag, you must consider the Doctrine of Signatures. For centuries people around the world have believed that a plant's use in healing can be determined by its shape, color, taste, smell, and other observable properties. The sixteenth-century doctor and alchemist Paracelsus noted that the leaf of an herb used to treat liver was shaped like the liver, and the Christmas rose, which was used to treat age-related disorders, bloomed in the winter. In Chinese medicine *lian qiao* (forsythia fruit), which resembles a chambered heart, is prescribed for heart ailments.

What holds true for medicine also holds true for magic: the properties of an item show its use in spiritual tools. A man who wanted to "spice up" his sex life might add a dried long pepper to his mojo bag. Because of its phallic shape and heat, it would do double duty in drawing the sexual power desired. A woman who wished to do the same thing might put in a dried Scotch bonnet pepper that had been split to resemble the *yoni*. A gris-gris bag to bring in more money might include a pinch of marigold or some other yellow flower petals; their golden color would help to draw gold. Someone who wished to snare a lover might put in a piece of honeysuckle vine, while a charm for fertility might include a piece of the fast-growing kudzu vine.

Animal parts are also believed to contain some of the animal's essence and can be added to one's mojo bag. A black cat bone was considered one of the most powerful things one could add to a mojo hand. Rather than killing a feline for its bones, using a bit of a black cat's hair is just as effective and far more humane. A bag to ensure your partner's loyalty might include a pinch of dog hair, since few animals are more faithful than man's best friend. A rattlesnake rattle or shark tooth could be an effective addition to a protection hand, while a raccoon's penis bone, otherwise known as a "coon dong," is said to bring not only success in love but good luck in gambling. (One might argue that it was hardly lucky for the raccoon, but the same could be said of the ever-popular rabbit's foot.)

Inorganic materials can be used as well. Lodestones and magnets are commonly added because it is believed they help to "attract" the bearer's desire, be it love, money, or luck. Small images or figurines representing your goal can be placed in the bag. A mojo hand to encourage your partner to marry you might have tiny bride and groom figurines inside, tied together with white thread. Tiny dice or cards might go in a gambling mojo, while a mojo hand to help you close the deal on a new home might include a Monopoly house. Iron pyrite (fool's gold) can be added to draw money, as can silver coins. And holy items are popular both in Africa and America. Depending on your ancestors' religious persuasion, you could use verses from the Qur'an or Torah, holy cards or blessed medals, or excerpts from the Book of Psalms or Gospel.

One custom that hearkens back to Africa is the use of certain kinds of dirt. "Foot track magic" uses the dust from your target's footprints to form a link with that person. If you want to make a love mojo, you might combine that dust with sweet or pleasant items. If you want protection from (or revenge against) your target, you might combine the dust with an iron chain link and some manure from an ill-tempered dog; you would then bury it where your target would be sure to step over it, thereby adding another layer of foot-track magic. Dust from outside a bank would be a good addition to a money-drawing mojo hand, while a healing gris-gris could use hospital dirt. (And if you live near where your ancestors are buried, nothing will kick up your gris-gris bag like a pinch of dirt from their grave. This will bring your magic under the care and protection of your ancestors and add their power to anything you seek to accomplish!)

In America mojo hands are traditionally made using small flannel bags. Red bags are most common but you can use any color based on the Gamache candle chart (chapter 20) or your personal preferences. Traditionally an odd number of items is added to the gris-gris bag, no less than three and no more than thirteen. After the items are gathered and placed in the bag, it is then fed using one or more of the methods described above. Some rootworkers and Voodoo queens recommend you keep the mojo hand beside your skin for at least a week so that it can become attuned to your energy. Do not do this with bags designed for negative magic, but keep them in a safe place where they will not be disturbed.

There are many ways to create and feed a mojo hand. All conjure men and Voodoo queens have secret methods that they swear by, using ingredients passed down to them by their sainted ancestors or spirit guides. Because New Orleans Voodoo has never been a hermetically sealed system, these often incorporate items from other traditions or cultures. Your improvisation may use things not commonly used by other practitioners; the important thing is not following someone else's recipe but creating an item that meets your needs and works for you.

That being said, a few items are legendary for their power. One of the most famous is the root that no rootworker will be without—the High John the Conqueror Root—an item fabled in song and story. To those who don't know what they are looking for, it's a wild vine resembling a morning glory and found throughout the United States and South America. But those who dig deeper will discover that this humble vine has a powerful—some might even say royal—root.

High John the Conqueror Root
and Its Relatives

Herbalists will caution you to avoid eating even small quantities of *Ipomoea jalapa* root. It is a powerful purgative and laxative that will restore your "get up and go"—but not in the way you might prefer. (It is rarely used even in cases of severe constipation, since its beneficial effects are invariably combined with nausea, cramping, and diarrhea.) But despite this, "Jalop root" and related species are highly sought after by rootworkers and Voodoo practitioners for their multifaceted magical powers. According to folk legend, High John the Conqueror (chapter 17) ultimately gained his freedom and returned to Africa. But before he departed he left the Jalop root behind so that other slaves and their descendants could benefit from his cunning and magical skill.

The Jalop root resembles a testicle and is most commonly (but not exclusively) used by men. The root is placed in a flannel bag and regularly anointed with an appropriate oil. High John Oil, which contains pieces of Jalop root and amplifies the root's unique spicy smell, is a favorite, but other oils may be used depending on the root owner's intentions.

For love spells, a woman might anoint a Jalop root with a bit of her menstrual blood, then carry it in a red sack along with a Queen Elizabeth root and a lock of hair or other item belonging to her lover, so that he might always be "pussy whipped" and amenable to her commands. She could recharge this with menstrual blood, vaginal fluids, or Follow Me Boy Oil. A man who wants to be more appealing to women might anoint his High John the Conqueror root with Lodestone Oil and keep two magnets within the sack so as to make him more "magnetic" and charismatic.

Gamblers will frequently anoint their root with Red Fast Luck Oil, Van Van Oil, or Triple Strength Algiers Oil (chapter 21); with Hoyt's Cologne; or even with their lover's urine! Because High John was famous for winning bets against impossible odds, it is believed that feeding his root will cause some of that luck to pass to the bearer. As Muddy Waters sang in 1964:

Oh, I can get in a game, don't have a dime,
All I have to do is rub my root, I win every time
When I rub my root, my John the Conquer root
Aww, you know there ain't nothin' she can do, Lord,
I rub my John the Conquer root[4]

Among the items that might be added to a High John the Conqueror mojo hand for gambling luck would be dice, silver coins, or a rabbit's foot, all placed in a small green flannel bag. This bag would be carried with you whenever you were going to be wagering and kept fed with the oil of your choice. And if you're not a gambler but just want to make more money (and who doesn't?), you can carry your High John root in your pocket with dollar bills wrapped around it. This will encourage High John to send prosperity in your direction.

For luck in family matters, look for a Dixie John or Low John (*Trillium* spp.) root. If you are arguing a great deal or if you want to conceive a child, Low John can be a powerful helper. In herbal medicine it is used to regulate difficult menstrual periods and postpartum hemorrhaging. Magically it is considered a powerful root for women seeking a lover or wanting peace in their homes. Where High John is most commonly used by men, Dixie John is generally used by women. Put it in a white sack and feed it with Blessing Oil, Peaceful Home Oil, or Dixie Love Oil (an old-time Hoodoo formulation that incorporates Dixie John root with several other sweet-smelling ingredients).

And if you find yourself in court, you may want to call on the aid of galangal (*Alpinia galanga* and related species), otherwise known as Chewing John or Little John to Chew. Although it resembles ginger, galangal root has a more complex flavor, with hints of sweetness and balsamic notes. Before a trial, defendants chew a tiny piece of galangal and then discreetly spit it on the floor. This is said to incline the judge and jury in their favor. Others say that Chewing John can help you find work if carried in your pocket. Still others praise its taste and use it for cooking. It is a common ingredient in many Thai dishes, most notably Tom Kao Gai soup.

Whatever magical powers the various John roots may or may not possess, they certainly provide their users with a faith and self-confidence that something better is coming. Disenfranchised and disempowered people who learned survival skills and gained inspiration from stories of John the Conqueror gained the courage to triumph over obstacles with the aid of his magical plants. Zora Neale Hurston noted that hundreds of thousands if not millions of black Americans (and a fair number of white folks) carried a John the Conqueror root. It "MEANS SOMETHING TO THEM," she said. "I mean the people who carry it, are acknowledging some sort of divinity."[5]

24

FORETELLING THE FUTURE

Folks in New Orleans may live for today, but that doesn't mean they aren't concerned about tomorrow. The future is a scary place, especially if you're living from paycheck to paycheck or just wishing you had a paycheck to live from. Inside information may make the difference between avoiding a crisis and getting crushed by it. As a result, many New Orleanians call on the services of a diviner to get them through tough times and provide them with leads for a more prosperous future.

Divination has long played an important role in African cultures. The Yoruba peoples have divination by cowries, coconut pieces, and the Table of Ifa, a complex system involving palm kernel nuts thrown on a consecrated surface. The Bantu peoples use knucklebones or small tablets to foretell the future. The Mande use sand divination, while the Xhosa diviners of southern Africa speak to the ancestors and spirits in shamanic trance. While many of these specific techniques were lost during the Middle Passage, the descendants of these prophets incorporated new methodologies into their practice.

Crystal Balls

For centuries the Romani people have been persecuted, enslaved, and vilified by dominant cultures that considered them born criminals and thieves. But they have also been romanticized as free-spirited, hot-blooded, happy wanderers who possess great spiritual wisdom along with an innate talent for dance and music. It is not surprising that many black Americans identified with their suffering, or that many African American fortune-tellers incorporated and still incorporate "Gypsy"* imagery into their practices. Many readers and root doctors claimed a touch of Rom ancestry or affected Rom styles of clothing—flowing dresses, brightly colored turbans, and abundant gold jewelry. They also incorporated one of the favorite tools of the "Gypsy fortuneteller"—the crystal ball.

In doing so, they were appropriating a cultural item that the Roma had themselves appropriated only a few years earlier. Wealthy medieval and Renaissance magicians frequently counted crystal gazing spheres among their tools. The notorious Elizabethan magician, mathematician, and spy John Dee used a crystal "shewstone," or gazing stone, to compile his influential Enochian manuscripts. But with the rise of the Industrial Age and the Victorian interest in Spiritualism, more reasonably priced crystal balls became a popular tool for inducing mediumistic trance. Large glass or crystal balls became a popular part of the stage mentalist's paraphernalia and soon became identified with diviners of every stripe, including Roma readers.

The crystal ball is merely a tool used for *scrying,* or seeing visions in a medium. Mirrors were often used for this purpose (hence the magic mirror used by Snow White's evil stepmother in the fairy tale and the mirrors placed on Kongo nkisi statues [chapter 22]). So were bowls of water darkened with ink, sometimes called "witches' mirrors." By gazing intently into a translucent surface, scryers calm their minds and enter a hypnagogic state. The limited visual input of a uniform field of color causes the brain to produce images and patterns amid the blankness—a phenomenon that paranormal researchers call the Ganzfield Effect, a German term meaning "complete field."

To use a crystal ball, sit quietly in a darkened room; candlelight is good for this, as the flickering light will also serve to encourage a trance state. Make sure you are comfortable and relaxed but not so relaxed that

---

*The word *Gypsy* is considered offensive by most Rom. *Rom* (singular) and *Roma* or *Romani* (plural) are preferred terms.

you fall asleep. Now gaze into the center of the crystal. Don't strain yourself; watch intently but not intensely. In time you will see clouding within the crystal. Watch the clouds and let them drift. In time they will form images, then sequences of images. Don't try to interpret them or force them to appear. They will come when they come. You may want to use a tape recorder to describe what you see, or you may want to write down brief notes. If the latter, don't get too detailed as that may break you out of the trance state.

The ability to scry requires a certain innate talent. It requires practice to separate true visions from wish fulfillment and even more practice to learn how to interpret those images correctly. Some pick up crystal gazing immediately, while others require more practice, and a few are never able to master the art. (John Dee required the services of a scryer, Edward Kelley, since he had no gift for seeing visions.) If you've spent hours staring into a crystal ball with nothing to show for it but headaches, don't despair. You may be able to benefit from another technique popularized by Romani fortunetellers—*tasseomancy,* or foretelling the future in tea leaves.

Tea Leaf Reading

Although in America tasseomancy is most commonly associated with the Roma, it was also extremely popular among English, Scottish, and Irish psychics and fortunetellers. All that is required is a cup, some hot water, and a bit of loose-leaf tea prepared in a pot and poured into a white cup so that some tea leaves remain in the brew.

Sip the tea slowly, savoring the flavor. (You should be sure to use a good tea, and be advised that once you've enjoyed properly made tea, you may never return to tea bags again!) When you are almost finished, hold the cup in your left hand and swirl the leaves three times round in a clockwise direction. Then turn the cup upside down on the saucer and let the remaining liquid drain away.

Turn the handle of the cup toward the *querent* (the person seeking information). If you are reading for yourself, turn the handle so it faces you, then lift the cup and examine the inside. The leaves, and the white porcelain spaces that show between the leaves, are then scanned like a Rorschach blot for symbols and images. You may see houses, human figures, animal shapes, letters, or other forms in the cup. These can then be interpreted through intuition or in accordance with one of the many guidebooks on the subject. (Cicely Kent's *Telling Fortunes by Tea Leaves* and *Tea-Cup Reading and Fortune-Telling by Tea Leaves* by "A Highland Seer" are both in the public domain and available on the Internet.)

If you don't like tea, you can also read the grounds in a cup of Turkish coffee. The methodology is similar. Oenophiles can read the dregs in the bottom of a glass of red wine, while beer lovers can read the patterns in the foam that remains after they have consumed their drink. (This may prove particularly useful when you are doing a late night bar crawl through the Quarter and want to chat up that attractive person across the room. If you have a hard time focusing on the suds, consider it an omen that you should go home.) And if you want to take your tasseomancy to the next level, you can purchase specially designed cups that feature zodiac signs or images of playing cards on the inside. These will allow you to combine cartomancy or astrology with your leaf reading.

Cartomancy

There is controversy as to whether playing cards originated in China, India, or the Islamic world. But what we do know is that by 1377 a Paris ordinance forbade card games on workdays and that on May 14, 1379, Duke Wenceslas of Luxemburg and Duchess Joanna of Brabant spent four peters, two florins (the cost of eight sheep) to purchase "a pack of cards."[1] The Italians enjoyed *tarocchi*, trick-taking games that resemble a more complex version of the modern Spades. The various trumps represented the social classes of medieval and Renaissance Italy, along with religious concepts and figures, like the Last Judgment and the Pope. The suit cards comprised swords, coins, cups, and wands from one to ten, along with court cards representing royalty.

While there is ample evidence of gambling and gaming with cards from the late fourteenth century onward, there is less of a record of cards being used for divination. A 1540 book by Francesco Marcolino de Forlì entitled *Le sorti intitolate giardino d'i pensieri* (*The Oracle called Garden of Thoughts*) detailed a method of drawing nine cards from the coins suit and checking them against oracular verses printed elsewhere in the book. Later evidence suggests that several Venetian women were accused of witchcraft for using trump cards in magical spells.[2]

Then, in 1781, Antoine Court du Gébelin claimed that the Tarot originated in ancient Egypt. The trumps, according to him, represented the survival in pictorial code of their ancient religion, preserved by the pharaoh's priests. He believed Tarot cards were brought to Europe by the Gypsies (who were at that time believed to originate from Egypt, hence the name). There they were treated as mere game pieces until the time was ripe for their secrets to be revealed—and du Gébelin, of course, was the man to reveal them. Later research would indicate that the Rom originated in India rather than Egypt and that Egyptian religion bore little resemblance to the "secret wisdom" du Gébelin had "discovered" in the Tarot. But the legend survived despite the facts, and the use of cards for divination became popular with the spiritually advanced and with those seeking to present themselves as such.

Although Tarot cards were associated with the Rom and ancient wisdom, most New Orleans readers used regular playing cards for their work. The *Jeu Lenormand* style of reading, which removed cards two to five from the deck and assigned specific meanings to each of the remaining thirty-six, was common among Francophone natives, while Anglophone readers might use the same style and call it "Gypsy Witch." Still others might use the cards as props for a "cold reading" or as an aid to their intuition. Today many readers still swear by the Lenormand method, claiming it produces less esoteric and more down-to-earth readings than the Tarot. Those wishing to learn the method may wish to pick up a pack of "Madame Lenormand's Mystic Cards of Fortune" or the "Gypsy Witch Fortune Telling Playing Cards" and study the accompanying brochures.

In 1992 Louis Martinié and Sallie Ann Glassman created a Tarot deck that paid homage to the city of New Orleans and the spiritual practices found there. *The New Orleans Voodoo Tarot* reimagined the four suits as the Four Cults of Voodoo—Santeria, Petwo, Congo, and Rada. The interpretations of the various cards were influenced by Thelema, Kabbalah, and Western ceremonial magic as well as by African American, Haitian, and Cuban mythology. The lwa of Haiti mingled with the Orishas of Cuba and New Orleans historical figures like Doctor John (chapter 10) and Marie Laveau (chapter 14). Glassman's artwork is powerful and evocative, and the accompanying text from Martinié includes suggested offerings and meditations.

Like the *Thoth Tarot* (a deck influenced strongly by Aleister Crowley's philosophy), the *New Orleans Voodoo Tarot* requires serious study and concentration. Those accustomed to the standard Rider-Waite deck may find it confusing or off-putting. But those who are willing to put in the effort of meditating upon the various images and studying the systems that influenced Martinié and Glassman (and reading Glassman's later text on the images, *Vodou Visions*) will find their efforts are richly rewarded. While their deck owes more to the contemporary New Orleans Voodoo espoused by Charles Massicot Gandolfo (chapter 4) than to historical practices, it is still a powerful and useful tool for divination, meditation, and spiritual growth.

Dream Interpretation and Policy Books

In Genesis 41:1–41, Joseph rises to prominence in Egypt through his skill at interpreting Pharaoh's dreams. Ailing Greeks would spend the night in the temple of Aesculapius at Epidaurus, hoping that they would dream a cure for their illness. Carl Jung believed dreams provided direct communication with the subconscious mind and the world soul, which he called the "collective unconscious." Dreamers in New Orleans generally aimed for a less lofty goal. They believed that by correctly reading their dreams, they might find their lucky numbers.

Louisiana has a long if not always honorable tradition of gambling. In 1868 the Louisiana Lottery Company received a twenty-five-year charter as the state's sole legal lottery provider. (Numerous attempts to challenge this monopoly were defeated with the help of another time-honored Louisiana tradition, bribing legislators.) By 1878 it was the only legal lottery in the country; as a result, over 90 percent of its revenue was coming from outside the state. In 1895 an act of Congress prohibited the interstate sale of lottery tickets, and the Louisiana Lottery was disbanded. An investigation of its business revealed corruption on a scale that shocked even hardened Louisianans. By 1900 thirty-five states had constitutional prohibitions against the operation of lotteries.[3]

But this did not stop entrepreneurs from running "policy" rackets. Bettors could buy a policy of four numbers from a numbers runner or at a policy shop (which was often a tavern or other public establishment). Those who picked the winning number received a payout, which was typically 600 to 1. Since the odds of winning were 1,000 to 1, this meant that bookies were able to make a tidy sum even after paying overhead to runners, shopkeepers, and police officers. During the 1880s, policy booths ran openly in the streets of New Orleans, taking bets ranging from a few pennies to $40. After the turn of the century, they went underground but remained popular with black and white clients alike.

To gain an advantage in the game, players turned to their dreams. But though they might not have been acquainted with Freud or Jung, they knew that the language of dreams was often subtle and symbolic. This led to a thriving business in policy dream books, which translated dream images into lucky numbers. The grandmother of these, *Aunt Sally's Policy Players Dream Book,* was first published in 1889 (and remains in print today!) but competitors soon produced their own dream guides. A few of the more popular ones include *King Tut Dream Book, Policy Pete's Dream Book,* and *Stella's Success from Dreams* (not to be confused with *Stella's Lucky Seven Star Dream Book*).

It was never entirely clear how these books distilled numbers down from imagery. Policy Pete suggested that a dream of coffee meant you should pick 098, while if you dreamt of a coffee shop you would go with 633. (Presumably if you were drinking coffee in the shop, you would make two bets to be on the safe side.) But *Mother Shipton's Gipsy Fortune Teller and Dream Book* warned that dreams of coffee portended misfortune or meant that you should bet on 11, 12, and 39. *Rajah Rabo's Dream Book* (first published in 1932) advised that if you dreamed of a colored dope fiend, you should bet 037. A dream of a white dope fiend would mean betting 778.[4] But though their numerological reasoning might be opaque, bettors swore by their favorite policy books and scorned all others as pale imitations.

Many of the books also included advice based on the bettor's sun sign, numerological analyses of names and addresses, and other factors. Several included Napoleon's Book of Fate and Oraculum, a divinatory system that had reportedly been used by the Little Emperor after he discovered it during his campaign in Egypt. (The oracle uses scratches on paper to form random figures and is actually a simplified form of classical Arabic geomancy.) *The Old Gipsy's Dream Book and Fortune Teller* taught basic palmistry and a system of divination using dice as well as offering dream interpretation.

You may not be a gambler, but you can still benefit from writing down your dreams and studying them. Many cultures have believed that it is possible to speak with gods, spirits, and ancestors while asleep. And even the most die-hard secular atheist will have difficulty denying the creative potential of dreams. Paul McCartney awoke from a dream with a melody in his head; he transcribed it on the piano, and it became the classic song "Yesterday." Mary Shelley turned a nightmare into a classic novel, *Frankenstein,* as did Robert Louis Stevenson (*The Strange Case of Dr. Jekyll and Mr. Hyde*) and Stephen King (*Misery*). German scientist Friedrich Kekulé dreamed of atoms dancing in a circle and awoke to an understanding of the mystery of the benzene ring. American inventor Elias Howe dreamed of natives carrying spears with holes in the point and was inspired to create the sewing machine needle.

Working with dreams is almost as easy as falling asleep. Indeed, getting enough sleep is one of the most important things you can do to have both better dreams and better health. Researchers have found that people who get between seven and nine hours a night have lower rates of cancer, depression, and heart disease as well as improved memory and cognitive function.[5] Keep a pen and paper by your bedside and write down your dreams immediately upon awakening. In time you will see recurring themes and possibly even answers to problems that have long perplexed you in waking life.

PART FIVE

JUST VISITING
or Settling Down

25

VISITING
THE BIG EASY

Since before recorded history began, people have traveled to sacred sites in search of spiritual reward. The Greeks, and later the Romans, traveled to Eleusis to participate in the Eleusinian Mysteries. Egyptians journeyed to Karnak to honor Amun, Mut, and Khonsu at the Ipet-Isut (Most Select of Places). Today many in India travel to the Ganges to bathe in its sacred waters, while devout Japanese undertake *junrei* to holy Shinto and Buddhist sites throughout their country. Muslims travel to Mecca and Medina for the *hajj,* and devout Christians and Jews visit sites in what they both call the Holy Land.

It may seem odd to consider a visit to a notorious party town like New Orleans a pilgrimage, but historically pilgrimages were not just grim, joyless quests. Chaucer's *Canterbury Tales* chronicled the stories of a number of pilgrims visiting the shrine of St. Thomas Becket. While the *Tales* include edifying religious discursions, they also include bawdy humor like "The Miller's Tale." It is quite clear that many of the travelers were there to have a good time and a good laugh while they fulfilled their spiritual duties. There's no reason your journey to the Big Easy cannot be both entertaining and enlightening.

Voodoo Shops and Stops

It's not difficult to find Voodoo dolls, candles, and purported gris-gris bags in the French Quarter. Just about every tourist trap stocks them alongside the Mardi Gras beads, shot glasses, and T-shirts. But if you want a better experience of New Orleans Voodoo (and if you're reading this book you almost certainly do), there are a few places that you definitely want to visit.

After you've seen the elaborately decorated shrines at Priestess Miriam Chamani's Voodoo Spiritual Temple on 828 North Rampart Street, you can check out her Cultural Center for some shopping. (Her selection of African statues and masks is particularly impressive.) From here it's just a walk across the street to Louis Armstrong Park and Congo Square. Congo Square became famous for the Sunday dances with slaves from various African nations showing off their native rhythms and playing music that would later become New Orleans jazz. (If you visit in November, be sure to check out the Congo Square Rhythms Festival, where you can enjoy African food and African drumming beneath the palm trees.)

The New Orleans Historic Voodoo Museum (724 Dumaine Street) is also worth seeing. While you may want to take some of the historical claims presented with several grains of Gulf Coast sea salt, the displays are stunning (see color plates 6 and 16). (Gandolfo and his predecessors knew how to make the most out of a small space.) If you're lucky you'll get a chance to see Jolie Vert, a large and lovely albino Burmese python who serves as the space's ceremonial snake. You may even be able to schedule a reading with Dr. John T. Martin, the resident psychic.

Anna Parmelee, the "Root Queen" of Erzulie's (807 Royal Street), draws on the herb magic teachings of her Portuguese grandmother, hatha yoga, Egyptian magic, European witchcraft, and astrology, among other occult strains. With rootworkers, paleras, and initiates of Haitian Vodou on staff to offer readings and services, Erzulie's offers a mélange of services with roots in Europe, the Caribbean, and elsewhere—a spiritual gumbo that is pure New Orleans. Erzulie's has a particularly nice selection of magical soaps and homeopathic tinctures.

It's difficult to miss Island of Salvation Botanica (835 Piety Street): enormous brightly colored paintings of various saints and spiritual figures decorate the outside. They're the work of Sallie Ann Glassman, mambo and artist. Her store features many of her statues, paintings, and other hand-crafted items, which can become the centerpieces of your altars or just great decorations for your house. Island of Salvation is a bit out of the way, located not in the French Quarter but in the nearby working-class neighborhood of Bywater. But it's well worth the walk for a chance to learn about New Orleans Voodoo from one of the city's most respected practitioners.

The folks who run Voodoo Authentica (612 Rue Dumaine) also organize Voodoofest, a Halloween celebration of New Orleans Voodoo and culture featuring speakers, drummers, and entertainment that highlights Voodoo's many contributions to New Orleans. Even if you can't make it to the Crescent City for Halloween, you're sure to find plenty of interesting stuff at their shop. Their Rootwork Spa Orisha Collection will help you get in touch with the Orisha of Lukumi and Cuban Santeria—spirits who have become increasingly important in New Orleans since the 1970s and whose importance will only become greater as the city's Latin population grows.

Reverend Zombie's Voodoo Shop (725 St. Peter Street) is worth visiting for the enormous collection of statues. One of the only American distributors for plaster statues made by Brazil's Imagens Bahia, this shop offers images you won't find anywhere else in the country (see plate 4). The establishment also carries a wide selection of occult books, while the adjoining tobacco shop offers a fine selection of cigars and smoking accessories. (If you call ahead you can book a reading with Mary "Bloody Mary" Millan, a famous New Orleans tour guide and spiritual worker who has forgotten more about the city than most people will ever know.)

Marie Laveau's House of Voodoo (739 Bourbon Street) is located near the intersection of St. Ann Street and the site that the original Marie Laveau called home. (Another New Orleans luminary, Fred "Chicken Man" Staten [chapter 10], briefly operated a shop here.) Several of the psychics who work at this store claim that Laveau's ghost still haunts the place and occasionally assists them in Tarot and palm readings. You may not see the Voodoo Queen's ghost when you visit, but you're sure to be impressed by the Marie Laveau altar and by the selection of souvenirs, herbs, and Voodoo paraphernalia.

Restaurants

If you want to make a culinary pilgrimage, you couldn't ask for a better city than New Orleans. The city's food culture is legendary, and great meals can be had in any price range. Since one cannot live on Voodoo alone, you might as well enjoy the Big Easy's cuisine while you're there.

Expensive

The Brennan family has created a culinary dynasty. Brennan's (417 Royal Street) is the home of Bananas Foster and considered one of the city's finest restaurants (see plate 1). One of its main competitors is an establishment run by another branch of the Brennan family, Commander's Palace (1403 Washington Avenue). Both are New Orleans institutions and will be well worth the price of a visit. (Expect to spend around $80 a person at Brennan's and around $100 at Commander's Palace. The Brennan's breakfast and Commander's Palace jazz brunch will be a bit less expensive but no less enjoyable.)

Another New Orleans favorite, Antoine's (713 St. Louis Street), has been serving locals and tourists since 1840. With fifteen dining rooms, each more romantic and charming than the last, this is a great place to propose marriage, celebrate a special anniversary, or just treat yourself. Oysters Rockefeller was created at Antoine's, and you'll find oysters served there in many fabulous ways, but be sure to save some room for dessert. (Given that the restaurant's Baked Alaska is the size of a football, you may want to save a lot of room!)

K-Paul's Louisiana Kitchen (416 Chartres Street) offers sophisticated versions of classic Cajun and Creole fare. Sweet potato pecan pie is touched up with a dollop of Chantilly cream; fried green tomatoes and molasses bread are served up along with crawfish étouffée and what some call the world's best gumbo. Run by the famous chef Paul Prudhomme (who invented the blackening technique and who still produces some amazing blackened fish), it is popular with visitors and locals alike. If you want to find out why Prudhomme is a culinary legend, you had best make reservations first, especially if you want a place on the balcony or in the enclosed patio.

The Green Goddess, located at 307 Exchange Place, adds a New Orleans twist to an international menu. That old British standby, bangers and mash, is reimagined with mashed sweet potatoes and a local duck sausage; an El Salvadorian pupusa features a filling of crawfish, black beans, banana blossoms, and queso fresco. Chef and owner Chris DeBarr won Best New Chef of 2006 from *New Orleans Magazine* for his work at the Delachaise wine bar and has carried on with his innovative cooking at the Green Goddess. Prices here are more modest than the tab at some of New Orleans' more famous restaurants ($15 to $25 an entrée), but the food has received rave reviews from critics throughout the city. (As an added bonus, its menu is vegetarian friendly for those herbivores seeking a Crescent City dining experience.)

Inexpensive

You could start breakfast with the traditional coffee and beignets at Café du Monde (800 Decatur Street). But if you're looking for something a bit more substantial, how about a nice bowl of phở? This beefy broth and noodle soup is becoming an American dinner favorite, but in Vietnam it is considered the perfect way to start the day. Since the Vietnam War, Louisiana has been a favorite spot for refugees fleeing the communist government. Many Vietnamese have taken up the shrimping trade, while still others have opened restaurants. Jazmine Café (614 South Carrollton Avenue), Café Minh (4139 Canal Street), and Doson Noodle House (135 North Carrollton Avenue) are all good choices. A bowl of phở and a cup of sweet, strong Vietnamese coffee is a great way to recover from the night before.

Poor folks of any gender will appreciate the po' boy, one of the Crescent City's greatest contributions to inexpensive eating. The concept is simple—a sliced baguette stuffed with meat or seafood and dressed with roast beef gravy, Creole mustard, or mayonnaise. But the po' boy is more than just a sandwich: it's a way of life for New Orleans natives. Ask one hundred locals and you'll get one hundred recommendations for where to get the absolute best po' boy in the city. Among the names that come up frequently are Domilise Sandwich Shop and Bar (5240 Annunciation

Street), Crabby Jack's (428 Jefferson Highway in neighboring Jefferson), and Parkway Bakery and Tavern (538 Hagan Avenue).

But the po' boy isn't the only sandwich that made New Orleans famous. Sicilian immigrants brought muffolettos, round hearty loaves of bread with the texture of focaccia. Split horizontally, layered with a marinated mix of olives, onions, pimentos, and celery, then piled high with Italian cold cuts and provolone, they become the famous muffaletta sandwich. Central Grocery (923 Decatur Street) is said to be the home of this Crescent City delicacy, but Napoleon House Bar and Café (500 Chartres Street) and Chartres House Café (601 Chartres Street) are also renowned for their muffalettas.

Since Katrina, many Central and South American immigrants have arrived in search of work in the construction and recovery industries. This has led to a growing number of excellent and reasonably priced Latin restaurants. Tacos San Miguel (3517 20th Street, Metairie) has received numerous raves for its fish and tongue tacos, while Sarita's Grill (4520 Freret Street) offers Mexican/Nicaraguan/Cuban fusion food that will tickle your palate without troubling your wallet.

And if you happen to be in New Orleans on a Monday (or any other day), why not try a big bowl of red beans and rice. Originally red beans and rice were served on Mondays; they could simmer on the stove for hours while the women of the house were busy with their washing. But today they are good anytime, especially when they are flavored with andouille sausage. Dunbar's (501 Pine Street) is known for its beans, but also for its fried chicken, jambalaya, biscuits, and greens.

Music

Unlike many music clubs, Preservation Hall (726 St. Peter Street) doesn't offer a bar, reservations, or air conditioning. Despite this, crowds begin lining up outside the door well before the 8 p.m. shows. Once you get inside and hear the Preservation Hall Jazz Band playing New Orleans jazz standards, you'll understand why. Classically trained young musicians play alongside old-timers who learned at the feet of some of the city's jazz legends. "What we're doing is part of a continuum," says Director Benjamin Jaffee, "part of a tradition that is now in its fifth and sixth generation."[1] One of the city's most popular musical destinations, Preservation Hall is helping to ensure that New Orleans jazz continues on for many generations to come.

In 1977 the Fabulous Fo'teen, a group of music fans, founded a club for Henry Roeland "Professor Longhair" Byrd to perform in. At this time the brilliant pianist was working as a delivery man and suffering from several debilitating ailments. The club, named Tipitina's after one of his early compositions, gave him a venue and reintroduced his combination of rhumba, boogie-woogie, and Southern blues to a whole new generation of admirers. Alas, Professor Longhair is no longer with us, but Tipitina's continues to host local and out-of-town artists at its original 501 Napoleon Avenue address and at a new French Quarter branch on 233 North Peters Street.

Mulate's Restaurant (201 Julia Street) and the Cajun Cabin (503 Bourbon Street) offer nightly live performances by Cajun and zydeco bands, as do many other local bars. But for a down-home taste of Cajun entertainment, you may want to go down the road a piece to the Abita Springs Town Hall (22161 Level Street, Abita Springs). Once a month this establishment features Cajun entertainment from 8 to 10:30 p.m. by the Northshore Cajun Dancers. If you get there early, you can even get a free dance lesson starting at 7 p.m. To get an up-to-date copy of the schedule, check out the website (http://my.att.net/p/s/community. dll?ep=16&groupid=336806&ck=).

New Orleans and goth music go together like andouille sausage and red beans. Since wearing black during the daytime in the Crescent City is uncomfortable at best, the Dungeon (738 Toulouse Street) opens at midnight and closes at dawn. If you like decadence, elegance, and lots of attractive people in fetish wear, you're sure to love this place, but be sure you leave yourself time to get back to your coffin before sunrise. (And if you've partaken of the Friday night three-for-one drink specials, be sure you have a designated hearse driver!)

Café Lafitte in Exile (901 Bourbon Street) is one of America's oldest continually running gay bars. Before he was famous, Tennessee Williams cruised here, and if you're lucky you may just go home with a future Pulitzer Prize winner yourself. And if you just want to enjoy the music, why not stop by for "trash disco"? The '70s come alive again each Sunday at Lafitte; you can get down and boogie oogie oogie with locals and tourists of every persuasion. (If you feel like making music, Wednesday is karaoke night.)

Do you like rockabilly, swing, blues, and rootsy American music? Do you like bowling? If the answer to either of those questions is "yes," you need to stop by the Mid City Bowling Lanes (3016 South Carrollton Avenue). Owner John Blancher took over this old facility soon after returning from a pilgrimage to the town of Medjugorje in western Bosnia and Herzegovina, where the Virgin Mary (chapter 12) was reportedly appearing. He didn't get to see Mary, but his prayers for "something that would get my whole family involved" came true when he started booking musicians at his bowling alley. You'll be knocking down pins and knocking back cheap drinks in no time flat.

In the early part of the nineteenth century, New Orleans was the opera capital of America. Today the New Orleans Opera Company and the Louisiana Philharmonic Orchestra (LPO) continue to provide great performances of great works. Opera performances take place at the Mahalia Jackson Theater for the Performing Arts (801 North Rampart Street), while the LPO, the only musician-owned and collaboratively managed professional symphony in the United States, can be seen at First Baptist New Orleans (5290 Canal Boulevard) and at various other venues throughout Louisiana and around the world.

Cemeteries

We all end up there sooner or later, but in New Orleans people make a point of visiting before they become permanent residents. The Big Easy has long attracted tourists fascinated by the somber beauty of its many historical graveyards. If you're visiting, you'd be foolish not to explore the gorgeous necropoli that decorate the city's landscape. But you would be equally foolish to saunter about the New Orleans graveyards without exercising a bit of caution. The narrow alleyways of the graveyards and the ornate tombs provide many hiding places for muggers, rapists, and street criminals. To make matters worse, many of the city's most beautiful cemeteries are also located in or near high-crime neighborhoods. A nighttime séance in a Crescent City necropolis might seem romantic, but becoming a statistic is not. Most New Orleans cemeteries are best visited by day and in groups.

St. Louis Cemetery No. 3 (3421 Esplinade Avenue) was built atop a former burial ground for lepers. E. J. Bellocq, who became famous for his pictures of the notorious red-light district in Storyville, New Orleans, is buried here. St. Louis Cemetery No. 2 is the final resting place of Jacques Nicholas Bussiere de Pouilly, who designed many of the city's most ornate tombs, and it is claimed by some to be the true resting place of Marie Laveau (chapter 14). (Most, however, claim she is buried in the city's first cemetery, St. Louis No. 1, along with civil rights hero Homer Plessy and Bernard de Marigny, the French-Creole playboy who brought the dice game of *crapaud*—in English, craps—to America. Alas, his enthusiasm for gambling was not matched by his luck. To make up for his losses, he was forced to sell the land that now encompasses the Faubourg Marigny neighborhood.)

Greenwood Cemetery (5200 Canal Boulevard) was established in 1852 when a particularly nasty epidemic of yellow fever left burial sites in short supply. Its centerpiece is the Fireman's Monument, which pays tribute to the Fireman's Charitable and Benevolent Association, which established the cemetery. Other notable sites include the mass grave of six hundred Confederate soldiers, the society tomb of Lodge Number 30 of the Benevolent and Protective Order of Elks (complete with a large elk statue), numerous impressive cast iron tombs, and the grave of John Kennedy Toole, author of *A Confederacy of Dunces*.

St. Roch Cemetery No. 1 and No. 2 (1725 St. Roch Avenue) is considered one of the most beautiful in the city and is worth a visit for the St. Roch Shrine (see chapter 16). Be advised that it is also considered one of the most dangerous, since it borders on several high-crime areas. If you want to go you may be well advised to travel with a tour group or, at the very least, make sure you are out of the neighborhood well before dark.

Lafayette Cemetery No. 1 (1400 Washington Avenue) has been captured in many films and photo shoots. If you've seen *Interview with the Vampire,* you may recognize some of the tombs. While it is located in one of the safer sections of New Orleans, caution is still advised. (If you decide to go with a tour group, you'll have no problem finding a guide. This is one of the city's most popular cemeteries.) And if you work up an appetite walking around beautiful tombs, you're only a short distance away from Commander's Palace, where you can have a spectacular if somewhat pricey lunch.

While many in New Orleans opt for above-ground internment, orthodox Jewish law requires burial. But though they don't have so many elaborate mausoleums, there's plenty of history to be seen at Gates of Prayer No. 1 (4824 Canal Street), where tombstones date back to the nineteenth century, marking the historical progress of the city's sizeable Jewish community. Since this is New Orleans, you can expect at least a few impressive monuments. One of the most striking is the eleven-foot-tall lighthouse that marks the grave of Harry Offner, former president of Lighthouse for the Blind.

And if you want to hobnob with the crème de la crème of deceased New Orleans society, be sure to visit Metarie Cemetery at 5100 Pontchartrain Boulevard. The Josie Arlington tomb (chapter 19) is found here, but it is not the largest or most impressive pile of granite in the place. The honor for that goes to the Moriarty tomb, built in 1887 by wealthy builder Daniel Moriarty to pay tribute to his deceased wife. A sixty-foot-high (18.3 meter) obelisk surrounded by four women who represent Faith, Hope, Charity, and Memory (the last statue added after Moriarty was told there were only three graces, not four), the Moriarty tomb cost over $185,000 to erect and required the construction of a special railroad spur to haul in the massive slabs of marble.

26

MOVING TO NEW ORLEANS
Triumphs and Tragedies

Before it was a tourist town, New Orleans was a port city where goods from around the globe were bought and sold by people from every corner of the world. Some came here to establish themselves in a trade or a business. Others left their hometown's gray mediocrity for bright lights, beautiful scenery, and sparkling conversation. Many found what they sought: the Crescent City has always welcomed outsiders. If you have been studying New Orleans Voodoo for a while, you may be feeling the city's pull. Perhaps you have already paid a visit to the Big Easy and fallen head over heels in love. A nexus of spiritual and creative power, New Orleans has always called out to those spirits who could benefit from and add to its energy.

But though many people have profited from their association with the Crescent City, many others have found the city's influence more corrosive than salutary. New Orleans can be a dangerous place, spiritually and otherwise. Some have become too deeply involved in the party culture and paid the price for their overindulgence; some have become statistics in the city's notoriously high crime rate; others have found that the quirks of New Orleans culture soon went from charming to insufferable. If you are thinking about spending some time as a resident of New Orleans, you should give careful consideration to the drawbacks as well as the benefits. A study of those who have come before you may give you food for thought and assist you in making the right choice.

Tennessee Williams

When Thomas Lanier Williams moved to New Orleans in 1938, his future looked less than promising. His writing achievements were modest: a $5 third prize in 1927 for his essay "Can a Good Wife Be a Good Sport?"; a 1928 short story entitled "The Vengeance of Nitocris" in *Weird Tales;* and three plays staged during his time at three different colleges. His job history was even less impressive: his two-year stint at his father's shoe company was marked by his sullen incompetence and culminated in a mental and physical collapse. He suffered from alcoholism, depression, and a nagging fear that he would end up like his beloved but unstable older sister, Rose, who had spent much of her adult life in mental hospitals.

But New Orleans was good for Williams. He had spent years wrestling with his urges, saying later, "I was finally fully persuaded that I was 'queer,' but had no idea what to do about it. I didn't even know how to accept a boy on the rare occasions when one would offer himself to me."[1] The Crescent City was far more tolerant of homosexuality than his hometown of St. Louis or the various college campuses where he had studied. At the age of twenty-eight, Williams finally lost his virginity, and then he made up for lost time with what he called a period of "deviant satyritis." To mark his new life Williams began going by the nickname he had acquired in college for his thick Southern accent—Tennessee. From that moment forward Williams would be open about his sexual orientation—a courageous stance in a time when sodomy was still a criminal offense in most of America. Williams later described with some amusement the reaction of a few uptown debutantes invited back to his apartment in 1946.

> They seemed to like the bedroom. Who wouldn't? A bedroom is either the loveliest room of a place of residence or the most abhorrent: this one belonged to the first category.
>
> Then somebody turned to my apartment mate.
>
> "Now show us yours."
>
> "Oh, I—"

He probably knew that a scandal was brewing and would have wished to avoid it but I found it perfectly natural to say, "We share this room."

I thought the silence that followed my statement was not natural at all.

You see, the bed was somewhere between single and double . . .

Debutantes began to whisper to their escorts, there were little secretive colloquies among them and presently they began to thank us for an unusual and delightful evening and to take their leave as though a storm was impending.

I suppose it was better that way. My place in society, then and possibly always since then, has been in Bohemia. I love to visit the other side now and then, but on my social passport Bohemia is indelibly stamped, without regret on my part.[2]

Williams's first stay in New Orleans would be brief. A hoped-for position with the Works Progress Administration failed to pan out. Williams supported himself with various day jobs and spent his nights absorbing the atmosphere of the French Quarter. It was enough to pay his rent at a squalid boarding house on 431 Royal Street—at least most of the time— but though he felt the city was helping him to grow as a writer, he finally decided to seek fortune elsewhere. He headed to Hollywood and spent some time trying unsuccessfully to break into screenwriting. From there he moved on to New York, where he supplemented his income from grants from the Rockefeller Foundation and the American Academy of Arts and Letters with work as a waiter in Greenwich Village. Then, in 1944 *The Glass Menagerie,* a tribute to his dysfunctional family and his doomed sister Rose (who had recently been lobotomized), excerpted below, became an overnight sensation:

TOM: Not long after that I was fired for writing a poem on the lid of a shoe-box. I left St. Louis. I descended the steps of this fire escape for a last time and followed, from then on, in my father's footsteps, attempting to find in motion what was lost in space. I traveled around a great deal. The cities swept around me like dead leaves, leaves that were brightly colored but torn away from the branches.[3]

Menagerie premiered in Chicago, then came to New York in 1945 and won the New York Drama Critics' Circle award for Best Play of the Year. Seeking a follow-up to his sudden success, Williams turned his attention once again to the Crescent City for his next play, *A Streetcar Named Desire*.

BLANCHE: (near him, facing him) So late? Don't you just love these long rainy afternoons in New Orleans when an hour isn't just an hour—but a little bit of Eternity dropped in your hands—and who knows what to do with it?[4]

Blanche DuBois, *Streetcar*'s heroine, has come to her sister Stella's French Quarter apartment after losing the family's Mississippi plantation. While there she becomes embroiled in a simultaneously contentious and flirtatious relationship with Stella's husband, Stanley Kowalski. A Polish-American dockworker, Stanley has little use for Blanche's pretensions and efforts to deny her reduced circumstances. The play ends tragically, as Blanche is raped by Stanley and later sent away to a mental hospital. Its conflict between an old-money Southern belle and an urban laborer is both universal and deeply rooted in New Orleans culture and history. The play, and later the movie, cemented Williams as a major American playwright. It also launched the career of Marlon Brando, whose portrayal of Stanley Kowalski made him a star and helped to popularize the Method school of acting.

The year 1947 was important for Williams in another arena: it was the year he met Frank Merlo, a Sicilian-American Navy veteran. Merlo provided an island of stability and sanity for the tempestuous Williams. The two remained together off and on until Merlo's death from cancer in 1963. They lived together in Key West and New York, but Williams always considered New Orleans his spiritual home and returned to the city frequently. His final play, 1977's *Vieux Carré*, would return to the seedy boardinghouse where he made his start. By then his star had faded; his fondness for alcohol was now combined with an addiction to barbiturates. *Vieux Carré* opens with the Writer musing, "Once this house was alive, it was occupied once. In my recollection it still is but by shadowy occupants like ghosts. Now they enter the lighter areas of my memory."[5]

Today Williams enjoys an honored place in the lighter areas of the Crescent City's memory. Thousands of Williams fans descend on New Orleans every March for the Tennessee Williams/New Orleans Literary Festival, where they enjoy theatrical productions, literary panels, and the ever-popular Stanley and Stella Shouting Contest. Contestants, usually attired in sleeveless undershirts, compete to shout the most convincing appeal to the judges on the balcony of the Pontalba Apartments on Jackson Square. (In a nod to gender equality, women contestants are allowed to shout "Stanley!")

Emeril Lagasse

Had things gone a little differently, TV's most famous chef might be playing in bar bands up and down the coast of New England. But Emeril Lagasse turned down a percussion scholarship at the New England Conservatory of Music to pursue his other passion. "I just loved food," he explains. "Eventually, I had to make the decision, because hey, can't do both, because of the way the businesses are structured. I can enjoy both, but there's no way you could do both."[6] After getting a degree from the culinary school at Johnson & Wales University, Lagasse traveled to France to master the art of French cuisine. He then went on to work at high-end restaurants in Boston, New York, and Philadelphia, honing his craft through long, grueling hours spent behind a stove.

Then, in 1982, Lagasse was asked to step in as executive chef at Commander's Palace. This New Orleans institution was regularly listed among America's ten highest grossing restaurants, and its former executive chef, Paul Prudhomme, was America's most famous master of New Orleans cuisine. But the twenty-three-year-old Portuguese kid from Fall River, Massachusetts, was up for the challenge. "The Brennans asked me what I thought of all their great food," Lagasse said of the interview process. "I said it feels like home."[7] Lagasse's lighter style of cuisine, which he dubbed "Creolized Today," focused on quality local ingredients—something that has never been in short supply in New Orleans. In Emeril's words,

> New Orleans is one of the greatest cities in the world for food. There's a lot of tradition—between Creole, which is the city cooking, and Cajun or Acadiana, which is the country cooking. It's been there for over 200 years. You're not just going to go in there and get a paint brush and change things. There are a lot of cultural influences that make up Louisiana besides the French, the Spanish and the African American. There's a little Italian, there's a little Irish—it's really a great melting pot which is probably why we have the best gumbo on the planet.[8]

In 1990 Lagasse resigned his position to open his first restaurant, Emeril's, at 800 Tchoupitoulas Street in the Warehouse District. Many people questioned his decision to move to an up-and-coming neighborhood, fearing it would frighten the old-school gourmands who had given his food so many accolades at Commander's Palace. But Lagasse soon proved them wrong, as *Esquire* magazine declared Emeril's the 1990 Restaurant of the Year and *Wine Spectator* bestowed upon it the 1991 Grand Award. In 1993 he opened a second establishment, NOLA, in the French Quarter at 534 St. Louis Street. More casual than the white-tablecloth Emeril's, NOLA soon became a favorite with locals and tourists alike.

Already a local celebrity, Lagasse achieved national stardom when he joined the fledgling TV Food Network in 1993. His appearances on the syndicated program *Great Chefs of New Orleans* had caught the eye of network executives, and his *Essence of Emeril* soon became one of the Food Network's most popular programs. Lagasse shared his love of New Orleans cuisine with an infectious enthusiasm, with catchphrases like "Kick it up a notch" and "Bam!" Soon *Essence of Emeril* was joined by

Emeril Live! Lagasse used his innate sense of rhythm to work the audience into a frenzy, throwing in "Aw, yeah, baby!" and "Pork fat rules!" at just the right moment for maximum impact.

Lagasse soon turned his TV stardom into a one-man empire. Supermarkets stocked spice blends like "Emeril's Essence," "Bayou Blast," and "Emeril's Kick It Up Red Pepper Sauce." Bookstores sold tomes like *Louisiana Real and Rustic* and *Emeril's Creole Christmas.* With Emeril's New Orleans Fish House in Las Vegas (opened 1995) and Emeril's Orlando at Universal Studios (opened 1998), Lagasse expanded his restaurant holdings outside the Crescent City. Later he opened restaurants in Atlanta and Miami Beach as well. All those years of hard work had paid off in spades.

This newfound celebrity didn't lead to an easier schedule—Lagasse still regularly puts in eighteen-hour days. But it led to fame and fortune he could hardly have dreamed of when he was ten and working in a Fall River bakery. In February 2008 Martha Stewart's Omnimedia Productions purchased the rights to Emeril's cookbooks, TV shows, and licensed food products and cookware for a reported $50 million in cash and stock. Lagasse retained the rights to his restaurants, and he continues to hold forth on television while opening new establishments in Las Vegas and Florida and expanding to Gulfport, Mississippi, and the Bethlehem, Pennsylvania, Sands Casino.

But though he continues to diversify his holdings, Lagasse still calls the Crescent City home. His corporate headquarters, Emeril's Homebase, can be found at 829 St. Charles Avenue in downtown New Orleans. While his television programs are filmed in New York, they are produced at Emeril's Homebase. And since 2002 his charity, the Emeril Lagasse Foundation, has given $3.2 million to culinary, nutrition, garden, arts, and life skills programs in New Orleans and on the Gulf Coast.

Willy DeVille

Although he got his first break at New York's CBGB, Willy DeVille had little use for the punk rock scene. While he had the surly attitude and heroin habit of a punker, his musical interests were more diverse, incorporating Latin music, rhythm and blues, French cabaret, and Brill Building pop. Unfortunately, this meant that the music industry didn't know what to do with him. The albums *Mink DeVille* (1977) and *Return to Magenta* (1978) produced great critical buzz but no big hits. *Le Chat Bleu* (1979) so baffled executives that they released it only in Europe. (They finally released it in the United States after strong import sales and rave reviews from *Rolling Stone* and other publications, but by then DeVille had signed to Atlantic and the record received little promotion from the label.)

Alas, his albums at Atlantic (1981's *Coup de Grace* and 1983's *Where Angels Fear to Tread*) were even less commercially successful. DeVille was becoming increasingly bitter and withdrawn as he spiraled deeper into addiction. By 1986 he had split with his wife and was forced to file for bankruptcy. Although 1987 brought some triumphs when his "Storybook Love" appeared on the soundtrack of *The Princess Bride* and was nominated for an Academy Award, he was still creatively and commercially adrift, a perennial critical favorite in search of that lucky break that would catapult him to stardom.

Le Chat Bleu featured several collaborations with legendary Doc Pomus, who had penned classics like "Save the Last Dance for Me" and "Teenager in Love." While the famously crotchety Pomus once complained that DeVille could sit for hours strumming a guitar aimlessly without an idea in his head, DeVille learned many lessons at the feet of his idol. One was that songwriters should immerse themselves in a regional genre of music before attempting to write honestly in that form.[9] While he had flirted with Cajun music and hired Mac "Dr. John" Rebennack for keyboard duties on *Return to Magenta* and *Le Chat Bleu,* he decided that a more serious study was in order. And so in 1988 DeVille packed up his bags and headed off to New Orleans in search of a change of scenery and some new inspiration. In a 2006 interview, he said:

> I was tired of being "Willy DeVille." Walking out of my building and having to be the guy who was up on stage all the time, even when I wasn't performing. I wanted to get away from that. So I got

down there and it was this famous guy had come to town, and I didn't want that. So I decided to do an album with a bunch of the musicians from down there, the music of New Orleans.[10]

Victory Mixture (1990) featured an all-star cast of the city's finest musicians. Dr. John shared keyboard duties with two of New Orleans' finest pianists, Allen Toussaint and Eddie Bo. Crescent City bluesman Ed King played guitar, and the rhythm section from the Meters kept time on several tracks. DeVille reminisced in 1996, "I was just trying to get them money, the writers of the songs, 'cause they all got ripped off in the '50s and '60s. They were all fascinated, and Dr. John convinced them that they wouldn't get ripped off by this Northern white boy. That's when I crossed over to being a local here in New Orleans."[11]

Victory Mixture was also a hit with the critics, who considered it a return to form. DeVille purchased a house in nearby Picayune, Mississippi, with his new wife and began breeding Spanish horses. But he continued to spend time in the French Quarter playing with and learning from the city's many talented musicians. In the summer of 1992, DeVille toured Europe with Dr. John, Johnny Adams, Zachary Richard, and the Wild Magnolias in a well-received New Orleans Revue. The city's influence can also be seen on his 1995 releases *Big Easy Fantasy* and *Loup Garou* and on his new look, which traded in Lower East Side cool for nineteenth-century riverboat elegance.

In time DeVille grew restless in the Big Easy. Relocating to New Mexico, he finally kicked heroin. But this triumph was marred by tragedy when his second wife committed suicide. Soon after he was involved in a head-on collision that shattered his leg and left him on crutches for over three years. In 2003 he returned to New York with his third wife, Nina Lagerwall. There he was diagnosed with hepatitis C in February 2009. While treating that, doctors discovered in May that he had Stage 4 pancreatic cancer. On August 6, 2009, three weeks shy of his fifty-ninth birthday, Willy DeVille died in his sleep at New York's Cabrini Hospital.

Zackery Bowen

When he came back to New Orleans in 2004, Zackery Bowen might have hoped he would find some peace after years of bloodshed. A decorated soldier who had served in Iraq and Bosnia, Bowen had become disillusioned with the military and began intentionally flunking physicals. Ultimately he received a general discharge, thereby losing his veteran's benefits and becoming ineligible to receive post-combat counseling. His marriage had fallen apart during his tours of duty, and he was now estranged from his wife and their two children. But the California native had an easy smile, good looks, and a charming manner, and those were enough to get him steady work as a bartender in the French Quarter.

Working in the hospitality industry provided Bowen with an active social life. Alcohol flowed freely after hours, as well as other substances like cocaine. Sometimes when Bowen was in his cups he would become morose, alluding to an overseas incident involving a child. But those moods were rare. For the most part his friends saw the 6-foot 10-inch (1.83 meter) Bowen as a gentle giant who would rather tell a joke or perform a magic trick than fight. By the summer of 2005 he was becoming increasingly friendly with another French Quarter bartender, Addie Hall.

Hall had also relocated to New Orleans, leaving her family in Durham, North Carolina. Like Bowen, she would sometimes allude to darkness in her past, telling friends that her brother had raped her and she ran away from home when her family refused to believe it had happened. Hall was a ballroom dancer, poet, and student of religions who was given to all-night conversations. But where Bowen had a reputation for easygoing affability, Hall was known for her unpredictable temper and violent alcohol-fueled rages. Still, the attraction between the two grew during the hot days of summer and was consummated when Katrina hit.

Bowen's apartment was flooded, and Hall suggested he stay with her in her apartment on Governor Nicholls Street. While the rest of the city evacuated, Bowen and Hall joined a few others who stayed behind and rode the storm out. Cooking dinners by candlelight and serving drinks to their fellow diehard New Orleanians, they were interviewed and photographed by numerous journalists. "We're having a civilized hurricane," Hall told the *Mobile Register*. "It's actually been kind of nice," Bowen added. "And I'm getting healthier, eating right and toning up."[12] The pair told *The New York Times* (which included pictures of the photogenic couple in the September 9, 2005, edition) of how Hall would occasionally flash her breasts to passing police officers to ensure regular patrols. By the time the city returned to some semblance of normalcy, Bowen and Hall had fallen in love.

But what seemed like a storybook romance soon turned turbulent. The couple fought constantly, falling into a cycle of bitter drunken brawls and tearful reconciliations. Bowen, who called her his "Goddess of the French Quarter," left for Seattle at one point but soon returned. Later they moved in together, renting an apartment on 826 North Rampart Street above Miriam Chamani's Voodoo Spiritual Temple. Then, on October 4, 2006, Hall told landlord Leo Watermeier that Bowen was cheating on her, and she was kicking him out. Watermeier suggested they work their problems out and get back to him, then left as the couple continued squabbling. It was the last time he spoke to her.

Soon afterward Bowen was out partying and working at his new job as a grocery deliveryman. Between shots of Jameson's and lines of cocaine, he explained to friends that Hall had left him. Given their frequent arguments, few were particularly surprised. And while Bowen appeared to be consuming more substances than usual, folks assumed that he was engaging in the time-honored New Orleans tradition of drowning his sorrows. Then, on October 17, after drinking for a few hours at the La Riviera, the Omni Royal Orleans Hotel's rooftop bar, he jumped from the balcony. Police who arrived at the scene found a note in his pocket.

> This is not accidental. I had to take my own life to pay for the one I took. If you send a patrol to 826 N. Rampart you will find the dismembered corpse of my girlfriend Addie in the oven, on the stove, and in the fridge along with full documentation on the both of us and a full signed confession from myself. The keys in my right front

pocket are for the gates. Call Leo Watermeier to let you in. Zack Bowen.[13]

When patrol officers arrived, they found the head of Addie Hall, burned beyond recognition, in a cooking pot. Her arms and legs were in the oven, and her bloody torso, wrapped in a plastic bag, was in the refrigerator. Spray-painted messages on the walls urged "please call my wife" and "please help me stop the pain." In an eight-page confession Bowen explained:

She had stolen this apartment (ask Leo Watermeier. He'll explain that one), tried to kick me out, then would not shut the fuck up so I very calmly strangled her. It was very quick. Then after sexually defiling the body a few times I was posed with the question of how to dispose of the corpse. . . . I came home, moved the body to the tub, got a saw and hacked off her feet, hands and head. Put her head in the oven (after giving it an awful haircut) put her hands and feet in the water on the range. Then I got drunk(er) and some hours later turned off the stove, filled the tub with water and passed out. Eventually I finished taking apart the body: Sunday night I sawed off the rest of the legs and arms and put them in roasting pans, stuck them in the oven, and passed out. I came to seven hours later with an awful smell eminating [sic] from the kitchen. I turned off the oven and went to work Monday. This would be the last day I'd work.[14]

For twelve days Bowen had lived in the apartment with the remains of his onetime goddess. To avoid decay, he kept the air conditioning at 60°F (15°C). At first he had apparently entertained the idea of eating her: chopped carrots and potatoes were found on the counter. But then he decided, as he explained in the note, to "spend the $1,500 I had being happy until I killed myself. So that's what I did: good food, good drugs, good strippers, good friends and any loose ends I may have had. And had a fantastic time living out my days."[15]

AFTERWORD

DEEPWATER HORIZON AND THE INDOMITABLE SPIRIT OF LOUISIANA

On the evening of April 20, 2010, the *Deepwater Horizon* caught fire some 52 miles (83 km) south of the Louisiana coast. Two days later the ultra-deepwater, semi-submersible rig—a floating fortress the size of two football fields—sank beneath the waves, leaving a growing oil slick in its wake. Beneath 5,000 feet (1.6 km) of water the damaged well continued to spew out oil and natural gas for months. Not until July 15, 2010, would British Petroleum engineers finally staunch the flow, after an estimated 5 million barrels of oil had been released into the Gulf of Mexico.

The most immediately injured were the region's fish, shrimp, and oyster industries. According to the National Oceanic and Atmospheric Association, 3.2 million recreational fishermen in the Gulf of Mexico region took 24 million fishing trips in 2008, while commercial fishermen in the gulf harvested more than 1.27 billion pounds (500 million kilos) of finfish and shellfish.[1] Until the extent of the oil's impact became clear, much of the area was declared off limits to fishing. Some were lucky enough to pick up a bit of extra income assisting in the oil cleanup, although few were able to match their pre-spill earnings.

BP agreed to place in escrow a $20 billion fund to help address financial losses: within the first eight weeks of operation, the independently

252

administered Gulf Coast Claims Facility had paid out more than $2 billion to approximately 127,000 claimants.[2] Most of the claimants worked in the fishing industry, but others who were affected filed as well, including plumbers, dockworkers, electricians, and the owner of Mimosa Dancing Girls, a New Orleans strip club that catered to many fishermen and gulf workers.[3] But many found it difficult to provide requested documentation. The Gulf fishing industry operates largely on a cash-only basis, with a great deal of earnings unreported and untaxed. Unable to verify their income, many could not access the fund to recoup financial losses.[4]

Images of dead birds, petroleum-soaked tortoises, and tarball-slimed beaches did nothing to help the tourism industry along the Gulf. A Louisiana State Tourism Agency report suggested the state would lose $691 million in tourism money through 2013 as a result of the oil spill (although it suggested this would be somewhat offset by $395 million in additional business and government travel related to the disaster).[5] Data from the Louisiana Workforce Commission showed that after the spill new unemployment insurance claims filed by workers previously employed in the Accommodations and Food Service Industry, which includes hotels, casinos, restaurants, and bars, surged by 33.0 percent: new jobless claims filed by workers from other industries in Louisiana increased by about 10.6 percent over the same time period.[6]

To help break up the spill, BP used over 1.9 million gallons of toxic dispersants; many of these chemicals have been linked to a growing number of health problems in the area. After swimming in the Gulf, 22-year-old Paul Doom developed symptoms, including internal bleeding, severe headaches, and seizures. "I've had two blood tests for Volatile Organic Compounds [VOC's] which are in BP's oil and dispersants, and they both came back with alarmingly high levels," says Doom. "A toxicologist that interpreted my blood VOC results told me they didn't know how I was alive."[7] While BP originally asserted that the health hazards of exposure to dispersant chemicals and leaking crude "are very low" they later reworded that statement to: health risks "have been carefully considered in the selection of the various methods employed in addressing its spill."[8]

A growing number of people began casting a critical eye on the petroleum industry's role in "Cancer Alley," the 107-mile stretch between Baton Rouge and New Orleans that holds over 150 industrial facilities and oil refineries as well as numerous toxic waste dumps and other environmental hazards. Growing numbers of people called for an end to offshore drilling, especially in deep water: the Obama Administration invoked a temporary moratorium and later enforced tougher standards on deepwater drilling.

But despite the disaster's impact, the energy industry is not without its defenders in the region. Louisiana is America's number one producer of crude oil and the number two producer of natural gas: roughly 88 percent of the nation's offshore oil rigs are located off the Louisiana coast.[9] The high oil and gas prices that hurt tourism encourage further exploration in the Gulf, helping to prop up the local economy when the entertainment industry is soft. Closing down the wells and refineries might make the residents of Cancer Alley and the rest of Louisiana healthier in the long term, but in the short term it would definitely make them poorer.

Deepwater drilling involves untried technologies under extremely difficult conditions. Should it continue, another blowout is inevitable. Yet it also seems inevitable that exploration will continue. Billions of barrels lie beneath the waves, and while Louisiana politics and regulations may be notorious, the political and regulatory climate here is a huge improvement over most of the world's oil-producing regions. The oil industry brings with it large amounts of tax revenue and well-paying skilled jobs: these are difficult to resist in a state where poverty and unemployment have long been endemic.

We do not yet know the ultimate impact of this spill. The fishing industry has yet to recover fully from this body blow, or from damage to the oyster beds in 2011 caused by flooding along the Mississippi River causeways. Much as Katrina destroyed many of the poor and working-class neighborhoods of New Orleans, the *Deepwater Horizon* spill has caused enormous upheaval throughout southern Louisiana. It is unclear how much oil remains beneath the surface, how it will affect future catches, how it will play on the lives and livelihoods of the workers who have been plying these waters for generations.

Despite all these uncertainties, it seems likely that the industry will continue. Be they black, Cajun, or Vietnamese, these fishers and shrimpers are a tough and hardy lot. Cast out of their homes in Acadia or Saigon, driven into the swamps to escape the plantations or the Indian hunters, they found refuge in this steamy land and have put down roots in its brackish soil. They have faced down hurricanes and debt collectors; they will triumph, if not necessarily prosper, in the face of these latest adversities. As third-generation oyster fisherman Bryan Encelade puts it, "I just don't know where else to go. I can't live anywhere else. Louisiana is me."[10]

PART SIX

APPENDICES

APPENDIX I

GREAT NEW ORLEANS BOOKS, MOVIES, AND TELEVISION

Books

A.D.: New Orleans After the Deluge **by Josh Neufeld (2009)**
The suffering wrought by Hurricane Katrina was frequently beyond words. In his graphic novel *A.D.*, Josh Neufeld gives us the illustrated story of seven survivors as they try to rebuild their lives. His drawings of the storm bearing down on New Orleans will haunt your dreams, as will the tragedies and triumphs of the men and women he chronicles.

All the King's Men **by Robert Penn Warren (1946)**
Warren's story of Willie Stark, a cynical populist who rises to become governor of an unnamed Southern state, is based on the life of Louisiana Governor Huey P. Long. Like all the best Southern literature, it delves into the possibility of redemption despite humanity's innate depravity—a concept familiar to anyone who has spent time in New Orleans.

The Awakening **by Kate Chopin (1899)**
When it was first published, this tale of love and loss among vacationing New Orleanians was scorned as vulgar and unwholesome, and protagonist Edna Pontellier was derided as a narcissistic, unnatural adulteress. Today

258

The Awakening is recognized as a bold study of the limitations placed on women by societal expectations and feminine roles.

A Confederacy of Dunces by John Kennedy Toole (1980)

This picaresque tale of Ignatius J. Reilly and the various characters he encounters in the French Quarter is considered by many to be one of America's greatest comic novels. If Faulkner, Twain, and Rabelais went on a week-long bar crawl down Bourbon Street, they might have written this book.

The Feast of All Saints by Anne Rice (1979)

Many of *The Vampire Chronicles* are set in the author's hometown. This historical novel explores the lives of the free people of color in antebellum New Orleans. While there are no undead immortals in *Feast,* there is no shortage of the bodice-ripping, bosom-heaving, and deliciously florid descriptions we've come to expect from Rice.

Liquor by Poppy Z. Brite (2004)

The cuisines of New Orleans are well known. Those who toil in its kitchens have received far less attention until Brite turned his pen to chronicling the lives of Rickey and G-Man, chefs, lovers, and aspiring restaurant owners. If this one catches your fancy, don't miss their continuing adventures in *Soul Kitchen* (2005) and *Prime* (2006).

The Moviegoer by Walker Percy (1961)

New Orleans stockbroker Binx Bolling lives his life vicariously, with the films he watches more tangible than the details of his daily existence, until his life changes during a fateful Mardi Gras weekend. Many consider Walker Percy's debut novel an existentialist masterpiece on a par with Camus' *The Stranger* and Sartre's *Nausea.*

The Sound of Building Coffins by Louis Maistros (2009)

A Crescent City native with an enormous record collection, Maistros has created a dark, funny, heart-wrenching tale of fin de siècle New Orleans and legendary bluesman Buddy Bolden. A grim and beautiful work that will linger in your memory like a bayou sunset.

The Tin Roof Blowdown by James Lee Burke (2007)
When Katrina hits, Detective Dave Robicheaux is called from his post in nearby New Iberia to help out in the city he calls the "Whore of Babylon." The protagonist of seventeen novels, this is one of Robicheaux's darkest and most troubling outings as he finds himself battling against both evil and incompetence.

A Walk on the Wild Side by Nelson Algren (1956)
Nelson Algren chronicled grifters, pimps, prostitutes, perverts, and junkies in his novel, but never treated them with condescension or contempt. His humor may be pitch-black, but his compassion for the underdog always shines through. *Walk on the Wild Side,* his ribald tale of Dove Linkhorn's coming of age among the working girls of New Orleans, is one of his finest. (And yes, Lou Reed stole the title for his biggest radio hit.)

Movies and Television

Angel Heart (1987)
William Hjortsberg set his 1978 *Falling Angel* in New York. For his adaptation, screenwriter and director Alan Parker moved much of the action to Louisiana and added a liberal dose of New Orleans Voodoo to the proceedings. Strong performances by Robert de Niro, Mickey Rourke, and Lisa Bonet help make this film that rarest of birds—one as unnerving and unforgettable as the original novel.

The Big Easy (1987)
Ellen Barkin is a district attorney working to root out corruption on the New Orleans police force. Dennis Quaid is a NOPD lieutenant with a good heart but a Crescent City sense of ethics. The inevitable clash and equally inevitable romantic sparks that follow liven up this stylish and sexy thriller.

The Buccaneer (1938)

Long before Johnny Depp's Captain Jack Sparrow, Hollywood produced many big-budget pirate movies. This story of Jean Lafitte and his role in the Battle of New Orleans features legendary actor Frederic March at his most dashing and charismatic. While it adds the obligatory romance, the script by Harold Lamb (based on Lyle Saxon's 1930 *Lafitte the Pirate*) hews surprisingly close to the historical facts.

Eve's Bayou (1997)

Many New Orleans stories have used Voodoo for horror or shock value. *Eve's Bayou* treats it as an integral part of Louisiana Creole culture. Many films have used black life as fodder for comedy or as a call for social reform. *Eve's Bayou* is a serious drama that neither preaches nor treats its subjects as victims to be pitied. A film to be savored, with fine performances from Jurnee Smollett, Samuel L. Jackson, Lynn Whitfield, and Debbi Morgan, among others.

Frank's Place (1987–1988)

Although it only aired for one season, this comedy-drama of a Brown University professor (Tim Reid) who returns home after inheriting a New Orleans restaurant is still remembered for its handling of race, class, and social issues and its portrayal of life among working-class black Americans. While many have clamored for its release on DVD, licensing issues with the music used in many episodes have kept it out of circulation. Rumor has it that a release with a new soundtrack is pending.

APPENDIX 2

NEW ORLEANS MUSICIANS

If you want to capture the feeling of New Orleans, there's nothing like sitting down and listening to (or standing up and dancing to) some of the city's finest music. Here is a small selection of some of the artists who have made the Big Easy one of America's most tuneful destinations.

Sidney Bechet

He was the toast of Paris and called "le dieu" by existentialists, but soprano saxophonist and New Orleans native Sidney Bechet never received his due in his home country. After being deported from France in 1928 for his role in a gunfight, Bechet struggled to make ends meet and wound up working as a tailor in Harlem. His playing combined technical prowess with a passion and heat that matched his notoriously mercurial temper.

Henry Roeland "Professor Longhair" Byrd

Although his recordings as "Professor Longhair" were a major influence on musicians like Fats Domino and Elvis Presley, he never became a chart topper. By 1970 he was delivering groceries and hadn't played in years. Then he was rediscovered and became one of the city's most popular performers. Alas, he died at age sixty-two in 1980, on the eve of the release of his first album, *Crawfish Fiesta*. Several generations missed out on this major talent. You shouldn't.

Harry Connick Jr.

Singer, actor, pianist, songwriter: Harry Connick Jr. has worn many hats in his career. But whether he's filming a blockbuster in Hollywood or performing for audiences in New York, Connick has never forgotten that the Crescent City is his home or that he mastered his chops in the town where jazz was born. His music is more sedate than that of many Big Easy bands. Instead of beers on Bourbon Street, think cocktails and turtle soup at one of the city's many fine dining establishments.

Eyehategod

While New Orleans is best known for jazz, it has a thriving heavy metal scene. Among the local headbangers are Phil Anselmo of Pantera and Pepper Keenan of Corrosion of Conformity. Eyehategod is representative of the city's "sludge metal" sound: slow and steamy as a New Orleans summer, with plenty of jagged edges to keep you awake. Eyehategod's lyrics frequently feature loudly screamed ruminations on Big Easy topics like drug abuse, poverty, and violence. It's an acquired taste, but certainly a bracing one.

Al Hirt

Weighing in at more than three hundred pounds (140 kilos), Al Hirt became known as "the Round Mound of Sound"—and what a sound it was! His sweet trumpet tone led fellow musicians to say he had "honey in the horn." (Later this would be the title of his 1964 top ten album.) He took his French Quarter stylings to the world and helped define an era. Slip on a smoking jacket, mix yourself a drink, and let him transport you to a time when "swank" really meant something.

Branford and Wynton Marsalis

Wynton is not only one of America's foremost jazz trumpeters, he's also a brilliant classical musician and composer whose oratorio on slavery, *Blood on the Fields,* won the Pulitzer Prize in 1999. Branford is a great saxophonist who spent several seasons leading the Tonight Show band for Jay Leno and provided the soundtrack to *Sneakers* and *Mo' Better Blues.* Both are American treasures who have taken New Orleans brass in whole new directions.

The Neville Brothers

Art Neville was one of the original members of New Orleans' legendary Meters and is considered one of the founding fathers of funk. Aaron Neville's sweet vocals have catapulted him to the top of the R&B charts on numerous occasions. Charles Neville is a saxophonist who cites Charlie Parker and John Coltrane as influences. Cyril Neville has played congas with Edie Brickell, Bob Dylan, Willie Nelson, and Jimmy Buffet. Put them together and you've got some red-hot New Orleans funk and soul going on.

Louis Prima

The son of working-class Sicilian immigrants living in the French Quarter, Prima was famous for his trumpet, his scat vocals, and the shuffling "Gleeby rhythm" of his bands. Prima never let audiences forget he was an Italian kid from the French Quarter or that he learned much from fellow Crescent City trumpeter and bandleader Louis Armstrong. David Lee Roth paid tribute to him with a competent cover of his signature "Just a Gigolo/Ain't Got Nobody"—but there's no substitute for Prima's version of swinging New Orleans with a smooth Sicilian twist.

Queen Ida

Ida Guillory didn't start touring until she was over fifty. Until then she concentrated on raising her family and driving a school bus. But in the mid-1970s, with her children growing up, she pulled her accordion out of the closet and started entertaining her fellow Louisiana expatriates in San Francisco. The Cajun and Creole songs she remembered from her childhood struck a resonant chord with them and later with audiences around the world. In 1983 she was awarded a Grammy for her *On Tour* album.

The Radiators

Combining zydeco, jazz, and other New Orleans styles with straight-ahead rock and roll, the Radiators are one of the city's great party bands. The house band of the Krewe of Mystic Orphans and Misfits, the Radiators provide propulsive boogie-down entertainment at the annual M.O.M.'s Ball and regularly play out in their home city and elsewhere. They're not to be missed if you get a chance to see them live—and you likely will, given their relentless touring schedule.

Allen Toussaint

For nearly fifty years this New Orleans icon has been writing, producing, and performing on hits for artists ranging from Al Hirt ("Java" and "Whipped Cream"), Glen Campbell ("Southern Nights"), Labelle ("Lady Marmalade"), Devo ("Workin' in a Coalmine"), and Paul McCartney and Wings (*Venus and Mars*). Inducted into the Rock and Roll Hall of Fame in 1998, Toussaint is one of the Crescent City's most influential musicians. He has brought a taste of New Orleans to many recordings—and his solo music will bring the Big Easy to you.

APPENDIX 3

PRESERVING
NEW ORLEANS

If you would like to give something back to the city, here are just a few of
the many organizations preserving Crescent City culture and working to
support New Orleanians in need.

Backstreet Cultural Museum
1116 St. Claude Ave.
New Orleans, LA 70116
(504) 522-4806
www.backstreetmuseum.org
Located in Tremé, America's oldest historically African American neighborhood, the Backstreet Cultural Museum has preserved an enormous
collection of Mardi Gras and jazz funeral memorabilia, including some
incredible Mardi Gras Indian costumes.

LGBT Community Center of New Orleans
2114 Decatur St.
New Orleans, LA 70116
(504) 945-1103
www.lgbtccno.org
Long known as one of America's most gay-friendly cities, New Orleans
still has its share of homophobia, bigotry, and intolerance. The fine folks

at the LGBT Community Center are doing their part to improve matters. Why not do yours and help them out with a donation?

New Orleans Area Habitat for Humanity
P.O. Box 15052
New Orleans, LA 70175
(504) 861-2077
www.habitat-nola.org
Even before Katrina hit, New Orleans suffered from a housing shortage. After the storm, many longtime residents were priced out as rents on the remaining properties skyrocketed. Habitat for Humanity works with people in need to provide safe and affordable homes.

New Orleans Hope and Heritage Project
835 Piety St.
New Orleans, LA 70117
http://nolahopeandheritage.org/NOLA.html
Sallie Ann Glassman's charitable organization works to heal New Orleans and its people and to preserve the city's unique culture. This organization also holds the annual Anba Dlo (Beneath the Waters) festival on Halloween. If you're in the city, don't miss it.

New Orleans Musicians Clinic
2820 Napoleon Ave., Suite 890
New Orleans, LA 70115
www.neworleansmusiciansclinic.org
Being a professional musician may offer many benefits, but health insurance is rarely among them. Since 1998 the New Orleans Musicians Clinic has worked to provide medical care for Louisiana's professional entertainers and their families, regardless of their ability to pay.

New Orleans Musicians Relief Fund

102 W. Washington St., Unit 2

Bloomington, IL 61701

(504) 352-8876

www.nomrf.org

After Katrina many of the city's musicians were scattered throughout the country. Jeff Benanito, founder of New Orleans Musicians Relief Fund, wound up in Illinois with his family. That hasn't stopped him from offering aid to displaced musicians in and out of the Crescent City, and it shouldn't stop you.

Save Our Cemeteries

501 Basin St.

New Orleans, LA 70112

(504) 525-3377

www.saveourcemeteries.org

Save Our Cemeteries is a 501(c)(3) organization dedicated to promoting, preserving, and protecting the city's thirty-one historic cemeteries. If you want to get in good with the Big Easy's dearly departed, a donation to these folks may be just the ticket.

NOTES

Introduction

1. Jean Baudrillard, *Simulacra and Simulation,* trans. Sheila Faria Glaser (Ann Arbor: University of Michigan Press, 1994), 1.

Chapter 1. Born on the Bayou: The Rise of New Orleans

1. Henry Rightor, *Standard History of New Orleans, Louisiana* (Chicago: Lewis, 1900), 11.

2. David J. Weber, *The Spanish Frontier in North America* (New Haven: Yale University Press), 202.

3. Roulhac Toledano, *The National Trust Guide to New Orleans* (New York: John Wiley and Sons, 1996), 9.

Chapter 2. From Saint-Domingue to Washington: Revolution Comes to Louisiana

1. C. L. R. James, *The Black Jacobins: Toussaint L'Ouverture and the San Domingo Revolution*, 2nd ed., rev. (New York: Vintage Press, 1989), 86–87.

2. Richard Gott, *Cuba* (New Haven, Conn.: Yale University Press, 2005), 45.

3. William R. Lux, "French Colonization in Cuba, 1791–1809," *The Americas* 29 (July 1972), 57–61.

4. Thomas A. Klingler, *If I Could Turn My Tongue Like That: The Creole Language of Pointe Coupee Parish* (Baton Rouge: Louisiana State University Press, 2003), 80.

5. Karol Kimberlee Weaver, *Medical Revolutionaries: The Enslaved Healers of Eighteenth-Century Saint Domingue* (Urbana-Champaign: University of Illinois Press, 2006), 105.

6. Walter C. Rucker, *The River Flows On: Black Resistance, Culture, and Identity Formation in Early America* (Baton Rouge: Louisiana State University Press, 2008), 153–54.

7. Ibid.

Chapter 3. King Cotton, Lady Liberty, and Jim Crow

1. East St. Louis Action Research Project, "The Steamboat Era," The IBEX Archive, 2000, www.eslarp.uiuc.edu/ibex/archive/IDOT/idot11.htm (accessed April 5, 2011).

2. Jean M. West, "King Cotton: The Fiber of Slavery," Slavery in America, 2001, www.slaveryinamerica.org/history/hs_es_cotton.htm (accessed June 22, 2009).

3. Solomon Northrup, "There Is No Such Thing as Rest," in *Twelve Years a Slave: Narrative of Solomon Northrup* (Auburn, N.Y.: n.p., 1853), available at Excerpts from Slave Narratives, www.vgskole.net/prosjekt/slavrute/10.htm (accessed June 24, 2009).

4. Don B. Wilmeth and Christopher Bigsby, *The Cambridge History of American Theatre* (Cambridge: Cambridge University Press, 1998), 406.

5. PBS, American Experience, "Reconstruction: The Second Civil War," www.pbs.org/wgbh/amex/reconstruction/states/sf_timeline.html (accessed June 25, 2009).

6. "Thomas R. Myers Reminiscences, March 11, 1919," available at Louisiana Native Guards, www2.netdoor.com/~jgh/porthud.html (accessed June 24, 2009).

7. "Benjamin Butler's New Orleans 'Woman's Order,'" http://www.civilwar-home.com/butlerwomanorder.htm (accessed May 24, 2011).

8. Louisiana State Museum, "Reconstruction: A State Divided," 2006, http://lsm.crt.state.la.us/CABILDO/cab-reconstructionI.htm (accessed June 25, 2009).

9. John Simkin, "Andrew Johnson," Sparatacus Educational, 2004, www.spartacus.schoolnet.co.uk/USAjohnsonA.htm (accessed June 25, 2009).

10. Eric Foner, *A Short History of Reconstruction* (New York: Harper Perennial, 1990), 146.

11. John W. Blassingame, *Black New Orleans, 1860–1880* (Chicago: University of Chicago Press, 2007), 188.

Chapter 4. The (Re)creation of "New Orleans Voodoo"

1. Franz Boas, "The Instability of Human Types," in *Papers on Interracial Problems Communicated to the First Universal Races Congress Held at the University of London, July 26–29, 1911,* edited by Gustav Spiller (Boston: Ginn and Co., 1912), 103.

2. Zora Neale Hurston, *Mules and Men* (Philadelphia: Lippincott, 1935), available at Zora Neale Hurston's Mules and Men and E-Project, http://xroads.virginia.edu/~MA01/Grand-Jean/Hurston/Chapters/hoodoo1.html (accessed September 15, 2009).

3. Zora Neale Hurston, *Jonah's Gourd Vine* (New York: Harper Perennial, 1990), 147.

4. Michael North, *The Dialect of Modernism: Race, Language, and Twentieth-Century Literature* (New York: Oxford University Press, 1994), 176.

5. Joan Wylie Hall, review of *The Life and Selected Letters of Lyle Saxon,* by Chance Harvey (2004), University of Mississippi, www.olemiss.edu/depts/south/register/winter04/read_2.html (accessed September 28, 2009).

6. Robert Tallant, *Voodoo in New Orleans* (New York: MacMillan, 1946), 5.

7. Jerry Gandolfo, "Voodoo Charlie," New Orleans Historic Voodoo Museum, www.voodoomuseum.com/index.php?option=com_content&view=article&id=48 (accessed September 22, 2009).

8. Jerry Gandolfo, "Re: Cap Francois 1790's?" Genealogy.com, http://genforum.genealogy.com/haiti/messages/1972.html (accessed September 22, 2009).

9. Mary Hampshire, "That Old Black Magic," *The Big Issue in the North* (Summer 1999), available at www.maryhampshire.com/downloads/tbiitn-voodoo.pdf (accessed September 22, 2009).

10. Ibid.

11. Elizabeth Thomas Crocker, "A Trinity of Beliefs and a Unity of the Sacred: Modern Vodou Practices in New Orleans" (master's thesis, Louisiana State University, 2008), 42, available at www.scribd.com/doc/7986314/Voodoo-Practises-in-New-Orleans (accessed April 4, 2011).

Chapter 5. When the Levee Breaks: Hurricane Katrina

1. Peter Applebome, "Where Living at Nature's Mercy Had Always Seemed Worth the Risk," *New York Times,* August 31, 2005, www.nytimes.com/2005/08/31/national/nationalspecial/31charm.html (accessed June 17, 2009).

2. Barbara McCarragher, "Hurricane History in New Orleans," 2006, http://web.mit.edu/12.000/www/m2010/teams/neworleans1/hurricane%20 history.htm (accessed September 26, 2009).

3. John McQuaid and Mark Schleifstein, "In Harm's Way," *Times-Picayune,* June 23, 2009, www.nola.com/hurricane/content.ssf?/washingaway/part1. html (accessed September 26, 2009).

4. National Hurricane Center, "Tropical Depression Twelve," National Weather Service, August 23, 2005, www.nhc.noaa.gov/archive/2005/pub/ al122005.public.001.shtml (accessed October 7, 2009).

5. Johnny Kelly, "Hurricane Katrina's Dire Warning," Examiner.com, August 28, 2005, www.examiner.com/examiner/x-5181-Jackson-Weather-Examiner~y2009m8d28-Hurricane-Katrinas-dire-warning-August-28-2005 (accessed October 7, 2009).

6. Ann Gerhart, "Inside the Superdome: 'And Now We Are In Hell,'" *Washington Post,* September 1, 2005, www.washingtonpost.com/wp-dyn/content/article/2005/08/31/AR2005083102801.html (accessed October 7, 2009).

7. "4 Places Where the System Broke Down," *Time,* September 11, 2005, www.time.com/time/printout/0,8816,1103560,00.html (accessed October 7, 2009).

8. Phyllis Johnson, "Voices of Katrina: Phyllis Johnson, Superdome Survivor," *Houston Chronicle,* September 12, 2005, http://blogs.chron.com/katrinavoices/ archives/2005/09/phyllis_johnson.html (accessed October 12, 2009).

9. Scott Shane, "After Failure, Government Officials Play Blame Game," *New York Times,* September 5, 2005, www.nytimes.com/2005/09/05/national/ nationalspecial/05blame.html (accessed October 12, 2009).

10. Heather Burke, "New Orleans Gets More Troops to Stop Katrina Looting (Update5)," *Bloomberg News,* September 1, 2005, www.bloomberg.com/apps/ news?pid=10000103&sid=axLmRQqK.K0U (accessed October 12, 2009).

11. John Aravosis, "Lead Religious Right Group Promotes Theory That God Wiped Out NOLA on Purpose," AmericaBlog, September 2, 2005, www.americablog.com/2005/09/lead-religious-right-group-promotes.html (accessed October 12, 2009).

12. Tom Gross, "Mideast Dispatch Archive: Al Qaeda, Kuwaitis & Iranians 'Congratulate' Hurricane Katrina, and Thank Allah," Tom Gross: Mideast Media Analysis, September 7, 2005, www.tomgrossmedia.com/ mideastdispatches/archives/000476.html (accessed October 13, 2009).

13. Ami Isserof, "Hurricane Katrina and Ovadia Yosef's Racism—Enough Is Enough," Middle East Web Log, September 8, 2005, www.mideastweb.org/log/archives/00000379.htm (accessed February 12, 2010).

14. Jonathan Freedland, "The Levee Will Break," *Guardian,* September 7, 2005, www.guardian.co.uk/world/2005/sep/07/hurricanekatrina.usa9 (accessed October 13, 2009).

15. Media Matters for America, "Boortz: '[P]rimary Blame' for Katrina Goes to 'Worthless Parasites Who Lived in New Orleans,'" February 11, 2008, http://mediamatters.org/mmtv/200802010015 (accessed October 13, 2009).

16. Scott Benjamin, "In Katrina's Wake, the Blame Game," CBS News, September 7, 2005, www.cbsnews.com/stories/2005/09/07/katrina/main821705_page2.shtml (accessed October 13, 2009).

17. Deroy Murdock, "State of Damage: Blanco v. Big Easy," National Review Online, September 22, 2005, www.nationalreview.com/articles/215494/state-damage/deroy-murdock (accessed October 13, 2009).

18. Poppy Z. Brite, "Banned Books Night," Dispatches from Tanganyika: The Online Journal of Poppy Z. Brite, September 25, 2006, http://docbrite.livejournal.com/2006/09/25/ (accessed September 23, 2009).

19. Associated Press, "Hastert: New Orleans 'Could be Bulldozed,'" September 2, 2005, http://seattletimes.nwsource.com/html/nationworld/2002466132_kathast02.html (accessed April 5, 2011).

20. Barbara Mikkelson, "Working Very Well for Them," Snopes. www.snopes.com/politics/quotes/barbara2.asp (accessed April 5, 2011).

21. John E. Carey, "Katrina and New Orleans Demographics," Peace and Freedom II Weblog, September 3, 2007, http://johnibii.wordpress.com/2007/09/03/katrina-and-new-orleans-demographics (accessed October 17, 2007).

22. Jennifer Liberto, "Black Businesses Hit Hard in New Orleans," CNNMoney.com, August 19, 2009, http://money.cnn.com/2009/08/19/news/economy/New_Orleans_black_businesses/index.htm (accessed October 16, 2009).

Chapter 6. Mardi Gras

1. Roger Dunkle, "Lupercalia," A Day in the Life of an Ancient Roman, 2001, http://depthome.brooklyn.cuny.edu/classics/dunkle/romnlife/luprclia.htm (accessed October 20, 2009).

2. Henri Schindler, "Mardi Gras—Myth and History," Carnaval.com, 2004, www.carnaval.com/cityguides/neworleans/history.htm (accessed October 21, 2009).

3. Clarence A. Becknell, Thomas Price, and Don Short, "History of the Zulu Social Aid and Pleasure Club," Zulu Social Aid and Pleasure Club, 2002, www.kreweofzulu.com/Krewe-Of-Zulu/History-Of-the-Zulu-Social-Aid-&-Pleasure-Club.html (accessed October 21, 2009).

4. John Roach, "The Rich History of Mardi Gras's Cheap Trinkets," National Geographic News, February 21, 2004, http://news.nationalgeographic.com/news/2004/02/0220_040220_mardigras.html (accessed October 23, 2009).

5. Brian L. Dear, "The Zulu Coconuts of New Orleans," Coconut: The Web Guide to the Tropical World, August 1996, www.coconut.com/features/zulucoco.html (accessed October 23, 2009).

6. James Grout, "Saturnalia," Encyclopedia Romana, 2009, http://penelope.uchicago.edu/~grout/encyclopaedia_romana/calendar/saturnalia.html (accessed October 22, 2009).

7. Mark Sottek, "King Cake—A Rich Tradition," Mardi Gras Unmasked, 2009, www.mardigrasunmasked.com/mardigras2/KingCakeHistory/tabid/65/Default.aspx (accessed October 22, 2009).

8. Catherine M. Bell, *Ritual: Perspectives and Dimensions* (New York: Oxford University Press, 1997), 127.

9. Jeffrey Gettleman, "Parade Has Passed by One Carnival Tradition: Race-Based Clubs," *Los Angeles Times,* February 27, 2001, http://articles.latimes.com/2001/feb/27/news/mn-30735 (accessed October 23, 2009).

Chapter 7. Music

1. Shane K. Bernard and Judy LaBorde, "The Link Between the Acadians and Cajun Culture," Louisiana State University Health Sciences Center: Genetics and Louisiana Families, 2002, www.medschool.lsuhsc.edu/genetics_center/louisiana/article_acadianscajuns.htm (accessed July 12, 2009).

2. Gertrude "Ma" Rainey, "Louisiana Hoo Doo Blues," 1925, available at Lucky Mojo: Ma Gertrude Rainey, www.luckymojo.com/blueslouisianahoodoorainey.html (accessed July 20, 2009).

3. Alan Lomax, "Library of Congress Narrative: Ferdinand 'Jelly Roll' Morton," 1938, available at Southern Spirits: Ghostly Voices from Dixieland, www

.southern-spirits.com/morton-hoodoo-new-orleans.html (accessed July 17, 2009).

4. Gary Giddins, "Conversation with Gary Giddins," Jerry Jazz Musician, October 31, 2005, www.jerryjazzmusician.com/mainHTML.cfm?page= giddins-neworleans.html (accessed July 16, 2009).

5. "Buckwheat Zydeco: The Facts," Buckwheat Zydeco Online, 1999, www .buckwheatzydeco.com/bwzydecoourstory/bwzydecoourstory.html (accessed July 12, 2009).

Chapter 8. Food

1. Andrew Sigal, "Jambalaya by Any Other Name," *Petits Propos Culinaires* 84 (Winter 2007/2008), available at www.sigal.org/CulinaryHistory/Jambalaya/ Jambalaya_by_Any_Other_Name.htm (accessed December 9, 2009).

2. Stanley Dry, "A Short History of Gumbo," The Southern Gumbo Trail, 2007, www.southerngumbotrail.com/history.shtml (accessed December 10, 2009).

3. Ravi Kochhar, "All About Okra," 2006, www.neurophys.wisc.edu/ravi/okra (accessed December 10, 2009).

4. Claire Kowalchik and William H. Hylton, ed., *Rodale's Illustrated Encyclopedia of Herbs* (Emmaus, Pa.: Rodale Press, 1998), 86.

5. "New Orleans and Coffee," Louisiana State Museum, 2002, http://lsm.crt .state.la.us/coffee/coffee5.htm (accessed February 14, 2010).

6. Lyle Saxon, *Fabulous New Orleans* (New York, London: The Century Co., 1928), quoted in "New Orleans and Coffee."

7. Thibodeaux Comeaux, "Crawfish History," Frugé Cajun Crawfish, 2009, www.cajuncrawfish.com/page.cfm?sct=club&pg=history (accessed December 11, 2009).

8. Trade Environment Database, "TED Case Studies: 1997 United States-China Crawfish Tail Meat Dispute," 1997, www1.american.edu/TED/ crawfish.htm (accessed December 11, 2009).

9. Steven Hedlund, "Katrina Knocks Gulf Down but Not Out," *SeaFood Business* 24, no. 10 (October 2005): 24. Available at http://seafoodbusiness .texterity.com/seafoodbusiness/200510/ (accessed April 5, 2011).

Chapter 9. Voodoo Temples and Curio Shops

1. Carolyn Morrow Long, *Spiritual Merchants* (Knoxville: University of Tennessee Press, 2001), 145.

2. Ibid.

3. Marie Laveau, *Black and White Magic*, ed. Bivins N. D. P. (n.p.: International Imports, 1991), 14.

4. Zora Neale Hurston, *The Sanctified Church* (Berkeley, Calif.: Turtle Island Press, 1981), 21.

5. Lyle Saxon, Edward Dreyer, and Robert Tallant, *Gumbo Ya-Ya* (Gretna, La.: Pelican, 1991), 211.

6. Anthony B. Pinn, *Varieties of African American Religious Experience* (Minneapolis, Minn.: Ausburg Fortress Publishers, 1998), 45.

7. Miriam Chamani, "Diary of a Priest," Voodoo Spiritual Temple, 2009, www.voodoospiritualtemple.org/diary.htm (accessed December 9, 2009).

8. David Ian Miller, "FINDING MY RELIGION: Sallie Ann Glassman, a Vodou Priestess in New Orleans, on What Vodou Is Really About," *San Francisco Chronicle,* July 10, 2006, www.sfgate.com/cgi-bin/article.cgi?f=/g/a/2006/07/10/findrelig.DTL (accessed December 7, 2009).

9. Sallie Ann Glassman, telephone conversation with the author, December 8, 2009.

10. Sallie Ann Glassman, "La Source Ancienne Ounfo," Island of Salvation Botanica, 2009, www.feyvodou.com/lasource.htm (accessed December 7, 2009).

11. Andrew Fenner, "The Westgate Mistress: An Interview with Leilah Wendell," *Morbid Outlook*, www.morbidoutlook.com/nonfiction/articles/2003_08_westgate.html (accessed December 6, 2009).

12. Leilah Wendell, "A History of the Azrael Project and of the Westgate," Westgate: The Azrarel Project Online, 2007, www.westgatenecromantic.com/History.htm (accessed December 6, 2009).

13. Leilah Wendell, "Leilah Wendell," Westgate: The Azrael Project Online, 2007, www.westgatenecromantic.com/leilah.htm (accessed December 6, 2009).

14. Udo Blick, "And We Thought Vampires Were the Stuff of Our Dreams," True Blood Net, November 30, 2009, http://truebloodnet.com/thought-vampires-stuff-dreams (accessed December 3, 2009).

Chapter 10. Priests, Priestesses, Houngans, Mambos, and Chicken Men

1. Lafcadio Hearn, *Inventing New Orleans: The Writings of Lafcadio Hearn* (Oxford, Miss.: University of Mississippi Press, 2001), 79.

2. Richie Unterberger, "Liner Notes for Dr. John's *Gris-Gris*," 2009, www
.richieunterberger.com/drjohn.html (accessed November 17, 2009).

3. Kenneth R. Fletcher, "Dr. John's Prognosis," *Smithsonian*, March 1, 2009,
www.smithsonianmag.com/arts-culture/Dr-Johns-Prognosis.html (accessed
November 17, 2009).

4. David Evans, *Big Road Blues: Tradition and Creativity in the Folk Blues*
(Cambridge, Mass.: Da Capo Press, 1987), 121.

5. J. T. "Funny Paper" Smith, "Seven Sisters Blues: Parts 1 and 2," available at Lucky Mojo, 2003, www.luckymojo.com/number7.html (accessed
November 24, 2009).

6. Brenda Marie Osbey, "Faubourg Study No. 3: The Seven Sisters of New
Orleans," *Callaloo* 11, no. 3 (Summer 1988): 464–76.

7. New Orleans Historic Voodoo Museum, "Glossary," 2009, www
.voodoomuseum.com/index.php?option=com_content&view=article&id=
36 (accessed November 24, 2009).

8. House of the Seven Sisters Voodoo Shop and Museum, Brochure, quoted in
Erin Elizabeth Voisin, "Saint Maló Remembered" (master's thesis, Louisiana
State University, 2008), 58, available at http://etd.lsu.edu/docs/available/
etd07092008-223941/unrestricted/Voisin_Thesis.pdf (accessed May 19,
2011).

9. J. J. McCay, "'CHICKEN MAN' Prince Ke'eyama THE ONE TRUE KING
OF NEW ORLEANS VOODOO," Haunted New Orleans Tours, 2006,
www.hauntedneworleanstours.com/chickenman (accessed October 27, 2009).

10. Richard West, "Voodoo in Blanco," *Texas Monthly* (May 1975): 12–14.

11. Rick Bragg, "Jazzy Final Sendoff for Chicken Man," *New York Times*,
February 1, 1999, www.nytimes.com/1999/02/01/us/jazzy-final-sendoff-
for-chicken-man.html?pagewanted=all (accessed October 27, 2009).

12. Ibid.

Chapter 11. The Old Man at the Crossroads: Papa La-Bas

1. Robert Tallant, *Voodoo in New Orleans* (Gretna, La.: Pelican, 1983),
57–58.

2. Ibid., 103.

3. Ernest Borneman, "Creole Echoes, Part II," 1959, available at Jazz Studies
Online, http:// jazzstudiesonline.org/files/Creole%20Echoes%20Part%20II.
pdf (accessed January 8, 2010).

4. Henry Louis Gates, *The Signifying Monkey: A Theory of Afro-American Literary Criticism* (New York: Oxford University Press, 1989), 223.

5. Douglas Britt, "NeoHooDoo: Faith and Ritual in Art of the Americas," *Houston Chronicle,* June 20, 2008, www.chron.com/disp/story.mpl/ent/arts/theater/5848053.html (accessed January 10, 2010).

6. Carol McDavid, "Kongo Cosmogram," Levi Jordan Plantation, 1998, www.webarchaeology.com/html/kongocos.htm (accessed December 31, 2009).

7. Catherine Yronwode, "The Crossroads," Lucky Mojo, 1995, www.luckymojo.com/crossroads.html (accessed January 3, 2010).

8. David Evans, *Tommy Johnson* (London: Studio Vista, 1971), quoted in Catherine Yronwode, "The Crossroads," Lucky Mojo, 1995, www.luckymojo.com/crossroads.html (accessed January 3, 2010).

9. David Scotese, "Robert Johnson," The Mudcat Café, 1997, www.mudcat.org/rj-dave.cfm (accessed January 4, 2010).

Chapter 12. The Divine Mother: The Virgin Mary

1. Luigi Gambero, *Mary and the Fathers of the Church: The Blessed Virgin Mary in Patristic Thought* (Fort Collins, Colo.: Ignatius Press, 1999), 251.

2. Saint Iraneaus, "Against Heresies 3:22," New Advent, www.newadvent.org/fathers/0103322.htm (accessed February 14, 2010).

3. Leonard Foley, "St. Bernard of Clairvaux: Saint of the Day (August 20)," American Catholic, 1975, www.americancatholic.org/Features/Saints/Saint.aspx?id=1113 (accessed February 14, 2010).

4. Vincenzina Krymow, "Mary's Flowers," The Marian Library, February 29, 2008, http://campus.udayton.edu/mary/resources/flowers.html (accessed February 14, 2010).

5. Buddy Still, "Aug. 7, 1727 Ursaline Nuns Arrive in New Orleans," New Orleans History—Lake Pontchartrain, 2008, www.pontchartrain.net/templates/System/details.asp?id=40334&PID=495416 (accessed February 14, 2010).

6. Terry Jones, "Patron Saints Index: Our Lady of Prompt Succor," Patron Saints Index, 2008, http://saints.sqpn.com/mary0015.htm (accessed February 14, 2010).

7. Ibid.

8. Steve Leake, "Our Lady of Prompt Succor: Patroness of New Orleans," Da Mihi Animas, January 7, 2010, salesianity.blogspot.com/2009/01/our-lady-of-prompt-succor-patroness-of.html (accessed February 14, 2010).

9. Joshua Herne, "St. Dominic, Friar, Preacher, Champion of Orthodoxy," Telling the Stories That Matter, August 8, 2009, www.ttstm.com/2009/08/august-8-st-dominic-friar-preacher.html (accessed February 14, 2010).

10. Ibid.

Chapter 13. The Great Serpent: Li Grand Zombi

1. Joseph J. Williams, "Serpent Cult at Whydah," chap. 2 in *Voodoos and Obeahs* (n.p.: 1932), available at Sacred Texts, www.sacred-texts.com/afr/vao/vao04.htm (accessed November 4, 2009).

2. Henry C. Castellanos, *New Orleans as It Was: Episodes of Louisiana Life* (New Orleans: L. Graham and Son, 1895), 92–93.

3. "OLD SOUTHERN VOODOOISM; Amulets, Magic Potions, Witch Hazel, Serpents, and Toads. GRISLY ORGIES OF THE NEGROES. Curdling Incantations and Barbaric Rites—Bones of Dead Men for Luck—Sufferings of the Obi Man's Victims," *New York Times,* November 15, 1894, 20.

4. Milo Rigaud, *Secrets of Voodoo* (San Francisco: City Lights, 2001), 93.

5. Helen Pitkin, *An Angel by Brevet: A Story of Old New Orleans* (Philadelphia and London: J. P. Lippincott and Company, 1904), 196.

Chapter 14. The Voodoo Queen: Marie Laveau

1. Carolyn Morrow Long, *A New Orleans Voudou Priestess: The Legend and Reality of Marie Laveau* (Gainesville: University Press of Florida, 2006), 57.

2. Bonnye E. Stuart, *More Than Petticoats: Remarkable Louisiana Women* (Guilford, Conn.: Globe Pequot Press, 2009), 13.

3. Long, *New Orleans Voudou Priestess,* 51.

4. French Creoles of America, "Early Creole Houses of New Orleans: Early Homes of the Gens de Couleur Libre," Frenchcreoles.com, 2005, www.frenchcreoles.com/Early Creole Homes/Early Creole Homes index.htm (accessed February 7, 2010).

5. Long, *New Orleans Voudou Priestess,* 106.

6. Ibid., 107–8.

7. Lafcadio Hearn, *Inventing New Orleans: Writings of Lafcadio Hearn* (Oxford, Miss.: University Press of Mississippi, 2001), 70–71.

8. Robert Tallant, *Voodoo in New Orleans* (New York: MacMillan, 1946), 129.

Chapter 15. The Warriors:
Joe Féraille, St. Marron, and Yon Sue

1. Zachary Richard, "Joe Férraille," from the album *Couer Fidèle*, 2000, available at www.cdbaby.com/cd/zacharyrichard5.
2. Robert M. Salin and Sharon La Boda, *International Diary of Historical Places: Middle East and Africa* (London: Taylor and Francis, 1996).

Chapter 16. The Miracle Workers:
St. Expidité, St. Jude, and St. Roch

1. Michelle Delio, "St. Expedité: Patron Saint of the Nerds," Wired News, November 10, 2004, www.armeniapedia.org/index.php?title=St._Expedite (accessed June 25, 2009).
2. St. Jude Novena Blog, "Danny Thomas Puts His Life and Thoughts on Paper," June 21, 2009, http://stjudenovenablog.blogspot.com/2009/06/article-danny-thomas-puts-his-life-and.html (accessed July 8, 2009).
3. Ibid.

Chapter 17. The Bringers of Good Fortune:
St. Joseph, Assonquer, and John the Conqueror

1. Lyle Saxon, Edward Dreyer, and Robert Tallant, *Gumbo Ya-Ya* (Gretna, La.: Pelican, 1991), 92.
2. George Washington Cable, *The Grandissimes* (New York: Penguin Books, 1998), 74.
3. Samantha and Matthew Corfield, "Creole Voodoo Glossary," Spellmaker.com, 2000–2007, www.spellmaker.com/glossaryB.htm (accessed December 28, 2009).
4. Lyle Saxon, Edward Dryer, and Robert Tallant, *Gumbo Ya-Ya* (Gretna, La.: Pelican, 1991), 294.

Chapter 18. The Indians: Black Hawk and
the Black Hawk Spiritual Churches

1. Black Hawk, *Autobiography of Ma-ka-tai-me-she-kia-kiak, or Black Hawk* (Rock Island, Ill.: n.p., 1833), available at Project Gutenberg, www.gutenberg.org/files/7097/7097-h/7097-h.htm (accessed July 7, 2009).
2. Hans A. Baer, "The Limited Empowerment of Women in Black Spiritual Churches: An Alternate Vehicle to Religious Leadership," in *Gender and*

Religion, edited by William H. Swatos (New Brunswick, N.J.: Transaction Publications, 1994), 82.

3. Jessie Carney Smith, *Notable Black American Women,* book 3 (New York: Thomson Gale, 1995), 10.

4. Stephen C. Wehmeyer, "'Indians at the Door': Power and Placement on New Orleans Spiritual Church Altars," *Western Folklore* 66, no. 1/2 (Winter 2007): 15–44.

5. Andrew Herrmann, "Spreading the Spirit, Black Hawk Gets New Attention," www.highbeam.com/doc/1P2-4311973.html (accessed May 24, 2011).

6. Wehmeyer, "'Indians at the Door': Power and Placement on New Orleans Spiritual Church Altars."

7. Ibid.

Chapter 19. The Roots: The Dead

1. Lyle Saxon, Edward Dryer, and Robert Tallant, *Gumbo Ya-Ya* (Gretna, La.: Pelican, 1991), 321–22.

2. Charles Gayarré, *History of New Orleans* (New York: William J. Widdleton, 1867), 387–88.

Chapter 20. Candles

1. Zora Neale Hurston, *Mules and Men* (Philadelphia: Lippincott, 1935), available at Zora Neale Hurston's Mules and Men E-Project, http://xroads .virginia.edu/~MA01/Grand-Jean/Hurston/Chapters/paraphernalia.html (accessed January 25, 2010).

2. Henri Gamache, *Master Book of Candle-Burning* (n.p., Original Products, 1988), 3.

3. Colin B. Donovan, "Candles—Votive," Eternal Word Television Network, 2000, www.ewtn.com/expert/answers/candles.htm (accessed January 27, 2010).

Chapter 21. Oils

1. Patricia Rain, "Sex, Love and the Vanilla Bean," The Vanilla Company, 2006, www.vanilla.com/index.php/TROPICAL-FOODS/VANILLA/sex-love-and-the-vanilla-bean.html (accessed December 18, 2009).

2. Julie Bailey, "Alkanet Root and Powder Profile," Mountain Rose Herbs, 2000, www.mountainroseherbs.com/learn/alkanet.php (accessed December 18, 2009).

3. Catherine Yronwode, "Recipes for Potions Used in Spell-Casting," Lucky Mojo, 1995, www.luckymojo.com/spells/recipes.html (accessed December 18, 2009).

Chapter 22. Spirit Dolls

1. Zdenka Volavkova, "Nkisi Figures of the Lower Congo," Rand African Art, 1971, www.randafricanart.com/Nkisi_Figures_of_the_Lower_Congo.html (accessed February 17, 2010).

2. Patrick Bellegarde-Smith, *Fragments of Bone: Neo-African Religions in the New World* (Urbana-Champaign: University of Illinois Press, 2005), 194.

3. Sir James George Frazer, "Sympathetic Magic: Homeopathic or Imitative Magic," chap. 3, sec. 2 in *The Golden Bough* (New York: Macmillan, 1922), available at Bartleby, www.bartleby.com/196/6.html (accessed February 16, 2010).

4. Robert Joost Willink, *Stages in Civilisation: Dutch Museums in Quest of West Central African Collections, 1856–1889* (Leiden, Holland: CNWS Publications, 2007), 116.

Chapter 23. Mojo Hands and Gris-gris Bags

1. Jean Baptiste Léonard Durand, *A Voyage to Senegal; or, Historical, Philosophical and Political Memoirs* (London: Richard Phillips, 1806), 108.

2. Gwendolyn Midlo Hall, *Africans in Colonial Louisiana: The Development of Afro-Creole Culture in the Eighteenth Century* (Baton Rouge: Louisiana State University Press, 1992), 163.

3. Sylviane Anna Diouf, *Servants of Allah: African Muslims Enslaved in the Americas* (New York: New York University Press, 1998), 130.

4. Muddy Waters, *Folk Singer,* Chess, LP, 1964, remastered with extra tracks, CD, 1999.

5. Deborah G. Plant, *Zora Neale Hurston: A Biography of the Spirit* (Santa Barbara, Calif.: Greenwood, 2007), 92.

Chapter 24. Foretelling the Future

1. "Early References to Playing Cards," The World of Playing Cards, 1997, www.wopc.co.uk/history/earlyrefs.html (accessed February 23, 2010).

2. Paul Huson, *Mystical Origins of the Tarot: From Ancient Roots to Modern Usage* (Rochester, Vt.: Inner Traditions, 2004), 51.

3. Roger Dunstan, "History of Gambling in the United States," in *Gambling in California,* CRB-97-003 (Sacramento: California Research Bureau, 1997), available at www.library.ca.gov/crb/97/03/Chapt2.html (accessed February 21, 2010).

4. Rajah Rabo [Carl Z. Talbot], *Rajah Rabo's 5-Star Mutuel Dream Book for Lottery Number Play* (Mount Vernon, N.Y.: n.p., 1932; 1941), available at Lucky Mojo, www.luckymojo.com/rajahrabosmutuel.html (accessed February 22, 2010).

5. Mark Stibich, "Top 10 Health Benefits of a Good Night's Sleep," About .com, May 8, 2009, http://longevity.about.com/od/lifelongenergy/tp/healthy_sleep.htm (accessed February 22, 2010).

Chapter 25. Visiting the Big Easy

1. Phillip Lutz, "New Orleans Jazz Band Gets in Step with the Times," *New York Times,* December 31, 2009.

Chapter 26. Moving to New Orleans: Triumphs and Tragedies

1. Tanya Dean, "Tennessee Williams and the Catastrophe of Success," Long Wharf Theatre, 2009, www.longwharf.org/off_glass_williams2.html (accessed February 1, 2010).

2. Tanya Dean, "The Playwright: Tennessee Williams' Uncommon Tenderness," Longwharf Theatre, 2009, www.longwharf.org/off_glass_williams.html (accessed February 5, 2010).

3. Tennessee Williams, *The Glass Menagerie* (New York: New Directions, 1999), 97.

4. Tennessee Williams, *A Streetcar Named Desire: Play in Three Acts* (New York: Dramatists Play Service, 1947), 59.

5. Tennessee Williams, *Vieux Carré* (New York: New Directions, 1979), 5.

6. Gary James, "Emeril Lagasse Interview," FamousInterview.com, 1995, www.famousinterview.ca/interviews/emeril_lagasse.htm (accessed February 4, 2010).

7. Jack Hayes, "Lagasse Reigns Over the Palace," Nation's Restaurant News, September 4, 1989, available at BNET, http://findarticles.com/p/articles/mi_m3190/is_n36_v23/ai_7930833/ (accessed February 5, 2010).

8. Kat Kinsman, "Q and A with Emeril Lagasse," AOL Food, March 2, 2009, http://food.aol.com/emeril (accessed February 6, 2010).

9. Josh Allen Friedman, "Tell the Truth until They Bleed," WFMU, 2000, www.wfmu.org/LCD/23/docpomus.html (accessed February 1, 2010).

10. Richard Marcus, "Interview: Willy DeVille," Leap in the Dark, May 14, 2006, http://blogs.epicindia.com/leapinthedark/2006/05/interview_willy_deville.html (accessed April 15, 2011).

11. Sheila René, "Interview with Willy DeVille," Freenet, 1995, http://replay.waybackmachine.org/20090310234618/http://freenet-homepage.de/willy-deville/interview.htm (accessed February 1, 2010).

12. David Usborne, "Murder Most Mysterious: The House of Horror in New Orleans," *Sunday Independent* (London), October 6, 2006, www.independent.co.uk/news/world/americas/murder-most-mysterious-the-house-of-horror-in-new-orleans-420853.html (accessed February 6, 2010).

13. Ethan Brown, "Shake the Devil Off," Gambit: Best of New Orleans, August 29, 2009, http://bestofneworleans.com/gyrobase/Content?oid=oid%3A60492 (accessed February 6, 2010).

14. Ethan Brown, "Troubled Water," *Penthouse,* March 2007, 98.

15. Walt Philbin, Steve Ritea, and Trymaine Lee, "Katrina Survivalist's Descent into Madness," *New Orleans Time-Picayune*, October 19, 2006, http://blog.nola.com/tpcrimearchive/2006/10/katrina_survivalists_descent_i.html (accessed Feburary 6, 2010).

Afterword: *Deepwater Horizon* and the Indomitable Spirit of Louisiana

1. "Fish Stocks in the Gulf of Mexico Fact Sheet," Gulf of Mexico Sea Grant Programs, April 2010, http://gulfseagrant.tamu.edu/oilspill/facts_fish-stocks.htm (accessed May 31, 2011).

2. National Commission on the BP Deepwater Horizon Oil Spill and Offshore Drilling, chapter 6, "The Worst Environmental Disaster America Has Ever Faced," in *Deep Water: the Gulf Oil Disaster and the Future of Offshore Drilling,* April 2011, www.oilspillcommission.gov/sites/default/files/documents/FinalReportChapter6.pdf, 185.

3. Tim Webb, "Deepwater Oil Spill Victims, from Waitresses to Cabbies and Strippers, Plead for BP Payouts," *The Observer,* June 20, 2010, www

.guardian.co.uk/environment/2010/jun/20/deepwater-oil-spill-victims-compensation-bp (accessed May 31, 2011).

4. Renée C. Lee, "Fishermen Caught in a Quandry: Not Keeping Records Puts Industry at Risk," *Houston Chronicle,* July 4, 2010, www.chron.com/disp/story.mpl/business/deepwaterhorizon/7094194 (accessed May 31, 2011).

5. Ed Anderson, "Leisure Tourism in Louisiana Is Expected to Take a Hit after BP Oil Spill," *New Orleans Times-Picayune,* January 23, 2011, www.nola.com/business/index.ssf/2011/01/leisure_tourism_in_louisiana_i.html (accessed May 31, 2011).

6. Stephen Bronars and Jora Stixrud, "Assessments of Economic Loss Due to the Deepwater Horizon Disaster," 3rd Quarter, 2010, at Welch Consulting, http://web.welchcon.com/PDF/2010-3Q.pdf (accessed May 31, 2011).

7. Dahr Jamail, "Gulf Spill Sickness Wrecking Lives," Al Jazeera, March 9, 2011, http://english.aljazeera.net/indepth features/2011/03/201138152955897442.html (accessed May 31, 2011).

8. Elana Schor, "New BP Data Show 20% of Offshore Responders Exposed to Chemical That Sickened Valdez Workers," *New York Times,* July 4, 2010, www.nytimes.com/gwire/2010/07/09/09greenwire-new-bp-data-show-20-of-gulf-spill-responders-e-82494.html (accessed May 31, 2011).

9. "Energy/Petrochemicals/Plastics," 2011, Greater New Orleans, Inc., http://gnoinc.org/industry-sectors/energy-petroleum-plastic (accessed May 28, 2011).

10. Jordan Flaherty, "Mississippi Flood Renews Gulf Coast Anxieties," May 19, 2011, Al Jazeera, http://english.aljazeera.net/indepth/features/2011/05/2011519131959617935.html (accessed June 3, 2011).

INDEX

BOOKS OF RELATED INTEREST

Talking to the Spirits
Personal Gnosis in Pagan Religion
by Kenaz Filan and Raven Kaldera

Drawing Down the Spirits
The Traditions and Techniques of Spirit Possession
by Kenaz Filan and Raven Kaldera

The Power of the Poppy
Harnessing Nature's Most Dangerous Plant Ally
by Kenaz Filan

The Haitian Vodou Handbook
Protocols for Riding with the Lwa
by Kenaz Filan

The New Orleans Voodoo Tarot
by Louis Martinié and Sallie Ann Glassman

Vodou Shaman
The Haitian Way of Healing and Power
by Ross Heaven

Teachings of the Santería Gods
The Spirit of the Odu
by Ócha'ni Lele

The Diloggún
The Orishas, Proverbs, Sacrifices,
and Prohibitions of Cuban Santería
by Ócha'ni Lele

Inner Traditions • Bear & Company
P.O. Box 388
Rochester, VT 05767
1-800-246-8648
www.InnerTraditions.com

Or contact your local bookseller